Critical Marketing
Defining the Field

Edited by

Michael Saren
Pauline Maclaran
Christina Goulding
Richard Elliott
Avi Shankar
Miriam Catterall

AMSTERDAM • BOSTON • HEIDELBERG • LONDON • NEW YORK • OXFORD
PARIS • SAN DIEGO • SAN FRANCISCO • SINGAPORE • SYDNEY • TOKYO
Butterworth-Heinemann is an imprint of Elsevier

ELSEVIER

Butterworth-Heinemann is an imprint of Elsevier
Linacre House, Jordan Hill, Oxford OX2 8DP, UK
30 Corporate Drive, Suite 400, Burlington, MA 01803, USA

First edition 2007

Copyright © 2007 Elsevier Ltd. All rights reserved

No part of this publication may be reproduced, stored in a retrieval system or transmitted in any
form or by any means electronic, mechanical, photocopying, recording or otherwise without the
prior written permission of the publisher

Permissions may be sought directly from Elsevier's Science & Technology Rights Department in
Oxford, UK: phone (+44) (0) 1865 843830; fax (+44) (0) 1865 853333; email: permissions@elsevier.
com. Alternatively you can submit your request online by visiting the Elsevier web site at http://
elsevier.com/locate/permissions, and selecting *Obtaining permission to use Elsevier material*

Notice
No responsibility is assumed by the publisher for any injury and/or damage to persons or
property as a matter of products liability, negligence or otherwise, or from any use or
operation of any methods, products, instructions or ideas contained in the material herein.

British Library Cataloguing in Publication Data
A catalogue record for this book is available from the British Library

Library of Congress Cataloguing in Publication Data
A catalogue record for this book is available from the Library of Congress

ISBN-13: 978-0-7506-8066-0

For information on all Butterworth-Heinemann publications
visit our web site at http://books.elsevier.com

Typeset by Charon Tec Ltd (A Macmillan Company), Chennai, India
www.charontec.com
Printed and bound in The United Kingdom

07 08 09 10 11   10 9 8 7 6 5 4 3 2 1

Learning Resources
Centre

1328231X

Working together to grow
libraries in developing countries

www.elsevier.com | www.bookaid.org | www.sabre.org

ELSEVIER   BOOK AID
International   Sabre Foundation

Contents

List of Contributors

Dr Eric J. Arnould is the PETSMART Distinguished Professor in the Norton School of Family and Consumer Sciences at the University of Arizona. He holds a PhD in Social Anthropology from the University of Arizona. From 1975 to 1990, he worked on problems of economic development in more than a dozen West African nations. Since 1990, he has been a full-time academic. His academic research investigates service relationships, channels structure and market organization, households, consumer culture theory, and issues associated with the conduct and representation of multi-method research. Dr Arnould has written more than 40 articles and chapters that appear in the major US marketing journals, and other social science periodicals and books. He thanks Risto Moisio for significant intellectual contributions. The invitation to present at University of Wolverhampton and generous gift of a cardboard knight's helmet offered by two of the organizers of the Critical Marketing Seminar Series, Christina Goulding and Mike Saren, led to the development of this manuscript.

Olivier Badot is Full Professor at ESCP-EAP Paris, Senior Researcher at the University of Caen-Basse Normandie (IAE) and Visiting Professor at the School of Management of the University of Ottawa. His researches focus on retailing: he has developed a specific semio-ethnological approach to analyse the roles played by retailers in their environment and to audit their strategies and mix consistency. Prof. Badot has published around 20 (individual or collective) books and many scientific articles and reports. He holds two PhDs: one in industrial economics (ENST, Paris) and one in ethnology (La Sorbonne).

Shona Bettany is a Lecturer in Marketing at Bradford University. Her research interests are theoretically and methodologically defined, concerning ethnographic studies of consumption phenomena and critical approaches to marketing. She has written on reflexivity in consumer research, feminist approaches to consumer research and Afghan hound breeding and exhibition cultures. She has completed two major ethnographic projects over the past 6 years, an international ethnography of the making of marketing knowledge, linking academic identity to knowledge output in relationship marketing and an international ethnography of Afghan hound breeding and exhibition cultures, theorizing the processes by which complex distributed cultures enact cohesion and belonging.

Alan Bradshaw is a Lecturer in Marketing at the University of Exeter. His research interests include the commodification of music and culture and his articles can be found in the *Journal of Marketing Management, Journal of Macromarketing, Consumption, Markets* and *Culture* and *Marketing Theory*.

Douglas Brownlie teaches and researches in marketing subjects in the Department of Marketing at the University of Stirling. He previously did this at the University of Strathclyde, the University of Glasgow and University College Cork. He publishes on topics including consumer culture, critical marketing and marketing management.

Ampelio Bucci is the owner of MIES, a business consulting company in Milan working for Italian and international companies, mostly in the textile, fashion, design, furniture and publishing industry. In the 1990s, he was Director of the Fashion and Design Management Department at Domus Academy, Milan. Professor of Fashion and Design Management at IULM University, he coordinates exhibitions at the *Triennale di Milano* and at the *Biennale* of Venice. He is also a well-known winemaker. With his Villa Bucci, he has succeeded in maintaining the best of tradition, while revolutionizing quite a few of Italy's traditional winemaking tenets.

Miriam Catterall is a Senior Lecturer at the Queen's University of Belfast. Her research interests are in the areas of market research, consumer research and gender issues in marketing. She has published widely in international journals on these topics and is a Co-editor of *Marketing and Feminism: Current Issues and Research.*

Bernard Cova is Professor of Marketing at Euromed Marseilles – School of Management and Visiting Professor at Università Bocconi, Milan. Ever since his first papers in the early 1990s, he has taken part in postmodern trends in consumer research and marketing, while emphasizing a Latin approach (e.g. Tribal marketing). He has published on this topic in the *International Journal of Research in Marketing*, the *European Journal of Marketing, Marketing Theory* and the *Journal of Business Research.* He is also known as a researcher in BtoB marketing, especially in the field of project marketing.

Richard Elliott is Professor of Marketing and Consumer Research at the University of Bath School of Management, and a Fellow of St Anne's College, Oxford. He is a Visiting Professor at ESSEC Paris, Université Paris II, Bocconi Università Commerciale Milan, Thammasat University Bangkok and Hong Kong Polytechnic University. Previously he was the first person to be appointed to a Readership in Marketing at the University of Oxford and was a Deputy Director of the Säid Business School. He worked for 12 years in brand management with a number of US multinationals and as an Account Director at an international advertising agency.

Ross Gordon, BA, MSc is a Research Officer at the Institute for Social Marketing, Department of Marketing, University of Stirling. He researches social marketing theory and practice, with a particular focus on the impact of mass media communications on behaviour. His main interests within the Institute are the marketing activities of the alcohol industry, the impact of social marketing on the critical marketing debate and upstream social marketing. He has made contributions to the *Journal of Public Health Policy, Health Education* and *Public Health* and has also presented at the *Academy of Marketing*. His background is in politics having completed a BA in Politics and History and an MSc in Public Policy at the University of Strathclyde and worked in policy-based research previously.

Christina Goulding is Professor of Consumer Research at the University of Wolverhampton. Her research interests centre on cultural and subcultural consumption and in the development and application of interpretivist methodologies. Her publications have been in internationally recognized journals, such as the *European Journal of Marketing, Psychology and Marketing, Journal of Marketing Management* and *Consumption, Markets and Culture* and she is author of a book entitled *Grounded Theory* published by Sage.

Kathy Hamilton is a Lecturer in Marketing at the University of Strathclyde. Her research interests lie in consumer disadvantage especially low-income families. Of particular interest is the ways in which low-income families cope in a society that is increasingly dominated by consumption. Other interests include social exclusion, stigma management strategies and the relationship between consumer disadvantage and consumer agency.

Gerard Hastings is the first UK Professor of Social Marketing and Founder/ Director of two research centres: the Institute for Social Marketing (1993) and the Centre for Tobacco Control Research (1999). These are based at the University of Stirling under a joint venture agreement with the Open University. The Institute for Social Marketing researches the applicability of marketing principles, such as consumer orientation and relationship building to the solution of health and social problems. It also conducts critical marketing research into the impact of potentially health damaging marketing, such as tobacco advertising and fast food promotion. Gerard is an Advisor to the World Health Organization, and sits on the FCTC (Framework Convention on Tobacco Control) Cross Board Advertising Committee. He is also an expert witness in litigation against the tobacco industry, and provides regular guidance on social and critical marketing to the Scottish, UK and European Parliaments.

Paul Hewer recently accepted the position of Senior Lecturer in the Department of Marketing at Strathclyde University. Prior to this he had many happy years as a Lecturer in the Department of Marketing at Stirling University. His research interests lie in the area of consumer culture theory, especially theories of practice and consumer resistance. Outside of his cell, he is a keen cook but he hates following recipes with a passion. His wife refers to him as recipe-phobic, which makes the fact that he has published on the significance of cookbooks and recipes all the more alarming.

Dr Ingrid Kajzer Mitchell is a Lecturer at the University of Strathclyde. She has been a Visiting Lecturer at the Glasgow School of Art and at Goldsmiths

College, University of London, as well as organizing and facilitating Sustainable Innovation workshops with the Centre for Sustainable Design in Surrey, UK. Her research interests lie in the area of marketing and social change: marketing and sustainable development; consumers relationship to products; consequences of materialism; organizational change; and creation of alternative futures.

Pauline Maclaran is Professor of Marketing and Consumer Research at Keele University. Her research interests focus on the experiential, symbolic aspects of contemporary consumption and critical perspectives in marketing. In particular, her work has explored the utopian dimensions of fantasy retail environments, such as the festival marketplace. Her publications have been in internationally recognized journals, such as the *Journal of Consumer Research, Psychology and Marketing, Journal of Advertising* and *Consumption, Markets and Culture* and she has co-edited a book of entitled *Marketing and Feminism: Current Issues and Research.* She is also an Editor-in-Chief of *Marketing Theory*, a journal that promotes alternative and critical perspectives in marketing and consumer behaviour.

Gilles Marion is currently Professor at EM LYON (France) and Head of the Doctoral Program in Management with Lyon 3 University. His research interests include issues pertaining to marketplace ideologies and consumer's interpretive tactics, semiotic consumer research, marketing management history and marketing's effect on society. He has written several articles in English and French which bring together these research interests: *Contributions of French Semiotics to Marketing Research Knowledge, The Marketing Management Discourse: What's New Since the 1960s?*, and *Marketing Ideology and Criticism: Legitimacy and Legitimization.*

Laura McDermott is a Research Officer at the Institute for Social Marketing at Stirling and the Open University. Laura has studied and reported widely on social marketing and its effectiveness in changing health behaviours. Her work has also examined the effects of commercial marketing on the health and welfare of society. This includes a series of systematic reviews for the World Health Organization and UK Food Standards Agency studying the effects of commercial food promotion on children's dietary choices.

Liz McFall is a Lecturer in Sociology at the Open University. Her interests are centred upon economic life, work and consumption in the 19th century. She is the author of *Advertising: A Cultural Economy* and a number of articles exploring 19th century promotional culture, consumption and life assurance.

Ken Peattie is Director of the ESRC Research Centre for Business Relationships, Accountability, Sustainability and Society (BRASS), and is also Professor of Marketing and Strategy at Cardiff Business School, which he joined in 1986. Before becoming an academic he worked in marketing, information systems and strategic planning in the paper and electronics industries. His main research focus over the past 10 years has been the impact of sustainability concerns on corporate and marketing strategies, and on management education. He is the author of two books and a range of book chapters and journal articles on these issues.

Michael Saren is Professor of Marketing at Leicester University Management Centre. He is co-author with David Ford of *Marketing and Managing Technology* (Thomson Business Press, 2001) and co-editor with Douglas Brownlie, Robin Wensley and Richard Whittington of *Rethinking Marketing* (Sage Publications, 1999). He has been a convener of the Marketing Stream at the first five *Critical Management Studies International Conferences*, 1999–2007, a Member of the organizing committee for the *European Association of Consumer Research Conferences* in 2005 and 2007 and one of the 'Gang of Six' who ran the *ESRC* seminar series in Critical Marketing. He was Chair of the *7th International Relationship Marketing Colloquium* in 1999 and Chair of the *2003 European Marketing Academy Conference*. His latest book is *Marketing Graffiti: The View from the Street* (Butterworth Heinemann, 2006).

Jonathan E. Schroeder is Professor of Marketing in the School of Business and Economics, University of Exeter. He is also a Visiting Professor in Marketing Semiotics at Bocconi University in Milan, Visiting Professor in Design Management at the Indian School of Business, Hyderabad, and Associate Faculty, University of the Arts, London. His research focuses on the production and consumption of images, and has been published widely. He is the author of *Visual Consumption* (Routledge, 2002) and Co-editor of *Brand Culture* (Routledge, 2006). He is an Editor of *Consumption Markets and Culture*, and serves on the editorial boards of *European Journal of Marketing, Marketing Theory* and *Advertising and Society Review*.

Linda M. Scott is Reader in Marketing at the Säid School of Business, Oxford University, and a fellow of Templeton College. Prior to joining the faculty at Oxford, she spent 15 years at the University of Illinois, where her primary appointment was in the Department of Advertising, but where she also held joint appointments in Art and Design, Gender and Women's Studies, and in the Institute for Communications Research. She has published two books, *Fresh Lipstick: Redressing Fashion and Feminism* and *Persuasive Imagery: A Consumer Response Perspective*, as well as numerous articles.

Avi Shankar is a Senior Lecturer in Marketing and Consumer Research in the School of Management at the University of Bath. Prior to this appointment he worked at the University of Exeter, a veritable hot-bed of criticality. Avi's research interests focus on understanding some of the unintended consequences of living in a consumer culture, conceptualizing pleasure in consumer research and studies of identity and consumption. His work has been published in journals like the *European Journal of Marketing, Consumption, Markets* *and Culture* and the *Journal of Marketing Management* amongst others. When not writing these articles, that few people seem to read, Avi likes tending to his vegetable garden, cooking and flyfishing.

Pierre Siquier is Président of Du Groupe Ligaris, a major advertising agency in Paris who are responsible for the Help program, the anti-smoking campaign of the European Commission running between 2005 and 2008. His agency was also responsible for the campaign to introduce the Euro that ran in France between 1997 and 2002.

Robin Wensley is Professor of Policy and Marketing at the Warwick Business School and was Chair of the School from 1989 to 1994, Chair of Faculty of Social Studies from 1997 to 1999, and Deputy Dean from 2000 to 2004. He is convenor of the new Public Management and Policy subject group within the Warwick Institute of Governance and Public Management and was Co-editor of the *Journal of Management Studies* from 1998 to 2002. He is also Director of the ESRC/EPSRC Advanced Institute of Management Research. His research interests include marketing strategy and evolutionary processes in competitive markets, investment decision-making, the assessment of competitive advantage and the nature of choice processes and user engagement in public services. He has worked closely with other academics and practitioners both in Europe and in the USA. His books include (with D. Brownlie, M. Saren, and R. Whittington), *Rethinking Marketing: Towards Critical Marketing Accountings*, Sage: London, 1999 and (with B.A. Weitz) *Handbook of Marketing*, Sage: London, 2002.

Dr Brian M. Young is Senior Lecturer and Economic Psychologist in the School of Psychology at the University of Exeter. He has published extensively in the area of children and advertising with *Television Advertising and Children* published by Oxford University Press in 1990 and most recently, Young, B.M. (with Palmer, E.L.) (eds) (2003). *The Faces of Televisual Media: Teaching, Violence, Selling to Children*, 2nd edition, Erlbaum. Brian is Editor of *Young Consumers*, an Emerald Group journal.

Acknowledgements

The six editors – Pauline Maclaran, Michael Saren, Christina Goulding, Richard Elliott, Avi Shankar and Miriam Catterall – gratefully acknowledge the financial support from the UK *Economic and Social Research Council* for the organization of the seminar series in Critical Marketing on which this book is based.

Introduction: Defining the Field of Critical Marketing

The aim of this volume is to explore one of marketing's least visible sub-areas, Critical Marketing. There is a significant and growing stream of research and publications in the field of management and organization that takes an overtly critical stance. Many of these critical management theorists have been drawn together through the international conference series in Critical Management Studies that has been held bi-annually in the UK since 1999. Critical research in marketing however has lagged some way behind other academic management disciplines in its volume and visibility – so far. This book represents our attempt to begin to redress this balance and raise the profile of Critical Marketing research. It is the first book on Critical Marketing that provides a compilation of original contributions from well-known 'critical' authors within (and, sometimes, from outside) marketing. As such, it not only explores and debates what it means to be a critical marketer, but also provokes some rethinking of many taken-for-granted assumptions within marketing theory and practice. The idea for the volume arose from a series of Critical Marketing seminars, funded by the Economic and Social Research Council that took place in the UK between December 2004 and May 2006. These seminars were designed to bring together an international group of scholars from a variety of disciplinary backgrounds to foster a stronger critical forum within the academic marketing community.

The six editors of this volume have all been asked on numerous occasions 'So, what do you mean by "Critical Marketing"?' There is no easy answer to this question. There are many controversial debates surrounding the meaning and use of the term 'critical' and, consequently, also around the term 'Critical Marketing'. As organizers of the seminar series, it was not our intention to be prescriptive, or to tightly define our understanding of these terms in advance. Instead, we wanted the seminars to open up a space where scholars and marketing practitioners could discuss, argue and negotiate what it means to undertake critical work in marketing. The writings here, by some of the seminar series' keynote speakers and its participants, reflect this meaning negotiation and illustrate the difficulty of trying to pin down a concept that remains somewhat loosely defined and fuzzy around the edges. Although some readers may find the elusiveness of the term 'Critical Marketing' somewhat frustrating, we should recognize that language is never static; that meanings are constantly adapting and evolving to reflect the changing nature of the contexts in which they are communicated (Bahktin, 1984/1965); and the inability of any linguistic form to include, or exclude, all of its 'meaning' (Derrida, 1978).

Part of the problem in defining Critical Marketing is that academics are presumed to engage critically with ideas per se, and it is something of a tautology to describe someone as a critical academic. There is a growing number of management and marketing academics, however, who are proud to add the prefix 'critical' to their work: for example, critical consumer research (Belk, 1995), critical management (Alvesson and Willmott, 1992), critical public relations (L'Etang and Pieczka, 1996), critical accounting (Cooper, 1995), critical organization studies (Burrell and Morgan, 1979/1992) and, not least, critical marketing (Hetrick and Lozada, 1999; Murray and Ozanne, 1991).

In these cases the prefix 'critical' is used to signal that the authors subscribe to one of a number of radical philosophies and theories that seek to make explicit certain ideologies and assumptions underlying the production of knowledge, the management process itself, and the wider context of socioeconomic relations within which these activities occur. By exposing underpinning ideologies and assumptions, critical theorists seek to reveal the power relations and contested interests that are embedded in knowledge production (Catterall et al., 2002).

As various authors highlight in this volume, the term critical is most closely associated with Frankfurt School Critical Theory and with the work of Adorno, Marcuse, Horkheimer and Habermas. Murray and Ozanne (1991) have illustrated the relevance and application of the work of the Frankfurt School for marketing and their pioneering contribution has resulted in a tendency for some scholars to conflate critical theory and research with Frankfurt School Critical Theory. However, many critical scholars in management and marketing argue for a broader definition, drawing their inspiration from a number of philosophical and theoretical sources of which Frankfurt School Critical theory is only one. For example, other well-known critical perspectives include feminist theory, postmodernism, poststructuralism, psycholinguistics, deconstruction and radical ecology (Burton, 2001; Fournier and Grey, 2000; Holman, 2000).

Of course, these radical philosophies and methodologies do not sit as comfortably together as the portmanteau label 'critical' might imply. For example, Frankfurt School theorists have little in common with postmodernism, regarding the latter an ontological non sequitur and epistemologically inadequate, and many poststructuralists would reject critical theory as another misguided modernist quest for grand narratives. Many feminists would denounce all these perspectives because of their inherently phallocentric bias, believing that both critical theory and postmodernism have little to offer on the subject of bringing about improvements to the status of women and other marginalized groups. For some postmodernists, theory is the enemy, they are anti-theory, and therefore critique is an end in itself, an act of resistance to theory. By contrast, critical theorists (Murray and Ozanne, 1991), feminists (Bristor and Fischer, 1993) and some postmodernists (Firat and Venkatesh, 1995) embrace distinctly emancipatory objectives. In addition to critiquing dominant ideologies, they also seek to transform them, with the aim of creating a more equitable society, and giving voice to those who are marginalized by mainstream discourse.

In selecting areas to include in this volume we have had to make some hard choices. Some of the topics in this volume have had little attention in marketing literature at all, such as consumer disadvantage (Hill, 2001) and marketing ideology (Marion, 2004). There are other critical aspects of marketing which have been covered well already in other volumes elsewhere, such as feminist approaches (Catterall et al., 2000) and marketing ethics (Smith and Quelch, 1993), therefore we have not sought to replicate these themes in depth here. Other sub-fields of marketing have been published widely, but have not conventionally been regarded as 'critical', such as environmental marketing (Kilbourne, 2004) and social marketing (Andreasen, 1995). We have chosen to include contributions from these areas that emphasize particular perspectives of critique of both marketing concepts and practices in social and environmental terms.

The spirit of this volume, then, is to build on these seminal perspectives and create a more substantial (and, hopefully, substantive), cohesive identity for critical marketing, an identity that can embrace differences as well as similarities, discord as well as harmony. We hope that the many diverse parts of Critical Marketing will come together as a greater whole for our readers on the pages that follow, and that this collection of critical writings will convey the multifaceted and dynamic nature of critical marketing.

We have organized the book into three overarching sections that follow the themes that emerged as the main areas of debate within the seminar series: (1) *Being a Critical Marketer: Reflections from the Field*; (2) *Critical Debates: Questioning Underlying Assumptions* and (3) *Effecting Change Through Critique: Social and Environmental Issues*.

The chapters in Part One – *Being a Critical Marketer: Reflections from the Field* – reflect on what it means to be a critical marketer and cover in more detail many of the debates that we have touched on above. An excellent introduction for any researcher wishing to follow a critical path in marketing, they illustrate how both new and established Critical Marketing scholars have made sense of the complex issues surrounding 'doing' critical marketing. They are also a great source of bibliographic material for those wishing pointers to the main 'must reads' of critical theorizing.

The opening chapter by Linda M. Scott (Säid Business School, University of Oxford) draws on her own experiences of doing critical work as a rhetorician, the experiences of her friends and colleagues in America and the experiences of her own doctoral students. Her chapter reflects the diversity of understanding about what critical actually means from a variety of academic perspectives including marketing. Similarly Jonathan E. Schroeder (University of Exeter) considers the same question from a European, but predominantly marketing perspective. Both these chapters (Chapters 1 and 2) neatly encapsulate the varying interpretations of what it means to be doing critical work. They are interlaced with Linda and Jonathan's own comments and analysis as they discuss the various definitions of critical that are offered from a variety of illustrious academics. In Chapter 3, however, any 'fuzziness' in definition of the term critical comes swiftly to an end! Alan Bradshaw (University of Exeter) and A. Fuat Firat (University of Texas, Pan American) are clear and unequivocal that, for them, critical means the post-Marxist Critical Theory of the Frankfurt School. They argue against the dilution of criticality evidenced in the previous two chapters and go on to outline key Marxian concepts and argue passionately how these concepts still have much to offer the interested student who wishes to analyse contemporary consumer culture.

Continuing the ongoing negotiation of meaning around the aims of Critical Marketing, Douglag Brownlie (University of Stirling), Paul Hewer, (University of Strathclyde) in Chapter 4, return us to a more eclectic framework of critique which leaves spaces for many voices and not just those of card-carrying critical theorists. Arguing for sceptical reflexivity within our theorizing, they highlight the politics of representation that can undermine the critical marketing project. They like the performance of critical theory to a form of cooking and offer up their own recipe for doing Critical Marketing.

A key feature of all these initial chapters and, to an extent, all the chapters in this book, is an acknowledgement of the role of the author in the construction of knowledge. This reflexivity towards the social construction of knowledge often marks out and identifies work as critical. Chapter 5 by Shona Bettany (University of Bradford) elegantly traces this journey within her own doctoral work. For doctoral students attempting a critical thesis, the degree of reflexivity demonstrated by them is often a key criterion used when examining and assessing the thesis. This chapter deals eloquently with these struggles and hopefully should be a comfort to anyone experiencing their own ontological crisis during the doctoral process.

The chapters in Part Two – *Critical Debates: Questioning Underlying Assumptions* – challenge not only taken-for-granted aspects of mainstream marketing thinking and research, but also various assumptions about marketing phenomena that are often made by critical and cultural theorists from outside the marketing discipline. In Chapter 6, Bernard Cova (Euromed Marseilles) Olivier Badot (ESCP-EAP Paris) and Ampelio Bucci (MIES, a business consulting company in Milan) present a detailed account of the marketing panaceas and the underlying logics that have dominated the discipline for the past 20 years. In doing so they offer a critique of the very term 'marketing', questioning in the process its continued validity in relation to the full range of human activities that have become prime sites for study in this ever expanding discipline. In its stead, they propose the term 'societing', and put forward an argument as to its greater relevance to the dynamic and constantly changing world of contemporary market-based phenomena.

This chapter is followed by another that is equally provocative. Chapter 7, by Gilles Marion (EM Lyon), further explores and critically deconstructs the use of language within marketing, opening up questions regarding such taken-for-granted marketing axioms as 'consumer sovereignty'. Gilles suggests that traditional textbook definitions ultimately lead to a stifling of innovation and he calls for a reorganization of the language in order to establish a new mental representation of marketing and a different mind-set that accounts for both customer exploitation and consumer exploration.

Chapters 8 and 9, although taking two very different perspectives, both question the alleged power of advertising. Advertising is, of course, one of marketing's most critiqued areas, particularly by those outside the marketing discipline. In Chapter 8, Brian Young (University of Exeter) concentrates on advertising to children and demonstrates through close readings of scientific reports that the supposed power of advertising and other marketing practices to influence the behaviour of children is often based on very questionable evidence. He goes on to outline the elements of theory which should provide a more scientific basis for evaluating the effects of advertising on children. In Chapter 9, Liz McFall (The Open University) critiques approaches to advertising based on critical theory, and argues that a more contextualized account will yield greater insights into the effects of advertising. She reviews structuralist and poststructuralist explanations of the ideological, hegemonic influences of advertising and concludes that they over-state its power. Instead, Liz proposes an alternative approach that studies the institutional norms and practices of the advertising industry via ethnographic and historical methods.

Finally in this section, Chapter 10 by Eric Arnould (University of Arizona) questions another frequently made assumption about the inescapability of the market and lack of consumer agency. Taking as his focus the question 'Can consumers escape the market?', Eric interrogates some of the sociological dimensions of each of the component words of this phrase in an effort to assess the meaningfulness of the question. Among many other things, he suggests that the concept of agency is conceptually problematic and proposes that the anti-consumption ideology that seems to underly the overarching question is in fact a class-based ideology, one that is consistent with a long history of reformist ideology in the UK and USA ultimately traceable to our common Calvinist heritage. He uses his discussions to consider how the fundamental question of materiality and objectification tends to get unhelpfully bundled with markets and marketing in some critical sociology.

All the chapters in Part Two raise highly thought-provoking conceptual and theoretical issues and overturn many existing preconceptions. To be truly effective, however, critique needs to bring about some type of change, not only in ways of thinking, but also in ways of doing.

The chapters in Part Three – *Effecting Change through Critique: Social and Environmental Issues* – all explore key issues around effecting social and environmental change. In Chapter 11, Ross Gordon, Gerard Hastings, Linda McDermott and Pierre Siquier discuss the contribution to Critical Marketing that Social Marketing can make. They critically examine the effects of commercial marketing on the health and welfare of society and how these same marketing principles can be used to resolve social and health problems and to influence policy decision-making. Overall they argue that social marketing provides a coherent framework for marketers to think of the broader societal implications of their activities.

In Chapter 12, Kathy Hamilton (University of Strathclyde) argues that interest in the societal consequences of marketing does not appear to extend the
same degree of legitimacy to all consumer populations and that disadvantaged
consumer groups often remain excluded or at least under-represented in this
research stream. She wants to see critical marketers paying more attention to
these groups. Positioning her work alongside recent calls for 'transformative'
consumer research, she discusses how research of this nature aims to make a
positive difference in the lives of consumers, not only enhancing quality of life,
but also providing marginalized consumers with a voice.

Environmental sustainability is another pressing societal issue and Chapter
13, by Ken Peattie (University of Cardiff), raises key issues around the challenges that face marketers in implementing sustainable marketing. Ken highlights how progress towards sustainability calls for a radical change in how we
live and think and how marketers need to confront their assumptions about the
goals towards which they are working and the means they use to achieve these.
To this end, he makes suggestions for re-thinking and re-mixing the marketing
vision and proposes ways to 're-tool' marketing for sustainability.

In Chapter 14, Ingrid Kajzer Mitchell continues the central theme of effecting change through critique as she sets out to illuminate our understanding of
some of the fundamental change processes that occur when we seek to rethink
our practices in the light of contemporary environmental and social problems.
She discusses a series of change initiatives where professionals were invited
to subvert dominant marketing logic in order to think differently about products, consumers and the role of marketing itself.

Finally, in Chapter 15, Robin Wensley raises issues of relevance as he asks
can and should Critical Marketing influence practice and policy? In considering this question, he brings us back to what has been a recurrent theme
throughout the book, our own reflexivity as critical marketers. Importantly, he
reminds us that, if we are to espouse a critical approach to our own field of
study, we must to some degree at least, apply this to ourselves as well and
consider how any intervention in practice or policy is legitimized in terms of
our intentions and our own knowledge claims. He concludes (thankfully!)
that there is a clear basis for Critical Marketing to influence both policy and
practices as well as to achieve an indirect impact via our teaching practices. In
establishing a more cohesive identity for Critical Marketing, we hope that this
book will also play its part in that influence.

References

Alvesson, M. and Willmott, H. (eds) (1992). *Critical Management Studies*.
    London: Sage.
Andreasen, A.R. (1995). *Marketing Social Change*. San Francisco: Jossey-Bass.
Bahktin, M. (1984/1965). *Rabelais and His World*, trans. H. Iswolsky.
    Bloomington: Indiana Press.

Belk, R.W. (1995). 'Studies in the new consumer behaviour'. In D. Miller (ed.), *Acknowledging Consumption: A Review of New Studies*. London: Routledge, pp. 8–95.

Bristor, J.M. and Fischer, E. (1993). 'Feminist thought: implications for consumer research'. *Journal of Consumer Research*, 19(March), 518–536.

Burrell, G. and Morgan, G. (1979/1992). *Sociological Paradigms and Organisational Analysis*. Alsershot: Ashgate.

Burton, D. (2001). 'Critical marketing theory'. *European Journal of Marketing*, 35(5/6), 722–743.

Catterall, M., Maclaran, P. and Stevens, L. (2000). *Marketing and Feminism: Current Issues and Research*. London: Routledge.

Catterall, M., Maclaran, P. and Stevens, L. (2002). 'Critical reflection in the marketing curriculum'. *Journal of Marketing Education*, 24(3), 184–192.

Cooper, C. (1995). 'Ideology, hegemony and accounting discourse: a case study of the National Union of Journalists'. *Critical Perspectives on Accounting*, 6, 175–209.

Derrida, J. (1978). *Writing and Difference*. Chicago: University of Chicago Press.

Firat, A.F. and Venkatesh, A. (1995). 'Liberatory postmodernism and the reenchantment of consumption'. *Journal of Consumer Research*, 22(December), 239–267.

Fournier, V. and Grey, C. (2000). 'At the critical moment: conditions and prospects of critical management studies'. *Human Relations*, 53(1), 7–32.

Hetrick, W.P. and Lozada, H.R. (1999). 'Theory, ethical critique and the experience of marketing'. In D. Brownlie, M. Saren, R. Wensley and R. Whittington (eds), *Rethinking Marketing*. London: Sage.

Hill, R.P. (2001). *Surviving in a Material World: The Lived Experience of People in Poverty*. Notre Dame, Indiana: University of Notre Dame Press.

Holman, D. (2000). 'Contemporary models of management education in the UK'. *Management Learning*, 32(2), 197–217.

Kilbourne, E.E. (2004). 'Sustainable communication and the dominant social paradigm: can they be integrated?' *Marketing Theory*, 4(3), 187–208.

L'Etang, J. and Pieczka, M. (1996). *Critical Perspectives in Public Relations*. London: International Thomson.

Marion, G. (2004). *L'Idéologie Marketing*. Paris: Eyrolles.

Murray, J.B. and Ozanne, J.L. (1991). 'The critical imagination: emancipatory interests in consumer research'. *Journal of Consumer Research*, 18(September), 129–144.

Smith, N.C. and Quelch, J.A. (1993). *Ethics in Marketing*. Irwin, Homewood, IL.

Part I

Being a Critical Marketer: Reflections from the Field

1

Critical Research in Marketing: An Armchair Report

Linda M. Scott

I admit I experienced ironic amusement when asked to address the question, 'What exactly *is* critical marketing research?' in my talk for the ESRC Doctoral Symposium. I chuckled that marketing doctoral students put such a question to their advisors because I had recently asked the same of several colleagues and they too expressed uncertainty about what that term really meant. I already knew there was no answer that could command easy consensus.

As a rhetorician, I am disinclined to advocate 'correct' definitions, but instead prefer to locate the meaning of any term in the common usage of the community in which it appears. Being sensitive to the historical construction of academic inquiry, I also would rather point to the current moment in the practice of critical research, specifically in marketing, as a distillation of past theory, current agendas, evident mistakes, and future potential, than adhere too slavishly to some canonical body of theory or erstwhile political perspectives borrowed from other fields. So, I decided to approach the question by asking a sampling of community members what they thought 'critical marketing' was.

I assembled an informal list, comprised to some extent of the usual suspects (for instance, people who had already written on critical research in the marketing literature), but I also included scholars who work in other research streams, but whose general opinions I respect. And, I included a scattering of people who are not based in business schools but who have had enough interaction with marketing to have become opinion leaders. Some I asked are senior academics – journal editors and ACR Fellows, for instance, were well represented on my list – and some are new to the field. This was by no means an exhaustive list: only 41 people were on it. Because Jonathan Schroeder and I were dividing up the world, so to speak, for the speeches at the workshop, I only included North Americans. So, obviously, I failed to ask many who would have had important things to say. But the lecture was coming up soon and I needed a quick take on the question, so I asked a list of people I knew well enough to answer me right away, even during the Christmas break, and promised myself to bill this survey for what it is: a quick-and-dirty convenience sample.

In order to frame the parameters of the question and give permission for multiple viewpoints, I told the list I had been having conversations with several colleagues and found their ideas about 'critical research' varied among four definitions:

1 To some people, 'critical' just means 'interpretive' or 'qualitative'.
2 To some people, 'Critical' is capitalized and it explicitly means 'Marxist'.
3 To some people, 'critical' refers to a stance that is concerned with larger social issues or using marketing for socially progressive purposes.
4 To some people, 'critical' means research that is critical of more mainstream approaches to the study of markets and marketing.

Twenty-five people responded to my query and only a handful of them are quoted here. Importantly, none of them knew in advance what my conclusions would be or how I would ultimately use what they wrote. Therefore, though they all gave their permission to be quoted, the presence of a name here in no way indicates endorsement of my own perspective on critical marketing research.

As the emails began filling my inbox, it became clear that many answers had been strongly influenced by the personal experiences of the writers. The notion of 'critical marketing', it seems, is a flashpoint for many, holding the potential to ignite not only on politics, but also on methods, rigour, evidence, and academic freedom. Several expressed anger, disdain, or fear of reprisals if they criticized the critical. Others expressed passion and a strong sense of urgency for a global initiative. It seems important to recognize up front that this essay is built on the off-the-cuff, but often intensely felt, perspectives of those who were asked. Hence, I have called it 'an armchair report'.

In order to frame my own synthesis of these motley responses, I want to describe the particular armchair in which I sit. Though I have recently moved to England, my exposure to the situation in Europe is so limited that I can only speak from the American experience with critical research. Even in the US marketing academy, I have been an outsider, albeit one with some pretty good connections to insiders. Until very recently, I had never worked in a business school, though I have built my career by publishing in the marketing literature. All this time, I have worked out of a multidisciplinary appointment in the Communications College at the University of Illinois. My background, however, gives me a fortuitous perch from which to comment on this particular question at this specific time.

My own training is in arts theory, especially literary theory. In the American academy, literary studies, rather than the social sciences, was the original field of entry for critical theory. Because 'critical theory' and 'criticism' are what all literary types believe they do, it has long been the convention there to capitalize 'Critical' when referring specifically to a stance informed by Marxism (including theoretical influences ranging broadly from Marx and Engels to the Frankfurt and Birmingham Schools to Althusser and Gramsci). I will be following that convention here, for reasons I think will become clear.

Critical Theory was carried along when literary theory – including semiotics, rhetoric and poststructuralism – became fashionable in the 1980s as a lens for examining a range of cultural forms, but especially advertising and film. The combination bore a new subdiscipline, 'cultural studies', which was sometimes housed in English departments and sometimes in communications schools. I spent nearly 15 years working in a cultural studies environment considered by many to be paradigmatic: the University of Illinois was home to both the Institute for Communications Research, where I held an appointment, and a weekly series of salons called the Unit for Criticism and Interpretive Theory, where I was 'a regular'.

Both the literary approach and cultural studies were identified with qualitative research and, in communications where I was housed, this produced a confrontation over the practice of science and the use of quantitative methods very similar to the one that occurred later in marketing. In some ways, the identification of cultural studies with qualitative data grew predictably from its origins in English departments, where statistics are nonexistent, science anathema, and questions of evidence, to say the least, narrowly circumscribed. The influence of poststructuralism, along with works from the history and philosophy of science like Thomas Kuhn's *The Structure of Scientific Revolutions* (1962), gave a language and a strategy with which to take on the precepts of scientific research. However, though the fight over methods was intense, the focus on a Critique of capitalism (and its cultural forms) was the most salient feature in the rise of cultural studies.

Indeed, cultural studies was so often characterized by a Critical perspective that, by the 1990s, the two had become synonymous. Ultimately, the Critical agenda had to be clearly reflected (using whatever Theory was currently fashionable) in any scholarly work before it could be accepted for publication. Those who attempted to write outside the prevailing perspective or, heaven forbid, to disagree with it, were simply frozen out. On the ground, colleagues who seemed to think differently from the ingroup were, at best, ridiculed as being in need of reeducation. Thus, freedom of inquiry became substantially constrained. The growing attention to political correctness infected even the classroom, where some students chafed under the unspoken but palpable limitations on their freedom of expression. Subordinating evidence to politics slowly became the order of the day, leading to a pronounced erosion of both critical thought and liberal education. The Critique, with its unrelentingly negative hermeneutic, had a further tendency to look like despair, scoffing at hope and disdaining those who sought solutions that fell short of revolution.

Two areas in which the Critical turn had its most public successes and its most blazing failures were the analysis of images and the emergence of women's studies programmes. Since my research interests cluster around imagery and women's history – and since I held appointments in both women's studies and art at Illinois – I was in a position to observe both triumphs and tragedies.

Critical Theory has a perspective on visuals that is at once naïve and paranoid. Though many canonical works in cultural studies involve the analysis of images – John Berger's *Ways of Seeing* (1973), Laura Mulvey's 'Visual pleasure and narrative cinema' in *Screen* (1975), and Judith Williamson's *Decoding Advertisements* (1979) are three famous examples – the lack of expertise or narrow range of evidence that too often marked such works eventually contributed to a growing sense that Critical research was inclined to make grandiose claims on insufficient grounds and without consideration of alternative explanations. The iconophobia that characterized this discourse had an unpleasant Calvinist ring to it – and tended to alienate many whose field of study really *was* imagery (e.g. art and art history).

In the USA, women's studies has experienced extraordinary growth and institutional success since its inception in the 1970s. The New Left and Critical Theory, it can be argued, found their most unambiguous success in American academic feminism: the typical parsing notwithstanding, all the feminist theories acceptable in the academy are antimarket and anticapitalist (the term 'liberal feminist' became almost as insulting an epithet as 'antifeminist'). Women's studies remains one of the most popular undergraduate majors, in spite of a growing chorus of criticism from within the discipline itself. (Daphne Patai and Noretta Koertge's *Professing Feminism* (1995) is one example), from the emergent Third Wave (for instance, Rene Denfeld's *The New Victorians* (1995)), as well as, predictably, from the radical right. The range of critics belies the consistency of the critique: that women's studies has become exclusive, hostile to dissent, blinkered by politics whether the question is tenure decisions or reading lists, and stubbornly set against traditional questions of evidence, especially where the documentation at hand is scientific or quantitative.

As the Critical view moved into fields like sociology with strong traditions reliant on statistics (as in, for instance, demography) and research funding more closely tied to government, the question of evidence seemed to me to intensify, as did the acrimony over required political views. The publication and promotion scandals, the paradigm schisms that destroyed departments – these became the stuff of academic legend. The political too often became personal.

Keep in mind that this was all occurring against a historical backdrop bearing the most contradictory evidence imaginable: the fall of the Soviet Union, followed quickly by the market conversion of nearly every other Marxist regime in the world, and the declaration by a generation of economists that the ideal of a centrally planned economy had finally been proven unworkable.

Yet the situation in business schools was also eerily out of touch with reality. As critiques appearing in vehicles ranging from the *Harvard Business Review* to the *Chronicle of Higher Education* have observed, the American business school had grown, during this same period, into an insular institution of technocrats. In the face of corporate financial scandals at home and an exploding market economy that threatened to destabilize societies and environments all over the world, American business education and research had focused so narrowly their sights were now sunk deep, ostrich-like, and they could offer little to meet the challenges of either practice or ethics. Indeed, in marketing, the research ideal for 30 years has been producing practical tools that will indiscriminately help industry sell more stuff. I cannot imagine a situation that cries out more clearly for a critical perspective than these material realities.

Interestingly, marketing focused narrowly on science in a desperate bid for academic credibility. My own sense is that the academy outside business schools has no respect at all for their research specifically because it so totally lacks critical perspective. Regardless of the level of scientific rigour that may be flaunted, the determination of business schools to be the unquestioning handmaids of industry make them a laughing stock at the campus level of most universities. Never mind that business academics have the highest salaries and most generous endowments – in the eyes of their more traditional colleagues, these are just the material evidence of souls being sold.

Marketing has inherited this moment. With cultural theory impinging on the discipline as it has over the past 20 years, I think it was inevitable that a critical (if not Critical) point of view on markets would begin to emerge. Yet coming also on the heels of what has happened elsewhere in the academy, some ambivalence is just as inevitably created among scholars committed to positive change but also to rigorous research and mutual respect. I thought it understandable that the responses I received were often contradictory, but impassioned.

Responses to the suggestion that 'critical research' merely referred to interpretive research were summed up by Rich Lutz in only two words: 'NO WAY'. Rich, along with many others, referred to Marxism (whether or not capitalized) as a primary identifying feature of what they saw as Critical research (again, whether or not they themselves used a capital 'C'). Several also specifically declared the roots of Critical work to be in either the Frankfurt School, the Birmingham School, or both. Some listed related high theorists, like Althusser or Baudrillard, while others cited examples from our own literature:

> From my perspective 'critical' has the broader meaning of 'critical theory' in general. By this I mean the body of theory based on the work of people like Gramsci and Foucault which questions the nature of the work we do as social scientists. That means asking who benefits from what we do, and how we are, ourselves, part of the ideological apparatus of capitalism. For me that means broadening the

scope of research ethics to consider the historical power relationships in which our work is embedded.

Rick Wilk

... I see it as related to critical theory, the Frankfurt school, Julie
[Ozanne] and Jeff [Murray]'s work (when talking about work within
our ACR/*JCR* world), the Birmingham School, and thus tangentially
small-M (neo) Marxism. In a more general and less lit-bound sense,
I see it as research that is *critical* of contemporary (particularly laissez-
faire, unrestricted) capitalism. It looks at contemporary capitalism
and capitalist/consumer culture with an eye to questions of social
equity, environmental effects, personal freedom, international distribution of resources, and social progress.

Rob Kozinets

Interestingly, several others besides Kozinets specifically located the term in a
broadly Marxist tradition, but also provided further elaboration that many of
us would see as offering a much larger scope:

My view is that the word refers to a 'small m' Marxist sociological
orientation, in which the point of research is to confound the wishes
of elites that the sources of their hegemony be kept unexamined.

John Deighton

Deighton's definition was my personal favourite, partly because you can see
that the word 'elites' has the potential to encompass not just the leaders of
corporate capitalism, but those of other institutions, including the church, the
government, the patriarchy, and even the academy – all of whom figure in the
power relationships of both the market for goods and the market for ideas.
Cultural studies work has tended to downplay, if not downright ignore,
these other manifestations of power, in favour of a monocular focus on the
market as the most oppressive force in world history. This has been true even
in places like women's studies, where the logical focus on patriarchy in all
its forms is usually subordinated by attributing the oppression of women to
capitalism.

Craig Thompson, after warning against the circularity of trying to define
'critical' in terms of 'Marxian' only to confront the question of what counts
as 'Marxian' (which I can attest was the topic of many a cruel and pointless
debate at Illinois), also offered a broader, institutionally focused concept:

I tend to think of a critical analysis as one that explores institutional
power relationships (and struggles) and their role in the operation of
social hierarchies, differential control of capital (in its various forms),
and the asymmetrical distribution of resources. So, a critical marketing analysis would focus on institutional relationships that are

embedded in market relationships (involving brands, consumers, commercial discourses and settings, etc.).

Russ Belk listed both journalistic examples and current events, but also offered a narrative that accounted for an evolution away from specifically Marxist constructs:

> ... I see this area as having evolved from the Frankfurt school, especially with the demise of communism, to a perspective that is critical of the ill-effects of global capitalism. The WTO/WB/IMF/ G8 protests are one manifestation. MoveOn is another. *No Logo* is another. Subaltern movements are yet another. Others might stretch the label critical to a variety of other neo-liberal causes like environmentalism, downsizing/VS, dematerializing, etc., but I don't see these as sufficiently radical. Perhaps eco-sabotage could slip in. But most broadly I would see critical research and scholarship in marketing as challenging the neglected evils of the capitalist system, usually focusing on the seller side, but potentially focusing on the buyer side as well.

Whether neoliberal agendas are to be included under the rubric of critical marketing is, I predict, going to be at the heart of the matter going forward.

Theoretical sophistication also is already evident as a measure of membership under this umbrella: one respondent wrote, 'I am all for pluralism but sometimes you just gotta tell people that they need to read and gain some knowledge before they make authoritative pronouncements.' Several people mentioned the need to be well versed in the work of specific theorists. Already emergent, I'm sorry to say, is the belief that colleagues who don't agree with the Critical stance are simply uninformed, politically suspect, or cursed with a poor ability to comprehend complex social thought. The implication is that this view of the world has a monopoly on truth. That, to me, sounds too much like logical positivism. And fundamentalist Christianity.

Eileen Fischer, among others, offered a definition that focused on a challenge to the things as they are, including power relationships and prior assumptions in research. She also offers a helpful distinction between Critical qualitative research and other forms of qualitative inquiry:

> I think of critical research as research that challenges the status quo. That is, it holds up for examination assumptions and ideologies and power structures and practices that are taken for granted and that tend to reinforce patterns of stratification or privilege. Critical research is thus differentiated from constructivist (or hermeneutic) traditions of research that focus more on understanding understandings harboured by particular groups or individuals. Critical research looks at individuals or groups in social context and is concerned with the ways that the social context valourizes some practices assumptions,

interpretations of reality, etc. over others, often in ways that protect vested power interests. It doesn't have to advocate an alternative set of assumptions or practices, though some critical research does. Critical research need not be, but may be, qualitative.

Eileen's caveat about method clearly anticipates an environment in which most people expect critical research to be qualitative. I'm inclined to agree with Eileen that it is unnecessarily restrictive to think that Critical work may not be quantitative.

However, past confrontations between Critical scholars and scientists over the conduct of research were also evident in these remarks:

> It's my understanding that the milder form of Critical Theory holds that social science research methods are so fallible that they cannot produce valid findings, while the stronger form of Critical Theory holds that all researchers (including researchers in the physical and biological sciences) are so misled by their racist, sexist, capitalist biases that their supposedly scientific findings are nothing more than easily deconstructed propaganda. From either point of view, a critical stance toward academic marketing research would seem to be that, except as an easy target for deconstruction, none of it is worth reading.
>
> Bill Wells

One scholar offered a definition that, as with the literary critics who first confronted 'the Critical' in America, probably describes what we all think we're supposed to be doing:

> I think of critical inquiry as one where one strives to think fully and deeply about a problem. To my mind, critical thinking means probing an idea to comprehend and elaborate on it. The effort is intended to gain unusual insight into a problem or idea, which includes placing it in larger contexts, and considering it from multiple perspectives. It is also to see its implications and its underpinnings and antecedents. It is to note similarities to and differences between other ideas and issues.
>
> Larry Garber

Interestingly, Eric Arnould pointed out that this kind of definition also applies to science – and that the quandary of definition for marketing scholarship probably has roots in the past emphasis on practice:

> On the other hand, it is kind of a sad commentary or perhaps merely a reflection of the professional slant to marketing that we need an adjectival form. Since scientific inquiry is by definition critical inquiry, to the extent that marketing has pretensions to science, it should

entail critical inquiry. That means fundamental constructs should be subject to critique.

Jeff Murray, however, was anxious to stipulate the meaning of 'critical':

> It is interesting, there is 'critical,' which everyone is, e.g., 'your Cronbach's alpha is too low!' And there is 'the critical tradition' which really is something, but for some reason, when we say 'critical' everyone just thinks they can start making stuff up. We don't sit around and say, 'Well, what is your version of the cognitive/behavioral tradition?'

Jeff, of course, has a legitimate interest at stake in trying to make clear that the 'critical' tradition he has written about is clearly delineated and identified properly. I have the same impulse to protect rhetoric (especially against the encroachments of semiotics). However, I feel it is important to point out that, as was the case 30 years ago in literary studies, the appropriation of the term 'critical' for a particular political perspective has negative implications for the entire discourse. This rhetorical move necessarily implies that those scholars who are not theoretically compliant or politically congruent belong in a category marked 'not critical' – which, without further specification, implies that they are not only 'politically incorrect', but also just generally naïve and muddy-headed. Further, such a categorization also places any competing theory in the same bin ('not critical'), which is a rhetorical sleight of hand that many scholars rightly will not tolerate:

> ... for my money, all theory is critical or it's not good for anything. There is a presumption of superiority and specialness that is annoying, as if the critical theory camp somehow has powers of perception and conception that are simply lost on the rest of us. Add this to the fact that much critical theory is (mixed metaphor alert in effect!) boilerplate from the Foucault playbook and something delirious has been accomplished.
>
> Grant McCracken

There was also a clear subset of respondents who held (or alleged on behalf of others) that Critical research itself was shoddy, for reasons of sparse evidence, political grand-standing, fly-by theoretical judgements, or an unwillingness to critically examine *their own* constructs. Tom O'Guinn commented: '[Critical research] is now a term either so varied as to be meaningless, and/or increasingly problematic. Among the reasons: Too much baggage; collapsing under its own weight; too oppressive; and as practiced, intellectually sloppy, occasionally dishonest.' Barbara Phillips remarked on the potential polysemy in the phrase 'critical marketing' to describe the promotion of political agendas through thinly disguised 'research': ' "Critical marketing" usually means radical feminists or Marxists who don't bother to do good scholarship and write bad papers to promote their agenda.'

I want to note in passing that O'Guinn, Wells, and Phillips have each either worked or trained in a communications school. I think this actual experience with how Critical work was practiced may account for their less sanguine attitude towards welcoming the Critical into marketing. I often feel that people in business schools romanticize Critical Theory to the point they are unwilling to acknowledge its warts.

Getting back to the issue of research quality, several cautioned about the use of the term 'rigour' and the narrowness in application the term 'evidence' can have. Nevertheless, my feeling is that cultural studies did grow long on polemics and short on support in a way that ultimately discredited it. Too often, it seemed a Critical writer was ignoring evidence or alternative explanations in order to maintain compliance with political imperatives. It appeared that scholars had to stop being critical in order to be Critical.

This issue will be, I expect, another important one for us. The broadswipe pronouncements about consumers, markets, and media that have been made in cultural studies do not square with the rich, contextualized picture that consumer research has begun to assemble. It will be necessary to ignore much of what we have learned over 30 years to accept accusations blithely made by previous Critical works.

But evidence is always the biggest threat to theory. The messiness of historical details, the particularities of cultural difference, the exquisiteness of situated experience, the force of real action to effect change, all these things present the potential to falsify the grandiose. I have often wondered if this is why the high theories of literature were so late coming to my newly adopted field, history, and, once there, so ambivalently received.

Interestingly, another notable theme in these responses was the assertion that critical perspectives intended to give voice to those who otherwise are excluded:

> I think the essence of critical research, including in marketing and consumer behaviour, is to give voice to constituencies that are marginalized, oppressed, misrepresented, or otherwise neglected by dom-inant paradigms, perspectives, or power bases.
>
> John Schouten

In the 1990s, there was a small crisis in cultural studies in which some writers began to question the way Critical work tended to treat ordinary people as 'cultural dupes' (or sometimes 'cultural dopes'). In many respects, this criticism responded to the practice (borrowed from literature) of writing textual interpretations that simply projected audience manipulation without providing evidence. This arrogant tendency was, to some degree, corrected by challenges coming from scholars working in postcolonial or other subaltern environments. But talking to ordinary people about their responses to culture often created its own problems: their voices don't often reflect the perspectives dictated by Theory. The concept of 'false consciousness' was handy and close by as a theoretically acceptable tool for rejecting such feedback.

Georg Lukàcs (a literary theorist 'by trade') originally developed the concept of 'false consciousness' in his *History and Class Consciousness* (1971) (though first use of this term was by Engels). Lukàcs' aim was to explain why the proletariat did not have a Marxist viewpoint. Sadly, Lukàcs himself probably used this thought to rationalize his own work in enforcing conformity (especially of artists and intellectuals) in Stalinist Russia. 'False consciousness' has since been used in the American academy to dismiss the messy details that come from looking closely at history, listening seriously to members of oppressed groups, or, especially, hearing dissent from other intellectuals.

Ironically, some of the most effective intellectual dissent in cultural studies is now coming from the former Soviet countries, as 'postsocialism'. The ability to adjust our perspectives to accommodate new voices of this sort, as well later historical events, is something that I believe needs to be carefully protected. This, in turn, may also require willingness on our part to adapt or revise Theory – or even to retreat from past thinking.

David Mick, who along with several others (Morris Holbrook, Elizabeth Hirschman) said he had not heard the term much and so was hesitant to comment, offered an idea that seems to fall logically out of what John Schouten said: that critical research in marketing might take an 'antimarketer' view or might engage in advocacy research of some sort:

> ... In thinking about these [critical marketing] papers, they are not actually that 'critical' of established theories but instead open a window on people who 'are not like us' – the homeless, students from low-income blue-collar homes who do NOT go to university – and I think these papers challenge our assumptions of who 'consumers' are. These are just two examples that resonate with me. ... in the best or truest sense, I think 'critical marketing' means taking on unstated assumptions that lie dormant in marketing theory and marketing research. In the past, these have tended to come from a Marxist (e.g., 'capitalism is beneficial to society') or feminist (e.g., 'the portrayal of women in advertising is just normal') perspective, but these specific ideologies don't have to underlie critical marketing.
>
> David Mick

John Sherry, arguing for a 'big tent' definition of the term, suggested a general direction that, it was clear, many of these respondents would support:

> I think it's a polyvocal term, as you've indicated, an umbrella concept that embraces 'critique' in all its aspects. I tend to use the term mostly to hold marketing accountable for its intentional exclusions and its unintended or unanticipated consequences, as both a discipline and a practice: Here are some of marketing's shortfalls, here are some ways they can be rectified, and this is the way practice might be reformed.

The problem for some will, I expect, in the end circle back to the twin tests mentioned earlier; that is, is this essentially neoliberal programme 'radical enough' or is it theoretically sound (or pure) enough? Consider the following example. Jose Rosa, writing me after just debarking a long trip to Chile, remarked:

> Critical marketing, like societal marketing, is one of those well-intentioned labels that was quickly high-jacked by multiple interests. My take on the term is that it refers to the use of marketing tactics to advance the views and preferences of those who by using critical perspectives and methodologies have identified serious (or not so serious) flaws in our social schemata, or alternative perspectives that can produce social welfare and still be viable for businesses to undertake. The interest in responsible marketing to the 4.5 billion poor in the world by creating products that will be beneficial and can be marketed responsibly is one example of what I call critical marketing. Products aimed at poor people that can be sold without exploitation while at the same time giving them the sense of self-awareness that comes from making consumption decisions can be developed, but they require a perspective that is more profound, complicated, and respectful than what we are accustomed to finding in the marketing planning meetings at companies like P&G and GM.

Such a sentiment, though I personally find it laudable, is in direct contradiction to the central precepts of Critical Theory, as it is has been understood and practiced, at least in the USA these past 30 years. The inherent conundrum can be read in Russ Belk's observation that: 'To me, critical marketing is an oxymoron. Marketing panders, it is not critical. There are critical scholars in marketing, however . . . .'

The need to address the practice of marketing – in research, in action, or in teaching – is thus likely to pose a key point of difference between how Critical research unfolds in our own field as opposed to elsewhere. Others have had the luxury of being able to critique but not engage. We are not so rich in options. We have to engage – or live in total hypocrisy.

One legitimate agenda may be to undertake a critique of the Critique, rather than meekly shouldering all its antimarket assumptions and accusations. My research has suggested to me that Critical perspectives very often rest on a dubious historical narrative. As Eric Arnould pointed out, these same perspectives often wear cross-cultural blinders as well:

> Let there also be a marketing that is itself a critique of say, planned economies. Following in the shoes of much greater thinkers than I in anthropology, I have argued for instance that marketing is a long-standing category of economic action, not just something invented by agricultural distributors in the 1920s in the US.

As people in armchairs often do, I spent a lot of time reflecting on what I had heard. In the months since, I have also had several face-to-face exchanges that I think bear reporting briefly:

- At the ESRC Doctoral Symposium, Jonathan Schroeder recounts his conversation with a literature professor, who questioned his commitment to Critical work because 'after all, your students are just going to go to work for major corporations'. Jonathan's spot-on retort: 'So are yours.'
- After the symposium, I ask Miriam Catterall about the status of 'critical research' in the UK. I am dumbfounded to hear that marketing is behind management and accounting in moving to a critical perspective in British business schools. It is a wonderfully hopeful sign, but I must admit that, to me, 'critical accounting' is an inscrutable term.
- Sitting out a snowstorm at a bar in Boulder later that winter, Lisa Penaloza and I consider what will emerge if corporations start taking the world's ills into their own hands. We agree that, even if at first blush it seems like 'corporate social responsibility', we are not so sure we want the Phil Knights of the planet setting policy.
- Barreling through the budding hills of Virginia with Julie Ozanne, I discover that we share a common concern: the tendency for traditional Critical Theory to take an unrelieved negative view of the world and to devalue activist efforts as 'reformism' (or 'neoliberalism'). We agree that we simply are not content to sit on our hands and 'wait for the Revolution'.
- At the ACR Gender Conference in Edinburgh, my doctoral students, Catherine Coleman and Katherine Sredl, give talks that challenge the Second Wave feminists' critique of advertising for having constructed female consumers as malleable, weak, unable to resist. Katherine remarks to me that one of the advantages of a Third Wave perspective (which is less market-unfriendly than the Second Wave) for us as consumer behaviourists is that 'we can stop pretending we don't know what we know.'
- In the first 2 weeks of my new job at Oxford, we interview for two positions. The candidates include several anthropologists who have studied market relationships in Africa and between Africa and the UK. One of the things that is becoming very clear to me is that cultural studies' erstwhile opposition between 'market' and 'no market' is too simplistic to address either the local viewpoint or the geopolitical complexities. In particular, the unrelenting focus on industrial capitalism as the major source of oppression in the world fails to encompass the profoundly patriarchal practices of traditional, agricultural economies.
- One late August night in the French Alps, Pauline Maclaran, Darach Turley, my husband Jim and I sip some brandy and talk about the religious experiences of our youth. We come from vastly different backgrounds – a Protestant who grew up amid religious violence in Belfast, an Irishman who gave up the priesthood, a Croatian Catholic from steel-mill Chicago, and a Southern Baptist from the Civil Rights era. Despite these historical differences, we share a distaste for zealotry of any kind as the result of our early

experiences. Pauline tells of the crashing moment when she realized for the first time that the Catholics saw their own position as perfectly correct (just as the Protestants did). We nod; we all had this experience, only against different backdrops. Darach uses a term that haunts me for the next few days: 'the relativist imperative'.

The global market and its media have brought the suffering of the world closer to us all. In proximity, the details of difference can be daunting. But it is important to heed both the differences and the commonalities among the situations we observe – and not prematurely force everything we see through a single scope. And, I think, it is crucial to maintain hope, because without it, we will not be able to innovate, challenge, and create on the scale this moment demands. A negative set of glasses ultimately leaves us only in the dark.

To that end, I think it's important to invoke the broader historical world background, not only as a charge for moving forward with a globally responsible agenda towards markets, but for holding Critical Theory in a critical light. Human society was miserable, violent, and unequal long before industrialization. Indeed, the really oppressive institutions in history – religion, race, patriarchy – are still very much with us and we are wrong if we ignore or discount them. Much has also changed about industrial capitalism in the 140 years since Karl Marx published *Das Kapital*. And, much has gone down in the history of applying Marx's ideas to the social and economic organization of societies. Max Horkheimer founded the Frankfurt School in 1930, just as Joseph Stalin was succeeding Lenin; the path of the School away from closely followed Marxist principles coincides perfectly with the unfolding terror in Soviet Russia. Stuart Hall became the Director of the Birmingham School, intending to bring it back to Marxist orthodoxy, in 1968 – the same year that Soviet tanks rolled into Czechoslovakia to accomplish the same purpose. The rise of Critical Theory in English departments in the USA dovetails almost exactly with the Cultural Revolution in China, while the heyday of cultural studies co-occurred with the fall of the Soviets, the dismantling of the Berlin Wall, and the horrific 'heads up' provided by Tiananmen Square. So ostrich behaviour in the American academy has not been limited to business schools. To argue at this point that the only genuinely emancipatory concepts can come out of a mental apparatus that has been used (and was sometimes invented) to justify depriving, imprisoning, and executing millions is, at best, viciously myopic. The connections between Marxism and world events cannot, in my mind, be wiped away merely by using a small m.

I also think it is helpful to remember that, despite its gross inequities and shocking excesses, the world market is providing more people with a better standard of living and more economic autonomy than any social regime in history. With that more optimistic view, it may, perhaps, be permissible to allow for a more liberal and pluralist perspective to prevail at this juncture. To some degree, in fact, this would be the most radical step of all. I am inclined to agree with Grant McCracken, who wrote to me that, 'The really critical people are, in my opinion, the ones who occupy the excluded middle between mainstream economistic discourse and the predictabilities of the critical camp.' Revolutions, once they occur, can seldom be directed towards progressive outcomes – indeed, they can seldom be directed at all. And few of our colleagues are prepared to take the nihilistic view that a 'neoliberal' attempt at changing the impact and direction of markets is less tenable than cocooning up in an intellectual vacuum and waiting for the sky to fall.

Breaking out of the blinders of a service-to-industry mandate is long overdue in marketing. As small and marginal a group as we may be, I think we owe it to ourselves and to the field, not to mention the world, to try and rethink (and rework) markets into a more humane shape. But the pressing need for a coherent critique of capitalist excesses among marketing scholars runs into some contradictions when faced with the bleak directives typical of traditionally Critical work. To be sure, Critical Theory includes concepts, terms, frameworks, and lenses with lasting value. But it has also left behind a trail of shoddy research and collegial unpleasantness. And, as traditionally conceived, this body of Theory would cast 'critical marketing scholars' as self-delusional sell-outs and not much else. Marketing scholars need to re-evaluate Critical Theory carefully before adopting it, unchallenged and undisturbed (i.e. uncritically), into our own field. So it seems to me appropriate that the term 'critical research in marketing' is still in play in marketing. That liminal instant in which a new definition, and therefore a fresh ethic, may be served, is still hanging in the air.

Works Mentioned

Berger, J. (1973). *Ways of Seeing*. New York: Viking.

Denfeld, R. (1995). *The New Victorians*. New York: Warner.

Kuhn, T.S. (1962). *The Structure of Scientific Revolutions*. Chicago: University of Chicago Press.

Lukàcs, G. (trans. 1971). *History and Class Consciousness*. Cambridge: MIT Press.

Mulvey, L. (1975). 'Visual pleasure and narrative cinema'. *Screen*, 16(3), Autumn.

Patai, D. and Koertge, N. (1995). *Professing Feminism*. New York: Basic Books.

Williamson, J. (1979). *Decoding Advertisements*. London: Boyars.

2

Critical Marketing: Insights for Informed Research and Teaching

Jonathan E. Schroeder

This chapter offers insights into critical marketing by examining the role of critique in consumer research, management studies, and broader intellectual traditions. It draws upon the views of a range of marketing researchers – all engaged in critical work – to contextualize and animate what constitutes critical marketing scholarship. It calls for careful reflection on the goals and gains of critical marketing, offers useful working definitions, and derives several guidelines for critically informed research via examples and anecdotes. After a brief review of what it means to be critical, I turn to commentary from several scholars engaged in critical research, drawing out implications for research and teaching, and providing some directions.

Preliminary, Personal Introduction

Some kind of introduction seems in order, if only to frame this discussion with a few biographical details that may illuminate my own stance regarding critical marketing. I consider myself a social scientist whose work went through its own critical turn, reflecting broader intellectual currents inside and outside marketing scholarship over the past 20 years. My doctoral training is in experimental social psychology from University of California at Berkeley, where I was fortunate enough to meet Franco Nicosia, one of the architects of the field of consumer research, and an early proponent of sociological approaches to consumption (see Nicosia and Mayer, 1976). At Berkeley, I also met Alladi Venkatesh – he was on sabbatical reading social theory and postmodernism – who has encouraged me throughout my career (for a glimpse into his recent work, see Venkatesh and Meamber, 2006).

My dissertation was a rather typical social influence study, looking at advertising in terms of social psychological variables. My first faculty position was at the University of Rhode Island, where Nik and Ruby Dholakia introduced me to the macromarketing group, an important critical centre for theoretical work in marketing (see, for example, Dholakia and Schroeder, 2001; Firat et al., 1987). My early work with Barbara Stern introduced me to the possibilities of humanities-informed consumer research, and I slowly began to incorporate cultural issues – particularly art history and aesthetics – into my research (Stern and Schroeder, 1994). During a sabbatical in 1998, I was a Senior Research Fellow at Wesleyan University's Center for the Humanities, where I joined a seminar on Culture and Visual Representation, rubbing shoulders with leading scholars from Art History, English, History, and Theatre, all interested in visual issues, and somewhat willing to welcome an interloper from a business school into their midst. Shortly thereafter, Pierre Guillet de Monthoux – who had set up the European Centre for Art and Management – and was gathering together like-minded researchers, and organizing seminars and conferences – invited me to Stockholm. I stayed in Sweden for 5 years, and wrote my book *Visual Consumption* (2002) during that time, feeling a bit liberated from the journal-centric US system. I joined the University of Exeter's marketing group in 2004, and set about to continue its critical tradition, built up by the former chair Richard Elliott, and his colleagues James Fitchett, Andrea Davies, and Avi Shankar – all of whom have moved on, to be replaced by a new group of like-minded consumer researchers, including Janet Borgerson, Alan Bradshaw, Robin Canniford, and Eminigül Karababa.

Together with Janet Borgerson, I have published a stream of papers with a critical agenda (e.g. Borgerson and Schroeder, 2002; Schroeder and Borgerson, 2005), and continue to draw inspiration from interdisciplinary theory. However, I am a bit hesitant to employ the critical term to characterize my research, as it throws up so many red flags (critical is often simplistically linked to communism), particularly for marketing and management colleagues. However, I did dub a recent method paper 'Critical Visual Analysis' (Schroeder, 2006). All right, enough about me, but I hope this helps situate my own perspective, before we turn to my eloquent colleagues.

Critical

There are many strands of critical scholarship. Criticism, per se, forms a basic concern for many humanities disciplines, and criticism underlies much academic work. In particular, critical thinking refers to a movement within philosophy that influenced the teaching of philosophy and forms the basis for many foundation courses in a variety of fields. Moreover, a specific strain of theory, the Critical School of Social Theory, commonly called the Frankfurt School, emerged in the 20th century, concerned with critique of prevailing structures, values, and rationalities in society (see Arato and Gebhardt, 1978; Craib 1992, for a review). Other critical movements include the work of French theorist Michel Foucault (e.g. Gutting, 1994), Critical Race Theory (e.g. Gordon, 1997), and Feminism (e.g. Bristor and Fischer, 1993) to name but a few (see Linda Scott's contribution to this volume). Furthermore, criticism looms large within humanities, as in Literary Criticism, Art Criticism, Film Criticism, and so forth. With varying influence and effort, each of these critical dimensions has encroached upon management scholarship, and inform much culturally inflected work within marketing and consumer research.

Critical Management

Management scholar John Mingers (2000) identifies four different aspects of critical thinking that are central to management education:

1 the critique of rhetoric,
2 the critique of traditional thinking,
3 the critique of authority,
4 the critique of objectivity.

Critical thinking is most often associated with the *critique of rhetoric*, logical analysis within a broader scepticism towards statements and rhetoric. This type of critical thinking should be reflective and able to propose alternatives. The second type of critical thinking involves questioning tradition and custom – 'the way we do things around here'. Thus, the *critique of tradition* provides the necessary foundation for change, questioning long-standing, yet perhaps ineffective theories and practices, and developing new knowledge and traditions. The *critique of authority* operates at a deeper level to foster scepticism of one dominant viewpoint. This aspect of critical thinking is perhaps most difficult for the teacher or manager to foster. In a world of multiple stakeholders and cultural diversity, the critique of authority remains a key attribute of critical thinking. The fourth aspect of critical thinking – the *critique of objectivity* – questions 'the validity of knowledge and information that is available, and [recognizes] that it is *never* value-free and objective' (Mingers, 2000). Particularly for marketing scholars, it is essential to realize that information is not value-free, cannot be extricated from culture, and is always becoming outdated.

Critical management represents a fairly well-established perspective, particularly within the UK and continental Europe, with a biannual conference, several devoted journals, and a handful of critically oriented management schools. Although marketing contributes to each of these strands, critical marketing often lags behind the management arena (cf. Alvesson, 1994; Brownlie et al., 1998; Burton, 2001).

How do marketing scholars respond to the idea of critical marketing? To find out, I turned to a non-random, probably (most certainly) not representative, rather idiosyncratic, small sample, based on collegial contacts, research orientation, and a willingness to respond to my email. I think their thoughtful responses provide some clues. In the following sections, I reproduce verbatim comments – with their permission, I might add – from this assortment of marketing scholars that I think help articulate and illuminate critical marketing, and begin the process of establishing some common themes and tenets. I list each contributor's name, title, and affiliation, not to mark out rank and territory, but to document their institutional position and celebrate a few important nodes in the critical marketing network. However, it must be noted that not all respondents feel that their institutions have supported their critical work, so this should not be taken as validation, necessarily.

Critical Marketing: What Is It?

My first query concerned how to locate critical marketing, how to define it, and how these researchers thought about the general idea. The topic is not without some irony, as Gavin Jack, Reader in Marketing at University of Leicester reflects with this quip: 'Critical marketing – *now there is a thought!*' I think Jack's comment captures an oxymoronic flavour of this endeavour – isn't marketing about selling to support the system? How many times have we discussed marketing with disdainful colleagues who assume we focus on practitioners, peddling Pampers to the poor downtrodden masses? Thus, those of us interested in critical projects always keep in mind the position from which we work – generally in business schools, often amidst clueless colleagues with multi-attribute models that miraculously 'explain' consumers, the economy and the market.

Therefore, some definitions come in handy. Andrea Prothero, Senior Lecturer in Marketing at University College, Dublin, proposes researchers ask themselves several important questions. First, are you being critical of marketing as a discipline or as a practice? For example, are you concerned about unintended consequences of advertising, environmentalism, materialism, poverty, or other negative 'effects' potentially linked to marketing and the market system? Second, reflecting a more general view of critical marketing research, are you assessing the topic (whatever it might happen to be) in a critical manner. Prothero adds: 'critical need not be criticizing, or a personal criticism, rather, critical remains fixed to the traditions outlined above'. Detlev Zwick, Assistant Professor, Schulich School of Business, York University, Canada, makes this distinction:

> One of the differences between critical marketing and critics of marketing, it seems to me, is that the former accepts the function of marketing as an articulation of the expansion of capital in general

but see room for improving its workings with regard to social justice, gender equality, cultural autonomy etc., while the latter, simply put, reject marketing as one of the root causes of much the contemporary social and cultural ills in capitalist market systems.

Zwick places marketing firmly within broader issues of political economy, highlighting its connection with culture and economics, as a foundational element of critical marketing. He points to the useful – and intellectually central – distinction between critical marketing and marketing criticism. Furthermore, he connects marketing to several key social concerns: justice, equality, and autonomy, a move that signals the sociological and philosophical roots of critical marketing.

Pierre McDonagh, Associate Dean for Research at Dublin City University's Business School, seconds this cultural angle: 'For me being critical means writing and using what little wit or wisdom I possess to help others see the wider ecological, socio-political picture and highlighting the cultural significance of marketing in contemporary society'. For McDonagh, critical marketing clearly has a political agenda of change, pointing out the ills of marketing, and seeking to militate against them. Furthermore, in this perspective, teaching and research are joined to the critical agenda, and critical work informs curricular development.

Detlev Zwick, too, points to marketing and its effects as a central topic:

> For me, critical marketing as a scholarly (and potentially managerial) enterprise needs to investigate the effects and role of marketing practice on the constitution of injustice and inequality related to concepts of class, race, gender, and nation, for example. In other words, critical marketing must be a political project, and it should be so boldly and unequivocally.

Critical marketing, then, points to the inherent entanglement of marketing with society, with markets and culture, and with refusing to hide behind business-as-usual approaches to so-called objective research methods.

James Fitchett, Reader in Marketing and Consumption, University of Leicester, provided a tripartite definition, pointing out epistemological foundations of critical marketing, and echoing distinctions amongst various forms of critical work. First, he urges differentiating between managerial, or functional research on the one hand, and 'critical' research on the other. From this position, researchers can then discuss the purpose of research, and expectations for format and outcomes. Second, he distinguishes between Critical marketing research, and critical marketing research – where the former relates explicitly to Critical Theory of the Frankfurt School, and the latter represents a broader agenda characterized by:

- A tendency to prioritize theoretical and conceptual contributions.
- A tendency to adopt a macro orientated, multiple constituency approach.
- A tendency towards historical, sociological, and political readings of marketing.

- A tendency towards phenomenological modes of enquiry.
- A tendency to be generally sceptical towards the current marketing hegemony, characterized by a US style of writing and set of priorities.

Third, Fitchett mentions critical realism as a response to interpretivist or relativist rejections of positivism.

Aside from clarifying some finer, but useful distinctions regarding critical marketing, Fitchett introduces a geo-political element in his response, noting the dominance of the US in the production of marketing knowledge and scholarship – one that has accelerated with the advent of Research Assessment Exercises, where US journals rank highly, in many higher education systems.

In my experience of researching and teaching in both Europe and the US, I tend to agree that European models of management, and, to a lesser extent, marketing scholarship, connect more comfortably with historical, sociological, and political theory, and sit more easily within a broader intellectual history of ideas, In this way, critical marketing draws strength from these disciplines. Janice Denegri-Knott, Lecturer, Bournemouth Media School, Bournemouth University concurs:

> Most generally accepted definitions and discussions of critical marketing are espoused to the intellectual traditions that underpin it; mainly critiques advanced by the Frankfurt and Birmingham Schools. From the Birmingham School, however a more optimistic and rebellious stream has developed, mainly promoted by the works of [John] Fiske into consumer guerrilla tactics to manoeuvre within consumer landscapes.

Her comment characterizes the parallel research stream within cultural studies, which broadened literary and sociological research by including popular culture within its purview, usually from a distinctly critical perspective (cf. Fiske, 1989). At times cultural studies and critical marketing make for odd bedfellows, but generally they support each other.

As Denegri-Knott continues:

> Critical marketing, without constituting a monolithic or unitary body of thought, would come to represent a challenge to existing ways of conceptualizing marketing and consumer matter as well as the development of different analytical tools to assess the underlying contestations of subjectivities and discourses that are embroiled in the creation and re-creation of markets and consumer landscapes. While some existing work may be theoretically indebted to its Marxist theoretical legacy and the need to expose the dark side of marketing in order to erect a more egalitarian society, there is also an interest in understanding marketing as a creative rationality open to a critical assessment of its modes constitution and operation.

And this contestation need not be rooted in political opposition – challenging received wisdom and sacred cows remains a powerful strategy for intellectual work itself.

Denegri-Knott points to the theoretical foundations of our field, asking us to continually question, refine and reject, while remaining aware of how knowledge and power are formed, not found (see Cherrier and Murray, 2004; Desmond, 1997; Denegri-Knott et al., 2006). Further, she embraces the profound reassessment of consumption that has swept through the academy in recent years, refiguring the subject of consumption – largely outside marketing departments – and firmly establishing consumption as an interdisciplinary field, encompassing a broader array of scholarly interests than the usual suspects of economics, psychology, and marketing. As Gavin Jack states: 'critical marketing might also involve the import of multidisciplinary insights into consumption and power into the discipline'. In sum, critical marketing indicates critique on at least three levels: (1) marketing and its actions, (2) marketing as a discipline, and (3) marketing and the creation of markets, consumers and subjects – knowledge, in other words.

Implications for Research and Teaching

I see at least four implications from this set of comments. First, *pluralism* should animate critical marketing's research and thought. As should be clear, there is no one true definition of critical marketing. Rather, this complex term requires careful thought and assessment, combined with a clear understanding of its intellectual and political heritage. In other words, 'critical' has a history, and researchers embracing a critical approach owe this history more than a passing respect. Moreover, there is a growing literature within marketing and consumer research from critical perspectives, which also needs citing, commentary, and even critique. Journals such as *Journal of Public Policy and Marketing* (published by none other than the American Marketing Association), *Journal of Macromarketing*, with almost 30 years worth of articles, *Consumption Markets & Culture*, nearing its tenth anniversary, and *Marketing Theory*, with an explicit critical agenda, form a large corpus of relevant literature. Journals from allied fields, such as *Journal of Consumer Policy*, *Journal of Consumer Affairs*, *Journal of Consumer Culture*, and *Media, Culture and Society*, and many others, bring a generally critical approach to bear on consumption issues, and help maintain a plurality of critical voices, from both inside and outside marketing.

Second, critical marketing seems to imply focusing on *societal issues*. Marketing remains part of society, and researchers interested in critical work require tools developed to study societal processes. For example, a critical approach to advertising might shift focus to consider advertising as representation, rather than mere persuasion. This simple move alters pertinent research questions, methods, and implications, allowing theoretical connections to a wide range of related disciplines. This turn must be informed, of course, by how each discipline or research area handles critical issues. As Denegri-Knott puts it:

> Theoretically then, critical marketing goes beyond marketing theory and adopts a multidisciplinary character in order to appropriate and adapt conceptual tools best suited to understand marketing and a social reality. So called 'postmodern'/critical theorists are summoned here to help ground conceptual and empirical explorations.

Once again, distinctions prove useful, as critical often is conflated with other approaches, such as postmodernism. As Gavin Jack warns:

> One could ask the critical question of 'postmodern' marketing of what its political agenda actually was. Is it just playing smart epistemological games, or did it ever have a political interest? [. . .] we might take the idea that critical marketing involves a critique of the use of reason for understanding market relations, and a need to open out into alternative ontological domains.

This concern underlies a third issue, *researcher reflexivity*, which forms a basic tenet of critical work. Reflexivity, of course, marks an important aspect of all kinds of research. What then, might be different about critical marketing's reflexivity? Apart from reflecting about research methods, processes, analysis, and writing, my informants suggest that critical marketing research implies concern for research subjects, outcomes, and utilization of research findings. Isabelle Szmigin, Professor of Marketing, Birmingham Business School responds:

> I feel there is an important issue around the difference between the active and passive participant in our research studies and that even the 'best' researchers capture their own voice before that of their participants . . . One thing that we have tried to do in our Alcohol and Identity research is to all reflect on our own positions on alcohol and to then share them with one another in an open forum.

In this way, research itself may form part of a critique. Thus, topics, methods, 'subjects', clients, and audiences make up a larger research system in which critical marketing researchers operate, and should reflect upon (cf. Hackley, 2002).

Another profound and far reaching implication, that should be clear from the discussion and quotes, concerns how critical marketing research generally views marketing and consumption as *basic issues*, eschewing an applied approach of more managerially inflected work, joining other fields that construct themselves as foundational subjects, and arguing for an intellectual platform for engaged management scholarship. This constitutes a tall order, perhaps, especially given marketing's rather low brand equity in the scholarly pantheon (see Alvesson, 1994; Denzin, 2001; Kilbourne et al., 1997). As Detlev Zwick complains:

> Unlike other social science disciplines whose journals are full of critical analyses of marketing practice, our journals do not necessarily appear open to such work. – Where, for example, would one publish a paper that outlines the collapsing of organizational and individual forms of sexism in the hiring of marketing personnel (excluding OB and other management journals)? – Or work that documents the grossly racist attitudes that inform how advertising firms and their clients devise campaigns to target the 'black' or the 'Hispanic' market, etc.?

However, journals do accept well-done critiques, and I think the cultural agenda within consumer research opens possibilities for critical work. Of course, targeting management journals, such as the well-respected *Journal of Management Inquiry*, *Organization*, and *Organization Studies*, that appear more open to critique – and often have a wider audience than marketing outlets – represents another option.

Outcomes

So far, we have defined critical marketing, read over the views of several researchers, and drawn some implications for research and teaching. We can just hear our modelling colleagues, heads of schools, and reviewers asking – so what? What are your outcomes? I offer three outcome-based issues for us to consider: (1) research, and the importance of framing critical research by joining scholarly conversations; (2) publishing – where, how (why?); and (3) teaching.

As mentioned above, there are a growing numbers of journals open to, and even dedicated for, critical marketing research. As I see it, a key concern for young researchers centres on joining academic conversations, partly by situating their own work within ongoing journal debates, dialogues, or even diatribes. How is this done? By engaging with existing literature. I often review papers that confidently discuss the dearth of critical work in marketing. Not true! Claims like these do a tremendous disservice to those scholars who have gone before us, especially those who have staked their career on critical work, often focusing on non-traditional, oppositional, or alternative topics that their more mainstream colleagues may not respect. In this chapter, I have tried to cite a few references that I think are essential, and I have mentioned several journals that hold reams of critical literature. Furthermore, projects such as this book should do much to make available the extant critical marketing literature. In addition, I can recommend conferences such as the Heretical Consumer Research group (HCR), which meets before the annual Association for Consumer Research conference, the biannual Critical Management Studies conference (which generally has a critical marketing stream) and the annual Macromarketing seminar. It is not enough to bemoan a lack of scholarship, one must critically engage in the critical marketing literature itself, before blithely criticizing.

How does one publish critical research in marketing? Aside from the outlets mentioned, one approach calls for embedding critical work within a more traditional paper or topic. For example, in my paper 'The Artist and the Brand', which was published in the mainstream *European Journal of Marketing*, I framed a discussion about artists by discussing brand management – a classic 'new way to see an established topic' approach. This framing allowed me to discuss art as criticism, and present several critical artists as pertinent to the overall argument. I snuck in this phrase to illustrate how artists critique consumption: 'They point out potential dehumanizing processes of commodification, the sameness of the branded environment, and the debilitating effects of celebrity and its quest' (Schroeder, 2005, p. 1301). Perhaps not devastating to the status quo, but a nudge in the right direction, I think.

Why publish critical research? Some of most exciting, intellectually challenging work takes place under the critical banner, in my view, and critical projects carry the responsibilities of reflection and reassessment central to good scholarship. Business schools need critical marketing scholars. Moreover, critical researchers represent an eager, prolific bunch, with useful abilities in defining projects, writing papers, and establishing centres. As Gavin Jack comments, 'Critical marketing might also be seen as a career project for young researchers looking for a subject position within the marketing discipline as alternative'. However, Andrea Prothero remains sanguine about these prospects:

> The other piece of advice is to remember that in the UK there are not actually that many critical marketers out there so I personally believe it is actually quite a risky route to take (not that I think people shouldn't take it, but that they should be aware of the risks). It is really important that your supervisor is on your side and is supportive of what you are doing.

Prothero's remark reminds us of the shaky status of critical approaches, in both research and teaching, where it can be difficult to offer classes that contain critical content.

Institutional power in the academy largely rests in the curriculum – what programmes require, who teaches what, and which subjects require lecturers. Marketing, of course, generally implies practitioner oriented managerial classes and programmes, where critical courses may sit uncomfortably amidst finance, accounting, and statistics (cf. Hackley, 2001). Yet I find students receptive to critical, reflexive approaches, particularly those based on current, interesting research. Pierre McDonagh, who developed a successful master's level class 'Consumption, Markets and Culture', exhorts critical marketers to contemplate:

> Not just teaching 'how to do marketing' but considering the effects both positive and negative of marketing discourses and theorizing a positivity about changing marketing. Being critical for me is a way of enacting change in marketing; it is all about changing it.

A key strategy of developing critical perspectives within the classroom involves not just criticism, but reflection and analysis – important elements of any course.

Concluding Thoughts

Critical marketing calls for engaged thinking, joining broader academic, political, and social projects. Some critical marketing academics remain opposed to marketing, others see hope in consumer empowerment, still others find critical perspectives intellectually crucial. As marketing departments and business schools grow, hire more faculty with PhDs in non-business fields, and develop more management programmes while books, conferences, and journals proliferate, critical marketing represents a growing, vital movement that challenges received wisdom, slays some sacred cows, and upsets a few apple carts – worthy 'effects' for intellectual work. I end with a final comment from Janice Denegri-Knott, which I think succinctly sums things up with a productive and useful motto: 'I like to see critical marketing theory as marketing theory without the illusions'.

Acknowledgements

I would like to thank Janice Denegri-Knott, James Fitchett, Gavin Jack, Pierre McDonagh, Andrea Prothero, Isabelle Szmigin, and Detlev Zwick for their time and thoughtful replies, the participants at the ESRC Critical Marketing seminar held at DeMontfort University in December 2005, and also John Desmond, Avi Shankar, Janet Borgerson, Caroline Bekin, Alan Bradshaw, Doug Holt, Chris Hackley, and Campbell Jones for comments and insight into this project.

References

Alvesson, M. (1994). 'Critical theory and consumer marketing'. *Scandinavian Journal of Management*, 10(3), 291–313.
Arato, A. and Gebhardt, E., (eds) (1978). *The Essential Frankfurt School Reader*. New York: Urizen.
Borgerson, J.L. and Schroeder, J.E. (2002). 'Ethical issues of global marketing: avoiding bad faith in visual representation'. *European Journal of Marketing*, 36, 570–594.
Bristor, J.M. and Fischer, E. (1993). 'Feminist thought: implications for consumer research'. *Journal of Consumer Research*, 19(March), 518–536.
Brownlie, D., Saren, M., Wensley, R. and Whittington, R. (eds) (1998). *Rethinking Marketing: Towards Critical Marketing Accounting*. London: Sage.
Burton, D. (2001). 'Critical marketing theory: the blueprint?'. *European Journal of Marketing*, 35(5/6), 722–743.

Cherrier, H. and Murray, J.B. (2004). 'The sociology of consumption: the hidden facet of marketing'. *Journal of Marketing Management*, 20, 509–525.

Craib, I. (1992). *Modern Social Theory: From Parsons to Habermas*. Upper Saddle River, NJ: Prentice Hall.

Denegri-Knott, J., Zwick, D. and Schroeder, J.E. (2006). 'Mapping consumer power: an integrative framework for marketing and consumer research'. *European Journal of Marketing*, 40 (9/10), 950–971.

Denzin, N.K. (2001). 'The seventh moment: qualitative inquiry and the practices of a more radical consumer research'. *Journal of Consumer Research*, 28, 324–330.

Desmond, J. (1997). 'Marketing and the war machine'. *Marketing Intelligence and Planning*, 15(7), 338–351.

Dholakia, N. and Schroeder, J.E. (2001). 'Disney: delights and doubts'. *Journal of Research for Consumers*, 1(2), Available: http://www.jrconsumers.com/

Firat, F., Dholakia, N. and Bagozzi, R.P. (eds) (1987). *Philosophical and Radical Thought in Marketing*. Lexington, MA: Lexington.

Fiske, J. (1989). *Understanding Popular Culture*. New York: Routledge.

Gordon, L.R. (1997). *Her Majesty's Other Children: Sketches of Racism from a Neocolonial Age*. Lanham, MD: Rowman and Littlefield.

Gutting, G. (ed.) (1994). *The Cambridge Companion to Foucault*. Cambridge: Cambridge University Press.

Hackley, C. (2001). 'Towards a post-structuralist marketing pedagogy – or from irony to despair (a two-by-two matrix approach)'. *European Journal of Marketing*, 35(11/12), 1184–1196.

Hackley, C. (2002). *Doing Research Projects in Management, Marketing and Consumer Behaviour*. London: Routledge.

Kilbourne, W.E., McDonagh, P. and Prothero, A. (1997). 'Sustainable consumption and quality of life: a macromarketing challenge to the dominant social paradigm'. *Journal of Macromarketing*, 17(1), 4–24.

Mingers, J. (2000). 'What is it to be critical? Teaching a critical approach to management undergraduates'. *Management Learning*, 31(2), 219–237.

Nicosia, F.M. and Mayer, R.N. (1976). 'Toward a sociology of consumption'. *Journal of Consumer Research*, 3, 65–75.

Schroeder, J.E. (2002). *Visual Consumption*. London: Routledge.

Schroeder, J.E. (2005). 'The artist and the brand'. *European Journal of Marketing*, 39, 1291–1305.

Schroeder, J.E. (2006). 'Critical visual analysis'. In R. Belk (ed.), *Handbook of Qualitative Methods in Marketing*. Aldershot, UK: Edward Elgar.

Schroeder, J.E. and Borgerson, J.L. (2005). 'An ethics of representation for international marketing'. *International Marketing Review*, 22, 578–600.

Stern, B.B. and Schroeder, J.E. (1994). 'Interpretive methodology from art and literary criticism: a humanistic approach to advertising imagery'. *European Journal of Marketing*, 28, 114–132.

Venkatesh, A. and Meamber, L.A. (2006). 'Arts and aesthetics: marketing and cultural production'. *Marketing Theory*, 6(1), 11–40.

3

Rethinking Critical Marketing

Alan Bradshaw and A. Fuat Firat

Critical marketing implies that the institution of marketing itself is to be critiqued, most likely through the tools provided by critical theory. Yet those who hold such expectations may be disappointed to learn that critical marketing can remain in the service of marketing practitioners and seems to refer to theoretical and methodological pluralism rather than to a Marxian informed critique. To address this issue, we submit that it is timely to remember the potential benefits of the previously overlooked critical theory for critical marketing. In this chapter we explore these issues, taking a timely review of critical marketing literature, and in particular three landmark publications (Brown et al., 1996; Brownlie et al., 1999; Firat et al., 1987). In doing so, we problematize the assumptions underlying the evolution of critical marketing and demonstrate how a more critical theory engaged critical marketing might be realized.

An Emergence of the Critical Marketing Umbrella

The publication of this book indicates that critical marketing is thriving. Journals, such as *Consumption, Markets and Culture* and *Marketing Theory* call for submissions from critical and radical perspectives, the *Journal of Macromarketing* continues to publish articles investigating the impact of marketing upon society, and critical work regularly appears in such journals as *Public Policy and Marketing, Consumer Affairs, Consumer Policy, Consumer Research* and *Business Ethics Quarterly* (Catterall et al., 2002). Having reflected upon the wider contributions to the *Journal of Consumer Research* and *Advances in Consumer Research*, Arnould and Thompson (2005) claim that there is now a sizeable tradition within consumer research which is broadly critical. Add to this the landmark edited books setting forth the agenda (Brownlie et al., 1999; Firat et al., 1987) and it becomes clear that critical marketing is alive and well, if not moving from strength to strength, as an established tradition with its own heritage and journals.

However, what is understood to be critical is worthy of reflection. For example, in their call for papers for a critical marketing stream within the *International Critical Management Conference*, Saren and Brownlie conceived critical marketing as 'any approach drawing inspiration from the substantive critical traditions of, for example, feminism, Marxism, ethnography and symbolism, poststructuralism, hermeneutics, postmodernism and environmentalism' (cited in Burton, 2001). Indeed Saren and Hastings (2003) later broadened the net by including sustainability, ethics and even discourse analysis into the recipe for the critical marketing cake. The final fare-thee-well to a stable definition of critical marketing was served by Catterall et al. (2002) in their review of critical marketing in the curriculum. For the authors, critical marketing was defined as subscribing to radical philosophies and theories that explicitly seek to identify and question the ideologies and assumptions underlying the production and consumption of knowledge (p. 184). Questioning underlying assumptions was positioned as being useful for marketing scholars as it may help to 'shift the current technocratic focus in the curriculum toward one that better reflects the needs and concerns of marketing managers' (p. 186). By now, what is understood as critical marketing, albeit in the context of the curriculum, is not necessarily based on a critique of the schema of market systems, but rather a critique of conventional marketing paradigms and methodologies for being out of touch with the 'concerns of marketing managers' (Catterall et al., 2002, p. 186); critical marketing, it seems, becomes another form of marketing scholarship to be put at the service of marketing managers.

One issue of contention, then, relates to the issue of praxis and in particular, whether critical marketing should at all be concerned with improving marketing theory and practice, and with being of service to marketing managers. Alternatively, should critical marketing be concerned with expressing what is wrong with current marketing theories and practices; or even with the *existence* of theories and practices we know as marketing? We shall be addressing this issue of contention, however, we think that critical marketing that is true to its roots in the 'critical school of thought' must not and cannot assume the existence of marketing as a given; critical marketing cannot be 'critical' if it does not question the very foundation(s) of marketing's existence.

Despite the loose constitution, there have been various attempts to lay down an agenda or blueprint for a critical marketing tradition. The book *Philosophical and Radical Thought in Marketing*, edited by Firat et al. in 1987, sought to break

the mould of marketing scholarship, and radically deconstruct its limitations –
held to be tied to naïve empiricism, conceptual poverty, restrictive methodologies,
excessive specialization, unidimensionality, opprobrious instrumentalism and
a lack of human interest resulting in disillusionment for marketing scholars
(p. 374). The challenge for the editors was to allow 'many different yet critical
and vigorous perspectives and orientations to be heard' (p. xx) and in their
concluding chapter 'Rethinking Marketing', the editors discerned six ways of
being radical in marketing, including infusing humanistic values, responsible
practice, developing holistic and integrative frameworks, and deepening the
historical basis of the discipline.

In their reflection on why this would be a useful exercise, they argued that
their suggestions could help overcome the disillusionment within marketing scholarship. Yet rejecting praxis was not a core drive of the project. For
example, as Kotler (1987) remarked in his own submission to the volume,
'Humanism Pays', those organizations who embarked upon a more social-
minded policy may become more profitable. Of perhaps greater significance,
by trying to move beyond the exchange-centric paradigm, the authors sought
to expose the social construction of marketing itself. Marketing re-thought
clearly entailed moving beyond the micro-concerns of behavioural mapping
and instead should consider the institution of marketing itself.

A further landmark publication which addressed the perceived need to
reconfigure the marketing blueprint was Marketing Apocalypse – Eschatology,
Escapology and the Illusion of the End, edited by Brown et al. in 1996. This time the
objective was not to rethink marketing, but rather to check for a pulse because,
as the editors noted, there was a perception that the 'end of marketing was
nigh' (p. 14); as McDonagh and Prothero (1996) observed, at a time of widespread critique, they appeared to be facing the 'final curtain of the marketing
concept' (p. 44). For Brown (1996), marketing was entering a third era, having
already passed through the 'Pro-Science Area', with marketing conceptualized
along Newtonian principles of stability and measurement. The conventional
agenda for this pro-scientific and positivistic era was described by Holbrook
(1996) as being dominated by 'neo-positivistic managerially relevant studies of
decisions to buy goods and services' (p. 241). This notionally pro-scientific era,
according to Brown, gradually phased into an 'Anti-Science Era', marked by an
increasingly felt vote-of-no-confidence for the scientific model from within the
marketing scholarship community. In turn, Brown (incorrectly?) predicted that
marketing research would realize its third era of an artistic orientation com-
mencing around the year 2000.

By 1999, Brownlie et al. felt that the time had once again come round for
some Rethinking Marketing and edited a new book that attempted to 'show how
a critical approach to marketing thought can reveal new pathways for marketing scholarship, perhaps helping to prepare well-trodden paths for the act of
change' (Brownlie et al., 1999, p. 2). Echoing the drive of Firat et al.'s earlier project
in Philosophical and Radical Thought in Marketing, was the perceived importance of revealing the social construction of marketing, this time by stressing an emancipatory impulse within marketing which would be cognizant

of the subject's duty to a constituency beyond marketing managers and would include managed consumers and citizens alike. Again they attributed blame for the perceived lethargy of the subject to the discipline's 'heady cocktail of naïve scientism' (p. 13) and 'easy complacency of mainstream thought' (p. 2) which delivered a 'relentless pursuit of scientific respectability and narrow technical focus on the bottom line' (p. 2).

For Brownlie et al. (1999), one of the chief inspirations for *Rethinking Marketing* was the emergence of the field of Critical Management Studies (CMS). With this in mind, CMS proponents such as David Knights and Hugh Willmott were contributors to the volume. Consequentially, critical marketing was put into conversation with CMS, and indeed Brownlie and Saren have ensured that critical marketing exists as a stream within the annual *Academy of Management* conference.

Yet, despite the rhetorical commitment to emancipation, the envisaged future of critical marketing entailed the expression of doubt about hitherto taken-for-granted precepts and methods within marketing scholarship. Once again, having promised an introduction of a critical agenda, the editors seem preoccupied with delivering a departure from the positivistic and bottom line orientation of the subject and instead look forward to an era of increased methodological eclecticism and a reduced emphasis on immediate managerial implications.

An Emergent Trend

Consideration of how the critical marketing agenda has been outlined within three influential edited books indicates a clear trend. Namely, the evolution of critical marketing can be understood as attempts by the more creative marketing scholars to break the narrow precepts of their discipline and to open up the subject to methodological and theoretical pluralism. Therefore 'critical' in critical marketing entails being critical of the existing scholarly conventions as a precursor to a more theoretically and methodologically eclectic orientation. As Burton (2001) states: 'a particular line of empirical enquiry might lead a researcher to critically evaluate a particular model or position which would lead to critical discourse without using critical theory to frame the discussion' (p. 726), and this, we submit, is precisely what has happened in critical marketing.

This notion of research fuelled by methodological and theoretical antipathy is echoed in historical accounts of the evolution of consumer research (such as Brown, 1996; Gummesson, 2001; Holbrook, 1996; Shankar and Patterson, 2001) where it is repeatedly demonstrated that the research tradition has evolved as an alternative to the conventional, positivist, marketing paradigm. Therefore, we contend that critical marketing can be understood as a reactionary movement, incorporating a rich bricolage of research tools – perhaps best thought of in terms of what it is not, rather than what it is. It is this ambivalent lack of a theoretically grounded centre, we submit, that has lead to critical marketing evolving into an umbrella under which diverse research strands have gathered.[1]

Yet marketing scholars concerned about the potential failure of the project of Enlightenment – one of creating a social order that would enable all human beings to lead lives of dignity, equality and freedom to realize their independent wills and potentials to the fullest – and who think that the major reason for this failure may be the hegemony of certain interests based on capitalism's class structure, tend to think that the term 'critical' in critical marketing has been overly diluted. That one can offer a *critique* of the state of marketing practice or theory from a different perspective that is based on one of the varied critical traditions does not and should not, in the estimation of these concerned scholars, mean that a 'critical' analysis of or approach to marketing has been delivered. As we will argue in this chapter, for a critical approach to marketing, the analyses must contain certain elements that may be most closely related to the Critical Theory School of Marxist thought. If this is not the case, the true contributions that critical thinking can bring to a universal understanding of marketing will be thwarted. Furthermore, our ability to help transformations that can redirect human energies towards achieving the project of Enlightenment, based on such understanding, will be frustrated.

Against this rather diluted conception of 'critical', it may be helpful to return – in terms of our ability to provide more substantive insights into the conditions of contemporary life and marketing's role in it – to a consideration of the roots of the critical school of thought. We wish to argue that these roots may be rediscovered in a brief remembering of the Critical Theory school.

Critical Theory

Critical theory may be regarded as a post-Marxian school of thought mostly associated with the Frankfurt Institute of Social Research in the period preceding and following the Second World War and consisting of such influential theorists as Max Horkheimer, Walter Benjamin, Theodor Adorno and Herbert Marcuse. Perhaps the clearest statement of the critical theory agenda is *Eclipse of Reason* (Horkheimer, 2004), written in 1946 by the School Director, Max Horkheimer, in which he outlined his description of an increasingly reified domination, whereby the hopes of humanity represented by Enlightenment humanism become reconfigured as a pattern of mimesis and commodity fetishism in the face of an ever dominating capitalist landscape. Further influential texts from the school included the *Dialectic of the Enlightenment* written by Adorno and Horkheimer (1998), and *One Dimensional Man*, written by

---

[1] As a separate issue, it is worth considering what these diverse research strands have gained by falling under the critical umbrella. For example, Maclaran & Stevens (2002) have argued that feminism within the critical marketing mould has in part resulted in a paralysis of feminist critique of marketing.

Marcuse (2002). Other influential authors such as Walter Benjamin were in regular contact and correspondence with members and therefore may be thought as part of the critical theory movement, though not a Member of Faculty in the Frankfurt Institute of Social Research (Arendt, 1999).

The Frankfurt Institute of Social Research was primarily concerned with exploring Marxian and post-Marxian concepts, however, the historical backdrop to the Institute led to a reshaping of the group's ideals. To put those changes into context, one can mention how Marxist politics regressed into the violent authoritarianism of the Soviet Union. This period also witnessed the rise of the Third Reich and the corresponding intolerance for the Marxian basis of the Frankfurt Institute and its predominantly Jewish faculty. Meanwhile, there was the continued rise of mass media which allowed for a more sophisticated and seductive ideologically driven culture industry and commodity fetishism. Most of the faculty were able to flee to the USA, leaving Walter Benjamin behind to eventually commit suicide in Spain during his run from the Gestapo. In the USA, the Marxian inclinations of the surviving members resulted in suspicion from the FBI, which investigated and interrogated the members and, its boss, J. Edgar Hoover, referred to the exiled theorists as 'communazis' (Rubin, 2003). The response of the researchers to the suspicious and authoritarian zeitgeist was to eliminate praxis from their work and to instead emphasize the importance of critique as an exercise in its own right. Echoing the school ethos, Adorno argued that theory must not be subordinated to praxis, as it would contribute to a prohibition in thinking and hence a form of repression.

For some, the absence of praxis from social critique was intensely frustrating and in particular it was an ethos that came to jar violently with the student revolutionary zeitgeist of the 1960s (Becker, 1978). The Frankfurt faculty may have been vindicated in their lack of support for the student protestors, given the emergence of the murderous Bader-Meinhof group, however, for many on-lookers, the inability of critical theory to play a more practical role at the time resulted in a loss of credibility and disillusionment with critical theory (Jager, 2004). Furthermore, the critiquing of supposedly regressive popular tastes from such theorists as Adorno resulted in the characterizing of critical theory as overly elitist and inherently hostile (Craib, 1992). Latter critical theorists such as Marcuse placed less emphasis on the strict avoidance of praxis, illustrating that critical theory has not emerged from a 'unified chappelle' of thought.

Yet, at a time when the drum beat to war is still broadcast from propagandistic vessels of mass culture in the business of 'manufacturing consent' (Herman and Chomsky, 1995), a time when alienated consumers can only move from one market discourse to another (Firat and Dholakia, 1998; Thompson, 2004), a critical theory which explores the 'euphoria in unhappiness' from satisfaction of manufactured needs and pseudo-activity (Marcuse, 2002) seems increasingly relevant. As Bernstein (2002) noted, rather than understanding the critical theorists as routed to a violent era and therefore irrelevant to contemporary times, critical theory instead can be understood as having made a series of predictions concerning an inherent repression implied within commodification that continue to come to pass.

Despite this relevance, a lacuna seems to arise given the absence of a broadly Marxian or critical theory conceived agenda within critical marketing. Indeed, some critical marketing authors have gone to lengths to make clear that they do not regard themselves as primarily grounded within a critical theory framework. For example, Catterall et al. (2002) state that 'critical scholars in management and marketing draw their inspiration from a number of philosophical and theoretical sources of which Frankfurt School critical theory is only one'. At times it is even possible to get a scent of hostility towards critical theorists within Brownlie et al.'s (1999) vision of an eclectic framework for critique which 'leaves space for many voices other than those of card-carrying critical theorists' (p. 9) – echoing a previous generation's suspicions of card-carrying communists. Meanwhile, whilst Brown did reflect that 'if the deeply hostile tenor of its literature can be tolerated, it is undeniable that marketing has much to gain from critical theory – from a more fully informed, self-reflexive stance than has been apparent hitherto' (Brown, 1995, p. 153), critical theory's influence has remained small. Given that critical theory took the impact of commodification upon life as a central concern, and the fact that the beginnings of a 'critical' approach to marketing are much indebted to a critical theory perspective, surprise might attend the realization that critical marketing has gained little by way of insight from critical theory.

In contrast to critical marketing, critical theory has played a much more central role in the continuing evolution of CMS. Despite a rich exchange of ideas between CMS and critical marketing, marked by the book *Rethinking Marketing*, the critical marketing stream within the *Academy of Management* conferences, research conducted by CMS personnel within marketing journals (such as Knights et al., 1994), or by scholars, such as Evert Gummesson whose input straddles the two subject areas (Gummesson, 2001), it might be said that CMS has a very different relationship with critical theory than critical marketing does. For example, seven of the nine chapters in the edited text *Studying Management Critically* (Alvesson and Willmott, 2003) are based upon critical theory. In the book, the editors reflect:

> Critical Theory comprises an important, but by no means a single, dominant strand in Critical Management Studies that continues to be an inclusive, pluralistic 'movement' where a diversity of critical approaches – from non-orthodox forms of labour process analysis, through varieties of Critical Theory to deconstructionism and approaches that have broader affinities with many contemporary social movements (e.g. feminism, environmentalism, post colonialism, etc.) is accommodated.
>
> Alvesson and Willmott (2003, pp. 2–3).

Similar to critical marketing, CMS is clearly not primarily concerned with working with critical theory yet it is much more overtly concerned with drawing from critical theory ideas.

By contrast, whilst critical theory is similarly one of many strands within critical marketing, it seems far from important within that mix, leading several scholars to note that despite the contention that critical theory has much to contribute to marketing, the research tradition has been mostly neglected (Brown, 1995; Burton, 2001). There have been exceptions of individual papers calling for a critical theory grounded approach (see Hetrick and Lozada, 1999; Murray and Ozanne, 1991; Rogers, 1987), but they do not seem to have stimulated much by way of critical theory inspired empirical research, despite regular citations of the Murray and Ozanne article. It is our contention that in this latest attempt to rethink critical marketing, it is time to imagine a more Critical Theory informed approach.

Critical Theory and Critical Marketing

We call for an undiluted critical theory approach to critically understand marketing which would explore marketing's history, its role in a certain social order, its practices and theories based in ideologies that emanate from a specific class structure enabling the political and economic necessities of a market system that has commodification as one of its core phenomena. This will be useful, we submit, for developing deeper and more rigorous insights into the human condition of this social order.

The potential of critical theory to impact upon marketing studies was outlined in particular by Murray and Ozanne (1991), who sought to develop critical theory into a five-step method that could be utilized by consumer researchers. These five steps included: a historical–empirical step to grasp the social and historical construction of existing conditions and a dialectical step that was held to entail a review of the inconsistencies between the objective social conditions and the intersubjective meanings. This dialectical interest in inconsistencies was also identified by Hetrick and Lozada (1999, p. 166). as a potential benefit of critical theory in marketing: 'societal members', they argued 'must understand the "true nature of their existence" before we demand that attempts be made at transformations of alienating social practices'. In this context, both Murray and Ozanne (1991) and Hetrick and Lozada (1999) emphasize a praxis-based outcome of a Critical Theory fuelled critical marketing, following a Marcusian brand of critical theory as opposed to more Adornian or Horkheimerean rejection of praxis.

To add to the Murray and Ozanne (1991) and Hetrick and Lozada (1999) contributions we call on critical marketers to pay more attention to such Critical Theory issues such as domination, reification, fetishization, commodification and alienation. All of these interlocking phenomena may be found within the act of consumption using the dialectic. For example, in Belk and Tumbat's (2005) review of the Cult of Macintosh, the authors noted that Macintosh users had fetishized, through mythology, their computers as somehow a registration of their anti-market anxiety. In this way, the spirit of counter-culture and rebellion had become reified (the process through which people or ideas become objectified) and packaged as a commodity, thereby the marketplace anxiety becomes re-routed towards what Franks (1997) refers to as a 'hip consumerism'. Under a critical theory lens, this is a classic example of a pseudo-activity as the consumer seeks emancipation through commodity fetishization (meaning that things become imbued with powers of fulfilling human desires) and consequently becomes more deeply integrated into a reified and dominated capitalist mould. Whilst Belk and Tumbat (2005) empirically investigated this process, their disinterest in a dialectical commitment – that is to unpacking the inconsistencies between the objective social conditions and the intersubjective meanings – resulted in not exploring the Cult of Macintosh as a negative dialectic (this refers to the process whereby the distinction between truth and objectified reality, as perpetuated by a dominant system, is reproduced). In this way, we submit that critical theory can add an important theoretical dimension to critical marketing.

Critical Theory does, indeed, provide us with the tools to critique the social, political and economic structuring of society by providing rigorous insights into the nature of the phenomena that construct and maintain these structures, informed by Marxist analyses. Marxist analysis is still, we submit, the best provider of insights about the modern order, built upon Enlightenment's principles, from within modern thought itself. This strength is attested to by the fact that simply all schools of thought mentioned as potential contributors to critical marketing, including Critical Theory, but also feminism, environmentalism, poststructuralism, symbolism, hermeneutics, among others, are all informed by Marxist theory. Critical Theory's strength is partially due to its Marxist roots, and partially to its insightful extensions of this analysis to recognize the more substantial role that phenomena, such as commodification, reification and consumerization that are significant to the continuity of markets, play in the hegemonic hold of the dominant ideology of the market system.

Recognition and understanding of these phenomena, best shed light on by the tools of Critical Theory, provide insights into the current resilience of the market system. Such insights seem to indicate that the marketization of human relations was a logical outcome of modern thought which intended to free the human individual from all impositions, natural or social. A 'market' relationship was imagined whereby each human being would be free of obligations to others except for the moment of exchange when one resource was transacted for another. The buyer and the seller need not know each other and need not have any relationship before or after the exchange. Once the exchange is completed, each can go their own way, having no obligations and free to do with the resource received in the exchange as one willed. Thus, the free will of each individual could be realized, as a result of liberation from all obligations to others. Then, within the resources that each individual had, s/he could decide, based on one's own will, where and how these resources would be utilized.

This idea further necessitated commodification, that is, the idea that the product one received in the exchange had no organic relations with anyone, including those who produced it and, thus, contained all the qualities that the one who acquires it is seeking in and by itself. All that a human being needed would or could be imbued in the 'commodity' one exchanged for – it would have all the qualities that the individual required, it was the commodity that had the power to satisfy one's needs. Thus, left alone with the commodities that s/he acquired, the individual could indeed be the sovereign, deciding what s/he needs and how to satisfy them.

With commodification, the human individual would further be freed from the necessity to produce all one needed or consumed; that is, s/he would become a consumer, because what s/he needed would now be contained in the commodities that s/he acquired. Marketization, commodification and consumerization completed the individualization, thus the emancipation of the human being (Slater, 1997). They also contributed to the growth of the market and its role in human lives, as well as the reverence for this institution called the market – thus the accolades for the 'free market' often heard from our politicians. In the end, these insights from critical analyses provide us with an appreciation of why the market has become such a powerful institution in contemporary society, and why so much human agency is abdicated to the market – an inhuman medium of practice.

Understanding marketing, as witnessed by its name, requires rigorous understanding of market(s) and the market system. Critical Theory's focus on phenomena that construct and maintain the ideological prominence of markets and the system that perpetuates them is, therefore, its clear advantage in critical marketing. It is this advantage that we need to harvest by not diluting the critical central significance of critical theory and its insightful contributions in critical marketing.

Indeed the issue of praxis seems to be fundamental to understanding critical marketing. Namely, if critical marketing is to remain relevant to the practice of marketing, then following a Critical Theory interpretation, it must necessarily be repressive. Consequentially, what Maclaran and Brown (2005) refer to as the 'emancipatory strand' within consumer research, namely those studies which are concerned with the attempts of consumers to either escape the market completely or renegotiate the basis of their marketplace participation, seems to feed into marketing practice as advertisers ironically seek to re-route the discourses of non-conformity and rebellion into marketing messages (Holt, 2002). The fear becomes, as Horkheimer put it, that 'thought today is only too often compelled to justify itself by its usefulness to some established group rather than by its truth' (p. 59). A rejection of praxis would insist on critical marketing that is purposefully of *no use* to marketing practice.

We are cognizant that the existence of a 'truth' is more questionable today than it was in Horkheimer's day. This should not, however, damage the ability of critical marketing in providing the most useful insights into modern marketing. The modern social order that markets and marketing are a key part of was, after all, constructed on the bases of ideologies that held a sacred belief in 'truth'. While we can expand our understanding of the conditions that created the modern social order through constructs that deconstruct these modern(ist) ideologies, further contextualizing the modern order in its history, understanding the modern order itself can probably not be better achieved than by being dissected using its own construct(ion)s. Critical Theory, and a critical marketing based on Critical Theory, therefore, does not lose usefulness in dissecting modern marketing.

As experienced by the Frankfurt School during the student uprisings, the analyses gained from critiquing the market can give rise to a call for praxis based on reconstructing the market, as was called for in both the Murray and Ozanne (1991) and Hetrick and Lozada (1999) treatises on Critical Theory and marketing. Indeed such deeper and more rigorous understanding drawn from a Critical Theory perspective could enable more successful interventions towards either accomplishing the project of Enlightenment or towards transforming the social order for purposes arising from such more robust insights. However, it must be recognized that Critical Theory, as purported by Horkheimer, and Adorno, implies a rejection of praxis and, therefore, critical analyses may also be seen as an exercise in its own right and not to become subject to a latter plan of action.

In that spirit, having provided analyses using Critical Theory, critical marketing might inspire radical reconstructions of marketing, including, and possibly most importantly, reconstructions of its very nature and purpose. A critical marketing orientation in this respect, in our estimation, would not propose modifications to improve marketing's role in making organizations serve and provide for consumers in order to better satisfy them or their desires and needs. Rather, it might inspire transformations that would empower people to shed their identities as consumers and perform a takeover of organizations and marketing to control and run them for their purposes. In effect, such critical marketing would not produce knowledge to be put to the service of marketing managers, it might, instead, put an end to marketing management as we currently understand it by turning people, who used to be consumers, into organizers of marketing. After all, the project of Enlightenment that Critical Theorists would like to complete (Habermas, 1983) is to understand all impositions that human beings endure, natural or social, that inhibit their ability to achieve lives with dignity, equality, justice and the freedom to fulfill their potentials to the fullest, according their own free will; which implies that they be masters of their institutions rather than simply be served by them.

Conclusion

As Hirschman (1991) has passionately argued, consumer researchers must never glance away from the 'dark side' of consumption, including matters of addiction and consumer disorder. So too, we argue, that critical marketing must not shy away from reviewing the dark side of commodification. Critical Theory can provide marketing with a lens to uncover domination, reification, alienation and fetishization that Critical Theorists were convinced lay at the heart of the commodification process. Incorporating Critical Theory into the critical marketing mix need not result in the cessation of the process of questioning received foundations, methods, principles, conventions or generally accepted findings in the marketing field. However it would entail this questioning should not lose sight of the idea that there exist systematic ideological biases, based in class formations and power structures, underlying these, and that a more substantive understanding of phenomena is possible. In turning to Critical Theory, it becomes necessary to rediscover the politics of truth as a means to progress criticality – as Fineman (1999) said, 'if everything is relative, what is the point of doing anything?' (p. 184). Embracing a Critical Theory orientation forces us to re-engage with such issues as fetishization and reification as inherent within a commodification system. This is how we conceive an imagined future of critical marketing.

Our purpose is not to suggest that Critical Theory is the 'only show in town' and consequently must dominate critical marketing, nor is it a call for all critical marketing research to stem from Critical Theory. Rather, it is to remind critical marketers of the importance of establishing Critical Theory as a pillar in the construction of critical marketing, and to offer a warning against the flow of critical marketing into, as Desmond (1997) put it, 'just another way of "doing" marketing'. Without a unifying pillar, we argue that critical marketing will continue in its project of unifying disparate research strands in a pseudo-genre which is at once ambivalent, reifying and ultimately removes us from a critique of the market; a critical marketing project in which marketing is never really critiqued at all.

Acknowledgement

The authors acknowledge the helpful advice of Olga Kravets in developing this chapter.

References

Adorno, T. and Horkheimer, M. (1998). *Dialectic of Enlightenment* (trans. by J. Cumming). New York: Continuum.

Alvesson, M. and Willmott, H. (2003). *Studying Management Critically*. London: Sage.

Arendt, H. (ed.) (1999). *Illuminations – Walter Benjamin*. London: Pimlico.

Arnould, E. and Thompson, T. (2005). 'Consumer culture theory (CCT): twenty years of research'. *Journal of Consumer Research*, 31(March), 868–882.

Becker, J. (1978). *Hitler's Children – The Story of the Baader-Meinhof Gang*, 2nd edition. London: Granada Publishing.

Belk, R. and Tumbat, G. (2005). 'The cult of Macintosh'. *Consumption, Markets and Culture*, 8(3), 205–218.

Bernstein, J.M. (2002). *Adorno – The Culture Industry*, Vol. 3. London: Routledge.

Brown, S. (1995). *Postmodern Marketing*. London: Routledge.

Brown, S. (1996). 'Trinitarianism, the eternal evangel and the three eras schema'. In S. Brown, J. Bell and D. Carson (eds), *Marketing Apocalypse – Eschatology, Escapology and the Illusion of the End*. London: Routledge.

Brown, S., Bell, S. and Carson, D. (eds) (1996). *Marketing Apocalypse – Eschatology, Escapology and the Illusion of the End*. London: Routledge.

Brownlie, D., Saren, M., Wensley, R. and Whittington, R. (1999). *Rethinking Marketing: Towards Critical Marketing Accountings*. London: Sage.

Burton, D. (2001). 'Critical marketing theory: the blueprint?' *European Journal of Marketing*, 35(5/6), 722–743.

Catterall, Maclaran & Stevens (2002). 'Critical reflection in the marketing curriculum'. *Journal of Marketing Education*, 24(3), 184–192.

Craib, Ian (1992). Modern Social Theory – from Parsons to Habermas. Hertfordshire: Harvester Wheatsheaf.

Desmond, J. (1997). 'Marketing and the war machine'. *Marketing, Intelligence and Planning*, 15(7), 338–351.

Fineman, S. (1999). 'Commentary'. In D. Brownlie, M. Saren, R. Wensley and R. Whittington (eds), *Rethinking Marketing – Towards Critical Marketing Accountings*. London: Sage.

Firat, F. and Dholakia, N. (1998). *Consuming People: From Political Economy to Theaters of Consumption*. New York: Routledge.

Firat, F., Dholakia, N. and Bagozzi, R. (1987). *Philosophical and Radical Thought in Marketing*. Massachusetts: Lexington Books.

Franks, T. (1997). *The Conquest of Cool: Business Culture, Counterculture and the Rise of Hip Consumerism*. Chicago and London: The University of Chicago Press.

Gummesson, E. (2001). 'Are current research approaches in marketing leading us astray?' *Marketing Theory*, 1(1), 27–48.

Habermas, J. (1983). 'Modernity – an incomplete project'. In H. Foster, *The Anti-Aesthetic: Essays on Postmodern Culture*. Washington: Bay Press, pp. 3–15 (trans. by Seyla Benhabib).

Herman, E. and Chomsky, N. (1995). *Manufacturing Consent: The Political Economy of the Mass Media*. London: Vintage.

Hetrick, W. and Lozada, H. (1999). 'Theory, ethical critique and the experience of marketing'. In D. Brownlie, M. Saren, R. Wensley and R. Whittington (eds), *Rethinking Marketing – Towards Critical Marketing Accountings*. London: Sage.

Hirschman, E. (1991). 'Secular mortality and the dark side of consumer behavior: or how semiotics saved my life'. *Advances in Consumer Research*, 28, 1–4.

Holbrook, M. (1996). 'On eschatology, onanist scatology, or honest catology? Cats swinging, scat singing and cat slinging and writs in a catalytic catechism for the cataclysm'. In S. Brown, J. Bell and D. Carson (eds), *Marketing Apocalypse – Eschatology, Escapology and the Illusion of the End*. London: Routledge.

Holt, D. (2002). 'Why do brands cause trouble? A dialectical theory of consumer culture and branding'. *Journal of Consumer Research*, 29(June), 70–90.

Horkheimer, M. (2004). *Eclipse of Reason*. London/New York: Continuum.

Jager, L. (2004). *Adorno: A Political Biography*. Conneticut: Yale University Press.

Knights, D., Sturdy, A. and Morgan, G. (1994). 'The consumer rules? An examination of the rhetoric and 'reality' of marketing in financial services'. *European Journal of Marketing*, 28(3), 42–54.

Kotler, P. (1987). 'Humanistic marketing: beyond the marketing concept'. In A.F. Firat, N. Dholakia and R. Bagozzi (eds), *Philosophical and Radical Thought in Marketing*. Lexington: Lexington Books.

Maclaran, P. and Brown, S. (2005). 'The center cannot hold: consuming the utopian marketplace'. *Journal of Consumer Research*, 32(September), 311–323.

Marcuse, H. (2002). *One-Dimensional Man*. London: Routledge.

McDonagh, P. and Prothero, A. (1996). 'Making a drama out of a crisis – the final curtain for the marketing concept'. In S. Brown, J. Bell and D. Carson (eds), *Marketing Apocalypse – Eschatology, Escapology and the Illusion of the End*. London: Routledge.

Murray, J. and Ozanne, J. (1991). 'The critical imagination: emancipatory interests in consumer research'. *Journal of Consumer Research*, 18(September), 129–144.

Rogers, E. (1987). 'The critical school and consumer research'. *Advances in Consumer Research*, 14, 7–11.

Rubin, A. (2003). 'The Adorno Files'. In N. Gibson and A. Rubin (eds), *Adorno – A Critical Reader*. Massachussetts, London: Blackwell.

Saren, M. and Hastings, G. (2003). 'The critical contribution of social marketing'. *Marketing Theory*, 3(3), 305–322.

Shankar, A. and Patterson, M. (2001). 'Interpreting the past, writing the future'. *Journal of Marketing Management*, 17, 481–501.

Slater, D. (1997). *Consumer Culture and Modernity*. Cambridge, UK: Polity Press.

Thompson, C. (2004). 'Marketplace mythology and discourses of power'. *Journal of Consumer Research*, 31(June), 162–180.

4

Concerning Marketing Critterati: Beyond Nuance, Estrangement and Elitism

Douglas Brownlie and Paul Hewer

Hitherto [wo]men have constantly made up for themselves false conceptions about themselves, about what they are and what they ought to be.

Marx and Engels (1985)

To problematize the status of knowledge claims in marketing, it is argued that an 'interesting' (Davis, 1971) critical theory of marketing will assert the provisional and interested nature of such claims. In seeking to reveal the power relations embedded in the operations of such claims, critical marketing practice will unmask the subtle work of conventions that frame the conduct of research and teaching practice. The cornerstone of this argument is that institutions of marketing instigate regularities of conduct and experience that come to constitute its subjects: this can be taken as a form of oppression that produces docile subjects which are little more than the fictive inventions of competing interests within the marketing academy. In critical management circles this is the 'spin' typically put on what is termed 'marketing'. However, in this chapter we are seeking to open up disciplinary space in a positive manner, without the unhelpful declamation of ambitious critterati. In our view the point of importing critical theory into marketing is to foster *sceptical reflexivity* within our theorizing. Of course, raising questions about entrapment within dominant paradigms and other totalizing systems that function as interpretation is fair game for an academic discipline. And if it stimulates informed debate, we welcome it, although debate has been part of the discipline's academic culture as long as we have been working in it: Can anyone remember the heated academic debates in the early 1980s about the early decision-support system that was known as the growth-share matric? So, although emancipation from the oppressive structures and strictures that bind scholars to institutionalized logics and norms may be the declared goal of the critical project, we suggest that the academic power games being played are strategic, interested, and elitist, masking claims to disciplinary territory and prestige. Clearly then, notions of emancipation are not only situated and utopian in character, but also undermined by the politics of representation that contain and enfold them.

Introduction

> Today, apart from its marginal role in reproducing the dominant social relations through the academies, it [criticism] is almost entirely bereft of a raison d'etre. It engages at no significant point with any substantial social interest, and as a form of discourse is almost entirely self-validating and self-perpetuating.
>
> Eagleton (1984, p. 108)

In her reviews of the character and status of critical marketing, Burton (2001, 2005) bemoans the slow development of critical discourse in marketing, attributing it to '[a] lack of a theoretical tradition and relatively poor knowledge of theoretical developments in other social sciences' (2001, p. 737). She broadly asserts that emancipation from the structures and strictures that bind marketing management scholars to normalized institutionalized logics, such as performative means-ends calculations and naïve scientism, should be the goal of a critical marketing project that seeks to redress the lack of critical theoretical discourse within the discipline. This chapter considers the claimed liberatory potential of critical marketing, arguing that notions of emancipation are not only situated and utopian in character, but also undermined by the politics of representation: this is another way of saying that if we are to realize the reflexive, de-naturalizing goals of critical marketing, we must theorize social contexts of marketing knowledge production. This chapter discusses how it might be that self-consciously motivated critical theorizing in marketing could make it possible to see and say different things than we are accustomed to: to interrogate our understanding anew, perhaps revealing new insights, or reminding us of past insights now forgotten. In this way we explore critical marketing's aim to open up collective disciplinary space for new voices and new sources of disciplinary capital, encouraging a theoretical pluralism within marketing that draws on the wider social sciences.

Reflexivity, De-naturalization and Non-performativity

The nascent stream of critical marketing scholarship claims that the basis of its contribution lies in a capacity to carry forward the project of reflexive theory building and critique within the discipline, through pedagogy and research practice informed by scepticism, or as Lyotard puts it, 'incredulity towards meta-narratives' (1984, p. xxiv). And while in marketing circles Lyotard's work has been assimilated and appropriated by the interests of a solipsistic brand of postmodernism, we use it here to make disciplinary space for a *radically relevant* body of critical practice in marketing studies. We argue that such practice shares with critical management an unwillingness to 'take received wisdoms and practices for granted' (Thompson, 2005, p. 365); it also shares what Fournier and Grey (2000, p. 18) describe as a commitment to 'uncovering the alternatives that have been effaced by management knowledge and practice'. In their view, 'writing in what has been written out' (ibid, p. 18) and other practices of de-naturalization are defining moments of critical practice. Also shared is a recognition of the creative tensions between scepticism towards, say, narratives that speak of how knowledge is situated within communities of research practice, and inspiration arising from efforts to rethink the plausibility of such narratives. Through illustrating the contested 'othering' of elite discourse on markets and consumers, we hope to suggest how a radically relevant marketing might lay claim to the mantle of critical practice while energizing other material practices within the academy.

While arguing that critically reflexive narratives may offer one way – not the only way – of imagining how the marketing academy *does* identity work through practices of theorizing and critique, we also explore how the knowledge claims constructed by such practices are interested and provisional – even if the disciplinary institutions that underpin economies of academic practice do not share those interests or horizons. Our argument draws on the perceptive comments of Parker (1995, p. 554) who concludes that a critical modernism, not postmodernism, usefully informs his radical analyses of organizations while at the same time offering him 'clear reasons for wanting to [continue to] write [about organizations]'. For while we argue that narratives compete for persuasiveness while speaking to the provisional nature of knowledge claims, they also position the material practices that constitute the marketing academy within discursive and institutional functions. This conveniently reminds us that the aim of critical marketing practice is to create a contestatory space in which 'the form of utterance or address speaks to otherwise unrecognized, or passively accepted, meanings, values, and beliefs that cultural production normally reproduces and legitimizes' (Solomon-Godeau, 1999, p. 240).

Drawing on critical social theory then, critical marketing perspectives seek to interrogate the functioning of settled knowledge claims and other orthodoxies within the institutions of the disciplinary formation we know as marketing – including those of armchair marketing critterati such as Morgan (1992, 2003), Alvesson (1994) and Alvesson and Willmott (1996). In this way it seeks to problematize uncontested practices by means of which credentialized knowledge claims are produced, distributed and consumed (Werner, 1991). Furthermore, the reactionary claims of those authors feed off venerable disputes within marketing about competing claims to knowledge expertise and legitimacy which frame the subject world of marketing in narrowly static and surprisingly naïve fashion. They appeal to the signifier 'critical' to perform the important function of disguising numerous implicit value judgements and strategic moves, while stabilizing the writing of their so-called 'critical theorizing'.

In the light of this we acknowledge a place for a body of critical practice within the field of marketing, whereby ruling illusions and their justifications, reproduced by convention and hierarchy, are subjected to a more active interrogation than the totalizing narratives of postmodern marketing permit. We argue that this calls for a more reflexive and historically informed critique of marketing than is currently available from mainstream 'critters' (Parker, 2002, p. 117) such as Morgan (1992, 2003), Alvesson (1994) and Alvesson and Willmott (1996) who, in their apparent rush towards the emancipation of the printed page, refuse to be distracted by the exploitative manoeuvres they offer up by way of 'oven-ready' critical content. This chapter discusses how it might be that critical marketing practice makes it possible to ask questions of context that interrogate our assumptions, perhaps revealing new positionalities, or repositionings of previous lines of thought: but importantly, encouraging new voices, new forms of cultural criticism capable of contesting the powerful subjectivizing processes of contemporary marketing discourse:

The Holy Theatre of Marketing

> The Holy theatre ... is the theatre of the invisible-made-visible: the notion that the stage is a place where the invisible can appear has a deep hold on our thoughts. We are all aware that most of life escapes our senses: a most powerful explanation of the various arts is that they talk of patterns which we can only begin to recognise when they manifest themselves as rhythms or shapes ....
>
> Brook (1968, p. 47)

The project of critical marketing is about 'seeing things' and making connections the 'marketing way'; that is, in a way that is admissible or socially acceptable within the social formation, discourses and practices that constitute the marketing academy. It is about what could be called the 'marketectures', or dominant discourses (Vargo and Lusch, 2004) that constitute forms of subjectivities or organizing visions within our field. It considers how we conjure up these visions through which we render ordinary, everyday experience comprehensible by representing it in terms of imagined acts and objects that we decide can stand for something we call 'real' acts and objects: that is, those that we impute to the lived experience of our informants as we say it represents itself to us through the distance of manufactured through objectification, categorisation, and discussion. It is also about how inscriptions organize us recursively in such a way as to sustain these conventions: that objects in the marketing world 'out there' are antecedent to our representations of them; and that our representations can be deployed as a neutral means of apprehending those pre-existing objects.

In seeking to destabilize the silent technologies or practices by means of which we 'do' objectivity in marketing, the critical marketing project aims to make available for inspection and decoration, not only the myth of objectivity itself, but also related assumptions regarding the neutrality of marketing knowledge-making practice. The paradox of all this is that while critical marketing is indeed said to be 'about' those things, this 'aboutness' is itself a discursive effect, an accomplishment of socially situated signifying practices. For in saying that some thing is 'about' some other thing, not only have we already called into being some act or object, but also we have fashioned an image of it from the repertoire of socially acceptable representational devices available to us. The relations between those so-called 'real' acts and objects and the images we use in talking or writing 'about' them are themselves representations. Objectification and its corollary objectivity are thus ways of saying something of some thing, of locating images in relation to other images within admissible scenes or 'marketectures'.

Starz in their Eyes

A path to the vibrant disciplinary reflexivity sought by critical marketing will then provide ways of thinking ourselves out of a social matrix whereby 'experience comes to us prepackaged' (McLaughlin, 1998, p. 203). Thus, the critical causal modelling or existential phenomenology project is also about how our imaginative works draw on the materiality of collectively sustained symbolic structures which organize our visions and bind us into sets of rules and orthodoxies that illuminate our imaginary, while leaving some space to be imaginative with our representations within admissible conventions (Geertz, 1973, p. 450). So, for instance, when we talk write about the so-called 'lived experience' of managers or consumers, we do so in the knowledge that our textual constructions are shot through with the imagery of admissible accounts governing rationalities, or inscriptions that frame what is seeable and sayable.

What such accounts would then depict is not necessarily how things *literally* are among consumers or managers, but of how, from a particular angle, they imaginatively are; or how, using a particular style of representation, say through speaking (privileging) the language of logical empiricism, causal modelling or existential phenomenology science, we can talk or write about them 'as if' they are. One of the key aims of the critical marketing project is to encourage a more reflexive approach to the making of truth claims within the discipline and also to widen the repertoire of strategic rhetorics available to those seeking to interrogate such claims and to position their counter claims. Lines of argument growing out of a body of unreflexive text have available to them a limited repertoire of positioning strategies which weakens the authority of the knowledge claims being forged. In the absence of a more reflexive research and writing practice, the marketing discipline seems doomed to perpetuate a narrow style of knowledge-making that is increasingly precarious. For instance, in discussing the contribution of the network approach to framing our understanding of market exchange, Hakansson et al. (2004) deploy the term 'marketing' as if there is no problem with its meaning. Indeed it is curious that, after almost 25 years of research and speculation, the IMP Group still seems unable or unwilling to theorize itself and the 'object' of its gaze in way that does not privilege the gaze of the researcher. For, in waxing lyrical about the value of framing market exchange through the lens of organizational relationships strategically, the authors leave uncontested the relations that mediate or frame their assertions regarding the penetrative power of the network perspective and the observations it affords. Yet, paradoxically, to legitimate their uncontested assertions, the authors employ a naïve rhetoric that privileges something they know as 'empirical observation' as the basis for passing judgement on knowledge claims, reverting to this cliché so often and predictably as to fetishize it.

Brownlie et al. (1994) argue that marketing's underlying framework of theory and concepts would benefit from critical perspectives. This is a line of thought of some standing within the discipline (cf. Alderson, 1957; Anderson, 1983; Arndt, 1980, 1985; Bristor and Fischer, 1993; Deshpande 1983; Dholakia and Arndt, 1985; Dholakia et al., 1987; Firat, 1992; Firat et al., 1987; Hetrick and Lozada, 1994; Murray and Ozanne, 1991; Murray et al., 1994; Ozanne and Murray, 1995; Arnould and Thompson, 2005; Brownlie and Saren 1997). In a general sense, it has been continued most recently by Burton (2001, 2005) who argues that the development of the discipline as a social science is being stifled by the tendency to take narrowly fixed positions of agreement about the character of marketing knowledge and its theorization. Drawing inspiration from Giddens (1993), this chapter understands that marketing theory is not just a way to frame meaning, it also 'constitutes a moral intervention in the social life whose conditions of existence the theory seeks to clarify'. In this sense Burton (2005) argues that what passes for marketing theory requires vigilant interrogation through the critical engagement of dialogic critique. Giddens sees this as 'the very life blood of fruitful conceptual development in social theory' (1993, p. 1), while Alvesson and Willmott (1996, p. 119) see it as contributing to the 'challenging and removal of discourses and practices that are incompatible with the development of greater autonomy and responsibility'.

In under-theorized fields like the discipline of marketing, illuminating how authors strategically deploy discursive conventions so to better occupy the higher ground, the authority of a particular mode of representation, is one contribution that critical marketing seeks to make. By expanding our awareness of the repertoire of styles of performing knowledge claims, of communicating and acting in wider policy contexts, critical marketing seeks to work through the 'status panic' that often infects the discipline when held to account in the company of the wider social sciences, where, as Alvesson trenchantly observes, 'marketing is used almost as a pejorative term' (1994, p. 291). In the world of the RAE (Research Assessment Exercise), this is increasingly important as the marketing academy takes serious efforts to jostle for position, status and respect in the highly competitive and under-funded world of higher education and its citation-driven jounral quality league tables. The tendency for one disciplinary area to trash another has to be seen in the context of higher educational politics within the framework of the RAE. Brownlie (2006) argues that marketing has to get over its crisis of confidence and that critical marketing has an important part to play in building the critical capacity of marketing scholarship through developing links with the critterati, especially those who have used Horkheimer, Adorno, Habermas and their likes as, tools to represent academics in marketing as co-opted slaves of the capitalist machine, reproducing delusion, oppression and false consciousness, etc. Although critters rarely admit it, such representations have oppressive and alienating consequences. We in marketing cannot separate the stance strategically taken by elitist critical management scholars on the veracity of their representations from the consequences they have for those of us employed to teach, research and consult in marketing subjects. Yet, there is a nice irony to be found here concerning the unreflexive and oppressive nature of some critical management scholarship of a so-called postmodern character. This is recognized by Tinker (2002, p. 424) when he writes that:

> UK postmodernism has become an upmarket spent-force as a critical activity [and] this is dramatically evidenced most recently by the postmodern text, *Management Lives,* used to teach nuance and estrangement to upwardly mobile MBAs studying at 'elite' British Universities located in centers of urban poverty, violence and deprivation.

Dormitive Framings

> To surmount the situation of oppression, people must first critically recognize its causes, so that through transforming action they can create a new situation, one which makes possible the pursuit of a fuller humanity.
>
> Friere (1996, p. 29)

Some of the more 'entrepreneurially minded' critical management scholars have not been slow to exploit the rhetoric of textually constructed 'critical distance' as a literary device for making strong assertions about the oppression wreaked by other disciplines upon the world – while claiming innocence for themselves! For instance, in a rather unforgiving, sanctimonious and myopic critique of what he calls 'consumer marketing', Alvesson (1994) claims that because this subject area is the dutiful servant of capitalism – cultural doping and mystification being among its more acceptable activities – society needs the intervention of critical theory in order to 'liberate parochial marketing academics' (ibid, 1994, p. 302) and the citizens they seek to orchestrate from the tyranny of calculated misrepresentation and narrow-mindedness that constitutes the field. He uses the metaphor of emancipation to evoke a process of transformation towards epiphany, an awakening to the institutionalized blindness embedded in the disciplinary formation of marketing. In this way the goal of emancipation is to help the blind (marketers) to 'see' through revealing the habits of thought and prejudices that guide their vision. In this sense 'sight' is the privilege of perspective: our 'gaze' is administrated by a technical and cultural apparatus, and it conforms to the norms of that social setting (Marcuse, 1964). It is not merely a matter of claiming to see things as others do not and of taking the trouble to say so, but of attributing to received disciplinary perspectives differential levels of consciousness. One person's acuity can be another's myopia and the paradox resides in the socially constructed nature of what we do or do not notice. As Thompson (1972, p. 24) writes 'In a town full of bedrock crazies, nobody even notices an acid freak.' The gaze is socially situated. It can become a penetrating gaze when turned in on itself to reveal ways in which our research gaze is the product of circulating technologies of self-governance embedded in interlocking marketing discourses.

The term dormitive is used by Goleman (1985, p. 24) to denote an obfuscation, or a failure to see things. He refers to dormitive frames as the forces that make for a waking sleep at the margins of awareness, or as the bends and twists insinuated into attention by the urge for security and comfort of habit. As Goleman (1985, p. 24) observes:

> if we can glimpse the edges that frame our experience, we are a bit freer to expand our margins. We may want to have more say over them, to consider whether we want the limits on thought and action so imposed.

After Firat and Venkatesh (1995), this chapter considers the liberatory potential of seeing things such as 'relevance' differently; of noticing what it is that we fail to notice about 'relevance' in marketing, even if it means that the pressures to conform to institutionalized expectations and conventions remain inescapable.

To think new thoughts, to render the familiar strange, we must first consider what makes the thinkable possible. Giddens (1993, p. 15) observes that 'modern institutions are unthinkable without systematic and informed reflection upon the conditions of social activity'. As Brownlie, Saren, Wensley and Whittington (1999) argue, marketing thought then calls for such systematic reflection upon the conditions of social activity within its gaze; and marketing re-thought, through critical perspectives, calls for the discipline to interrogate this normalizing gaze and to confront the strangeness of the familiar. Critical marketing can then be seen as an exercise in the surveillance of meaning (Baudrillard, 1983, 1990), a considered reflexivity which Mills (1959, p. 196) argues is an important component of what he calls 'intellectual craftsmanship'. In a similar vein, Cooper and Burrell (1988, p. 101) observe that:

> [i]n order to see the ordinary with a fresh vision, we have to make it 'extraordinary', i.e., to break with the habits of organized routine and see the world 'as though for the first time'; it is necessary to

free ourselves of normalized ways of thinking which blind us to the strangeness of the familiar.

The cornerstone of the critical marketing argument is that collective institutions of marketing instigate regularities of conduct and experience that come to constitute its subjects. The point of importing critical social theory is thus to nurture a sceptical reflexivity which raises questions about entrapment within dominant paradigms and other totalizing systems that function as interpretation Vargo and Lusch (2004). The critical marketing project is clearly about the renewal of what Habermas (1971, 1974) understands as the 'emancipatory impulse', the reflexive and sceptical urge, in this case, of marketing. Indeed, this chapter is an attempt to get beyond what might be known as the happy, business as usual marketing, beyond what Marcuse (1964, p. 84) refers to as 'The Happy Consciousness – the belief that the real is rational and that the system delivers the goods – [that] reflects the new conformism which is a facet of technological rationality translated into social behaviour.' However, to do so it is essential to speak of what Bauman terms the rise of interpreter and the fall of the legislator, since the return (if we've ever been away) to critical theory speaks as much of the aspirations, fears and imaginations of marketing intellectuals themselves as they seek out novel ways to survive in the citation-driven publication game that the rae has forged.

Moving Beyond Happy Marketing

Facts may seem black and white by the time they hit your TV screen, but professional teams sift through mountains of grey to get them there. You need positioning, like a product in the market – the jails are full of people who didn't manage their positions.

Pierre (2003, p. 34)

After Hopper et al. (1987, p. 438), the chapter argues that the value of critical perspectives 'resides in [their] capacity to reveal some of the basic assumptions and theoretical deficiencies of [conventional] approaches'. Thus, the critical marketing project is not attempting to draw attention towards 'new' marketing phenomena, but to the conditions of possibility of the 'new': how we might render different images of what we have already decided is knowable. In this regard critical marketing argues for a socially and historically located understanding of the discipline and the traditions that link the interpreter and that which is interpreted (cf. Arnold and Fisher, 1996; Burton, 2001, 2005; Holbrook, 1997). And drawing on the richly percipient work of Bristor and Fischer (1993) in the context of setting voices of feminist critique within consumer research, especially situating the presence of the researcher in the research, critical marketing also seeks to encourage voices that have been marginalized or excluded by disciplinary practices and the institutions which support them (Firat and Venkatesh, 1995; Murray and Ozanne, 1991; Ozanne and Murray, 1995). As Grey (1997, p. 593) comments:

The history of management studies, like the history of all disciplines, is one in which the contributions of some are recognised while those of others are occluded or marginalized. Although this may have an aspect of chance, more obviously it reflects distinct patterns of inequality. Thus those voices which are generally marginal in society are likely to be written out of any specific history.

Broadly speaking then, as Morgan observes, critical perspectives position marketing as a way of 'doing particular social relations' (1992, p. 136). In a revision of his work, Morgan (2003, p. 129) adds that the widespread penetration of marketing into the public sphere has become too important a part of collect-ive social life to be left solely to the naïve technocratic rhetoric and representations of the extant marketing discourse which has given us the hegemonic world of the 'governable consumer'. He concludes that critical approaches to marketing must 'be part of a wider attempt to reconstruct our understanding of the rela-tionship between self and society in a context where global problems of insecu-rity, risk and inequality cannot be solved on the basis of individual preferences' (2003, p. 130). And in this sense he bemoans the lack of substantive social cri-tique in marketing, especially in Brown's (1995, 1998) superficially seductive articulations of postmodern analysis. Morgan (2003, p. 119) argues that:

> the result [of postmodern marketing] is critique that ultimately lacks any purpose beyond its own local struggle to broaden the discipline of mar-keting. Any critique of 'society' or the social consequences of markets, marketing and mass consumption is lost . . . the result is critique with-out substance that is all about style and very little about content.

For some the aim of critical marketing is not merely to articulate criticism, but to explore the potential liberatory aspects of the tensions between current marketing thinking and criticisms of it (Bristor and Fischer, 1993; Firat and Venkatesh, 1995). Furthermore, it is not merely to reproduce the 'strong ver-sion' of Alvesson and Willmott's (1992b, p. 453) critical theory, with its total-izing attack on management ideology and promises of emancipation from false consciousness and 'frozen social relations'. Following Alvesson and Willmott's (1992b, p. 453) revealing attempt to reformulate the idea of eman-cipation in management and organization studies, this chapter suggests a more modest form of engagement with the discipline and its representations of the everyday practices of consumers or managers and the institutions that produce and mediate those practices. It favours an eclectic framework of cri-tique which leaves space for many voices in addition to those of card-carrying critical theorists. There is indeed much to be learned from letting consumers or managers speak for themselves, even if critical ethnographers have diffi-culty 'hearing' what is being said, for there is much to commend Lilley's (1997, p. 51) views that 'managers and critical management researchers may be play-ing similar games, with similar rules, for different teams'. The danger is that critical theorists would be unable to recognize emancipation anywhere but in their officially sanctioned showplaces; that, ironically, they would be blind to the possibility that the ardent claims of zealous critical management academ-ics and other wide-eyed, well-scrubbed children of the suburbs, are more a symbol of the contemporary culture machine's authority, than an agent of resistance (Frank, 1997, p. 154); that critical management and its local variant, critical marketing, would be silent in the face of its own unspoken claims to authority and privilege.

A critical marketing would then reassert the part to be played by active consumers and managers. It would of course seek to problematize the assumption that marketing managers and consumers act as the carriers of an impartial marketized rationality. It would show how marketing technology cannot provide a neutral way of looking at the world, irrespective of the intentions behind its deployment. It would show how the perennial debates about 'relevance' serve the wider political interests of the academy. It would raise awareness of how marketing discourse constitutes its object of analysis, consumers and managers, and is implicated in the production and reproduction of the existing social arrangements which constitute its domain of research. As Alvesson and Willmott (1992a, p. 4) suggest, it would also be motivated by 'an effort to discredit, and ideally eliminate, forms of management and organization that have institutionalized the opposition between the purposefulness of individuals and the seeming givenness and narrow instrumentality of work–process relationships', where, after Baudrillard (1975), we can consider markets as work organizations, consumption as a form of work, and consumers as an occupational group. As Morgan advises (1992, p. 154) it would develop a 'critique of existing social arrangements as much as a critique of marketing itself'. And it would seek to do so through developing a critique of the existing social arrangements that constitute the privilege and authority of critical perspectives. Rather than seeing 'emancipation' as a final end in itself, it would see it as an ongoing process, a state of mind that needs to be nurtured and sustained: for one person's emancipation is surely another's imprisonment, just as one person's totalizing ideology is another's free-thinking (Eagleton, 1991, p. 4); just as one person's convoluted dressage is another's straight talking; just as one person's alternative music is another's derivative product of the rebel ideology that fuels music industry marketing; just as the protestation of one person's counter-culture is another's repackaged ritual stomping; just as one person's worthless daub is another's venerated treasure; just as one person's reading of history is another's false consciousness; just as one person's attempt at levity is another's murderous insult. It would carefully consider the possibility of critique and how any critique could possibly be framed (Bauman, 1994; Grey, 1997; Grey and Willmott 2005; Parker, 1995) given a context in which the primary business of business is no longer producing goods or services, or exploiting labour, but the more important business of manufacturing culture (Frank, 1997, p. 157).

Let's Get Critical

> To instil into the Established Order the complacent portrayal of its drawbacks has nowadays become a paradoxical but incontrovertible means of exalting it.
>
> Barthes (1973, p. 45)

In his essay on the impotence of much contemporary criticism of dominant institutions, Barthes warns of the homeopathic effect of criticism that in effect quells or disables doubts about institutions through exposing their ills. He writes that through what he calls 'operation margarine': 'one inoculates the public with a contingent evil to prevent or cure an essential one . . . a little confessed evil saves one from acknowledging a lot of hidden evil' (ibid, p. 46). The public exposure of the problems of institutions is then a price worth paying if it immunizes the community against deeper social ills, ensuring stasis and conformity. Barthes argues that in this way the survival of the dominant order is ensured; and thus can criticism become the complicit bedfellow of conformity. Indeed, in his critique of postmodern marketing's critique, Morgan (2003) seeks to add the lustre of piety to his dark forebodings by arguing that when style itself becomes content, critique is the bedfellow of conformity.

The critical marketing project is 'in theory' not merely an attempt to bring the problems of the marketing discipline and its institutions to the public gaze through publication, although you could argue that careers may benefit from doing so. It is also an attempt to resist or disrupt the conventions that govern practices of interpretation and representation, through engaging in what Alvesson and Willmott (1996, p. 15) refer to as 'reconstruction and critique': where reconstruction 'mobilizes critical reason to diagnose prevailing conditions' (ibid, p. 15); and critique 'entails a process of self-reflection . . . designed to achieve liberation from the domination of past constraints' (Connerton, 1976, p. 20 in Alvesson and Willmott, ibid). In this sense critical marketing must at least offer ways of 'raising questions about dominant paradigms and resisting the totalizing systems that function as interpretation' (McLaughlin, 1996).

In our view one key point has been overlooked by students of the critical project in marketing: although the critical project may be dormant in the managerial domain of the marketing discipline where conflict is theorized away through the marketing concept, it is very much 'alive and kicking', and has been for many years, in the domain of consumer research. The reasons for this are available in the *Proceedings of the Association for Consumer Research* and related publications, including the *Journal of Consumer Research*, which records the debates that took place around the then mandatory managerial orientation of publishable research in consumer behaviour. We recommend Belk's (1995) comprehensive review of research in consumer behaviour for those who need to be brought up to speed. More recently we have had significant interventions by leading scholars such as Firat and Dholakia (1998), Denzin (2001), Kozinets (2002), Thompson and Troester (2002), Arnould and Thompson (2005) and indeed, Holt (2002). It is clear to the authors that the natural home for the critical project in marketing is in the domain of consumer studies, where the declared aim of liberatory practice is gaining wider recognition in the form of an emerging oppositional counter-culture. For instance, in his article on brands and consumer resistance, Holt (2002) reviews the stream of critical work in consumer research by way of theorizing resistance as consumer practice, or what Ozanne and Murray (1995) refer to as the 'reflexively defiant consumer'. Holt writes that 'consumers are beginning to break down market-ers' dominance by seeking out social spaces in which they produce their own culture, apart from that which is foisted on them by the market' (Holt, 2002, p. 72). His empirical study explores the commodification of personal sovereignty and how 'theories of consumer resistance – as a reflexive code-consciousness and fragmented self-production – are enacted in everyday life' (ibid, p. 73). In our view this is a good example of the critically informed reflexive scepti-cism that is available in narratives of the marketing discipline. Of course, this kind of writing practice is needed in other areas of marketing study, especially the managerial literature. So, in focusing on textbook representations of mar-keting management knowledge, we argue that armchair marketing critterati conveniently draw a veil around work that may interrupt or endanger the attainment of their ambitions.

Going Critical

> If we know in what way society is unbalanced, we must do what we can to add weight to the lighter scale . . . we must have formed a conception of equilibrium and be ever ready to change sides like justice, that fugitive from the camp of conquerors.
>
> Weil (1963, p. 151)

In adopting a 'critical stance towards the accepted managerialist assumptions' underpinning marketing, critical marketing seeks to problematize the sta-tus claims of marketing knowledge, exploring relations between power and knowledge within the discipline and their impact on norms, conventions and admissible practices in research, teaching and knowledge development (Catterall et al., 1999, 2002; Mingers, 2000). It points to important work in a range of cognate disciplines which explore the question of imbalance and related issues (Brownlie et al., 1993). The contribution of critical perspectives to management-related disciplines is perhaps most clearly developed within accounting (Power and Laughlin, 1992). In their lucid critique of research in management accounting, Hopper et al. (1987) discuss the 'failure to theorize accounting as a fully social practice', drawing attention to its narrow base in social science methodology. They question a number of features of main-stream management accounting research, prominent among them being: its theoretical and methodological base in neoclassical economics and function-alist organizational theory; the widely held image of the organization as a unitary and integrated system where resource allocation decisions are a mat-ter of information provision; the conventional representation of management accounting as a politically neutral, technical information service that can be abstracted from fundamental issues of ownership and control; and the wide-spread acceptance of the authority of managerialist assumptions. They go on to isolate a number of important problems in the discipline, including: the fail-ure to develop the idea that accounting is a set of practices which are both the medium and outcome of the politico-economic context in which accounting is embedded; the failure to consider the role of language in shaping accounting theory and practice; the failure to analyse the historical and cultural specificity of accounting practices and knowledge; and the growing evidence that 'conventional accounting knowledge is often not used in practice; and that when it is, it can induce undesirable and unsought consequences' (ibid, p. 438).

Hopper et al. (1987) not only reveal the potential of critical thinking to contribute to the development of research and theory within management accounting: their pathfinding work also suggests the potential of critical thinking to contribute to the development of several disciplines which share the basic assumptions of management accounting, including marketing. It is clear then, that as Sawchuck (1994, p. 95) comments, '[marketing] is a fecund terrain for critical thinking'; and that as Alvesson and Willmott (1996, p. 128) advise 'a critical theory approach to marketing can bring fresh insights and provide a more penetrating appreciation of its ethical and social significance'.

Importantly, Bartels (1976) and later Cochoy (1998), remind us that marketing has its origins as a discipline in studies of the impact of the monopsonistic buying power of intermediaries on the operations of agricultural markets of the mid-Western states of the USA during the late 19th century. Indeed at the turn of that century the 'marketing problem', as it was then known, referred to the 'suspected manipulation of prices for farm products by middlemen to the detriment of producers and consumers alike' (Benton, 1987, p. 422). The discipline of marketing emerged from studies of what steps could be taken to provide a civic framework within which markets would operate more effectively in the interest of producers and consumers too. And in this sense the early development of the discipline could be seen as contributing to the social good of society through exposing what Alvesson and Willmott (1996, p. 120) refer to as 'how structures of domination and exploitation shape and mediate [exchange] relationships'.

Through revisiting the emancipatory impulse of early marketing, critical perspectives also hope to remind us of the discipline's wider constituency of the managed, consumers and citizens alike, as well as the value of thinking historically (Jameson, 1991) about marketing thought (Fullerton, 1988; Hollander and Rassuli, 1993; Vink, 1992). There may be an imbalance in marketing scholarship which critical perspectives could help redress, for it does seem as if today's happy marketing discipline has lost its early direct involvement in the wider affairs of the community. The challenge posed by critical marketing is to be able to engage with more than one perspective, perhaps through dialectical tacking (Geertz, 1983; Thompson, 1997); to have a repertoire of more than one way of performing your knowledge; to recognize when the undecidable is being rendered decidable and for what purposes; and to privilege ideas knowingly. Towards this end there is an important role for critical thinking, as Eagleton (1984, p. xx) advises:

> [The task of criticism] is not to redouble the text's self-understanding, to collude with its object in a conspiracy of silence. The Task is to show the text as it cannot know itself.

So Long to the Marketing Legislator,
Hello to the Marketing Interpreter

In his book *Legislators and Interpreters* subtitled on *Modernity, Post-modernity and Intellectuals* (1987), Bauman charts the role of the intellectual within contemporary society arguing:

> For the better part of their history, Western intellectuals drew the blueprints of a better, civilized or rational society by extrapolating their collective experience in general, and the counterfactual assumptions of their mode of life in particular. A 'good society', all specific differences between numerous blueprints notwithstanding, invariably possessed one feature: it was a society well geared to the performance of the intellectual role and the flourishing of the intellectual mode of life.
>
> (ibid, p. 147)

Bauman's thesis is highly persuasive and relevant in the context of framing critical marketing practice. It centres on the idea that postmodern consumer culture has undermined what he terms the legislative role of intellectuals fashioning their overly prescriptive visions of the ideal society through the application of science, reason and rationality. Instead he suggests that the role of intellectuals has become reduced to that of generating simply 'good' interpretations. The contemporary intellectual predicament, or what we might term the academic condition, heralds a new form of theorizing, not borne of the legislating intent of yesteryear, but where the authority of academic interpretation is paramount. Or as Bauman spells out this project:

> The good interpreter is one who reads the meaning properly – and there is a need (or so one may hope) for somebody to vouch for the rules which guided the reading of the meaning and thus made the interpretation valid or authoritative; somebody who would sieve good interpretations from bad ones... What remains for the intellectuals to do, is to interpret such meanings for the benefit of those who are not of the community which stands behind the meanings; to mediate communication between 'finite provinces' for 'communities of meaning'.
>
> (ibid, p. 197)

This seems a useful way forward for critical marketing, that is to accept in other words the limits to our deeds, but to broaden our horizons theoretically. In resalvaging the import of critical theory to marketing we must consider what price must be paid. For us, the trade-off is the realization that the ground upon which critical theory was initially built is now much less certain, much less assured and that from such unstable and uncertain positions, what we term the conditions of academic knowledge, must bring forth a more humble and modest form of critical theorizing. At issue here is the sense of self-belief and assurance of the critical marketing project itself, especially the overly prescriptive and legislative form that this may sometimes take: 'Through the process of critique and dialogue, the critical researcher tries to help people imagine alternative social organizations that facilitate the development of human potential free from constraints' (Murray and Ozanne, 1991, p. 129).

Such emancipatory imaginings from Murray and Ozanne (1991) chimes with what we would argue is the position of the academic writing in contemporary culture. To understand this, we turn to Baudrillard who speaks of intellectuals as marginal characters largely distant from the drama of everyday life, but also as carriers of what he terms 'negativity', for whom 'opposition' is a cosy position to occupy, as he explains:

> I wouldn't be against envisaging a world without intellectuals as such. . . It would mean that the social order had eliminated every kind of discourse. On the other hand, it could mean a radiant and transparent world where there is no longer any need for thoughts, analyses, etc. We would envisage the end of the intellectual in an extremely optimistic or an extremely pessimistic version. Still, such as intellectuals are in this last century and a half of history, they cannot be denied the possibility of raving a little, of going in utopia, but intellectuals are carriers of a kind of utopia. This is the only positivity they can have.
>
> Baudrillard (1993, pp. 79–80)

So when we as intellectuals speak (or better 'rave on') it is always from this marginal position mediated through discourse, and no amount of medicine be it methodological or epistemological will serve to remedy this alienated location. But the value of this insight we argue is itself emancipating, since it serves to free us from the illusion of speaking for others. It also enables us to chart the future forms that a critical marketing project could take, a certain kind of 'positivity' in itself.

Performing Critical Theory

The time is through for more writing on the lamentable passing of the virtues of the Frankfurt School. To continue singing the praises of a critical consciousness is itself to rehearse the logic of emasculating irrelevance. It is now time to put our critical aspirations into action; to, in other words, move beyond the rhetoric, from questions of 'why', to questions of how'. To do so, it is necessary to spell out not simply what critical theory can bring to the discipline of marketing, but to chart the forms of knowledge and understanding which have adopted this perspective, to highlight in other words what forms of critical theorizing may look like. What does it mean in other words to do critical research? This kind of question takes us into the territory of doing critical theory, that is performing and practising this form of theorizing as marketing knowledge.

In this search we have consulted all the usual critters, turned to those instances of critmar within marketing which transcends that of merely rhetoric, and we believe ended up with what we see as a few useful examples of critical thinking in practice.

First things first, it is necessary to return to Bauman (1987), because to us, the critmar project is much more about understanding and interpretating the world around us, not theorizing for theorizing's sake, but rather theorizing for understanding rather than emancipation. For as Bauman argues emancipation, much like other beloved intellectual fictions such as resistance and community are created and sustained as much through our own interpretations and justifications rather than having any tangible objective presence in reality (Bauman, 1987, p. 148). Others faced with the self-same dilemmas of the critical theorist have resorted to verse, inventing resonant phrases like 'Ain't no black in the Union Jack' (Zephaniah, 1996, p. 76), or:

The world is like a flower
The sky is bright and blue
Me, egghead in the tower,
Can prove it's all untrue
And
It feels so good to feel so bad
I'm happy when I'm down and sad.

Guillet de Monthoux (2006)

For us, it is useful to envisage such an endeavour as a recipe, akin to a form of cooking. Recipes we believe are 'good to think with' since they provide a set of instructions to move forward, some might see them as too constraining, too systematic perhaps; others (and we include ourselves here) see recipes as enriching and edifying what we see and consume, revealing new understandings of texture and form, or as Rorty suggests in another context: 'help[ing] us break free from outworn vocabularies and attitudes' (1980, p. 12). As we have suggested in another context, it was Levi-Strauss (1970) who captured the notion of naturalizing 'nature', of rendering it in culture, by means of the metaphor 'cooking'. Moreover, as Williamson (1978, p. 103) writes, 'Levi-Strauss describes the cultural transformation of natural objects as a process of "cooking"... In cooking, nature, in the form of raw material (e.g. meat) enters a complex system whereby it is differentiated culturally (e.g. it may be roasted or grilled). In just the same way, images of nature are "cooked" in culture so that they may be used as part of a symbolic system... Once nature has been drawn into culture it is given meaning ... in this sense, nature has been transformed into "the Natural"' (quoted in Hewer and Brownlie, 2006). Cooking is thus a useful metaphor for thinking intellectual endeavours, for as Giard suggests: 'Tomorrow will be the day for another meal, another success. Each invention is ephemeral, but the succession of meals and days has a durable value. In the kitchen, *one battles against time*, the time of this life that is always heading towards death' (1998, pp. 168–169).

Strange Fruit

While the elder of the authors might get himself in the mood for the compensatory recovery provided by the practice of cooking by listening to the radical musical protests of Charles Mingus or nina simone, the younger author gets himself in the mood by listening to some Pulp, perhaps *Common People* to create the right ambience for the critical theorist, especially when Jarvis Cocker laments, ironically that:

> You'll never live like common people
> You'll never do whatever common people do
> You'll never fail like common people
> You'll never watch your life slide out of view
> and then dance and drink and screw
> because there's nothing else to do
> I want to live with common people like you . . .

Pulp (1995)

Now ready to cook, our recipe would start with the staple ingredients: a big dollop of Marx and Engels (especially *German Ideology*) followed by a sprinkling of Adorno and Horkheimer (maybe *Dialectic of Enlightenment* for starters) with Marcuse (*One-Dimensional Man*). To this mixture would then be added a splash of Habermas (go easy though with this, but it is essential to emancipate the other ingredients). To this mixture, why not gently cook in some De Certeau (*The Practice of Everyday Life*, Vols 1 and 2 are essential) and stir with the occasional Baudrillard (perhaps *Consumer Society*) just to improve the final taste of the mixture.

We refrain from giving exact measurements, it is better to learn by trial and error. But as with all recipes mistakes can occur, and are even to be welcomed, the cook like the critical theorist must be ready to 'think on their feet', differences of flavour will inevitably appear as it is in the messy sensuality and everydayness of the practice of cooking (and writing) that the results are revealed and we know whether our (and those of others) theoretical tastebuds have been aroused. Cooking in this sense is an embodied cultural practice akin at some level to praxis: 'that is a working out of philosophical conundrums by other means' (Miller, 1991, pp. 207–208). Cooking as a cultural practice is also a useful way of thinking and doing theory, since it alludes to the significance of performative embodied practices (Nash, 2000), and thereby connects us to the rhythms, rituals and playfulness of our labours to advance theory and understanding. We might argue that too much marketing theory remains 'uncooked', left in a raw unpalatable form with far too little engagement with broader social theory. For us, the performance of critical marketing becomes at its best a sustained engagement with theory and everyday practice (the link to the slow-food movement seems illustrative), a journey through which we 'do' critical theory, a journey in other words to cultivate our sense of taste and distinction as a discipline through practising and honing our critical imaginations.

Conclusion

> The ethical is thus the (back)ground of undecidability, while the polit-
> ical is the domain of decision(s), of taking the full risk of crossing the
> hiatus and translating this impossible request of messianic justice
> into a particular intervention that never lives up to this request.
>
> Zizek (2005, p. 434)

Critical marketing is then not an attempt to provoke unfettered sniping and declamation, nor is it a home for those with a grudge and an axe to grind. Although it shares a sense of wonder at the accelerating momentum of our discipline, it also seeks to give voice to an increasingly held feeling that something important is happening which embraces yet transcends marketing: reshaping its conditions of possibility, dissolving its ideology into the onward rush of the everyday (Berman, 1983, p. 91). You could argue that marketing, as a way of doing social relations, has escaped the gravitational pull of the academy and is itself already in global circulation as a cultural commodity and sign-vehicle (Sawchuck, 1994, p. 111), despite the foundational view of knowledge widely promoted in the academy. Perhaps these developments are outlining a defining moment in the evolution of marketing discourse. Or perhaps we are just witnessing the double hermeneutic at play, one consequence of which is, as Giddens (1993, p. 15) suggests, 'that original ideas and findings in social science tend to "disappear" to the degree to which they are incorporated within the familiar components of practical activities'. And as Knights (1992, p. 514) trenchantly observes 'once knowledge of the social world enters the public domain, the human conditions which rendered it possible are changed, thus undermining the original validity of such knowledge'.

We are caught in the ordering of the social that we seek to analyse (Law, 1994). And with the growing 'marketization' of social relations, we have argued that the internalization and naturalization of a complex set of practices will provide new forms of common sense, self-evident experience and personal identity which the discipline may not be equipped to interrogate, de-naturalize, or otherwise tease-out from underneath the stone of our collective unconscious (Deetz, 1996, p. 37). Generating a marketing gaze sufficient to this task of revelation and rejuvenation offers several opportunities to enrich and strengthen the discipline's contribution to social theory.

We labour within a culture that was not always sympathetic to the marketing discipline and have evolved a repertoire of rhetorical devices that, in anticipating resistance to our edicts, has made space for their realization. Yet, within a few years marketing practice has been taken to heart, enterprise culture pressing them into service towards the 'marketization' of many walks of life. Critical marketing is not concerned that this rhetoric might be punctured, but that its popularity highlights a paradoxical failure, for marketing remains firmly wedded to an 'ideological method' (Durkheim, 1982, p. 82). Through placing singular emphasis on the use of 'facts' to govern the derivation of theory, in the belief that facts mirror 'reality', this method can only provide inadequate accounts of the pre-understandings (Gadamer, 1989) that make it possible to identify an issue, let alone pass judgement upon it. In doing so this method is silent on how social relations are historically and culturally conditioned. It also disregards how research methodology and instrumentation are involved in producing and sustaining a particular construction of reality. Our understanding of the principles around which society organizes itself is changing. This offers critmar the chance to contribute to a more reflexive understanding of marketing as a discipline and to seek to (re)forge interdisciplinary links with areas of contemporary social theorizing, even if, as Knights and Willmott (1997, p. 10) declare, 'the culture and career ladders of academia endorse a defensive kind of disciplinary closure that inhibits critical self-reflection'. That the norms of marketing scholarship cannot be divorced from techniques of normalization which structure thought and discourse into mutually exclusive categories is not in doubt. And although we may share a common identity as members of the marketing tribe, we do not need to believe in the same myths about its past and present; and future past and future present.

References

Alderson, W. (1957). *Marketing Behavior and Executive Action*. Homewood, IL: Irwin, Inc.

Alvesson, M. (1994). 'Critical theory and consumer marketing'. *Scandinavian Journal of Marketing*, 10(3), 291–313.

Alvesson, M. and Willmott, H. (1992a). 'On the idea of emancipation in management and organization studies'. *Academy of Management Review*, 17(3), 432–464.

Alvesson, M. and Willmott, H. (eds) (1992b). *Critical Management Studies*. London: Sage.

Alvesson, M. and Willmott, H. (1996). *Making Sense of Management: A Critical Introduction*. London: Sage.

Anderson, P. (1983). 'Marketing, scientific progress and scientific method'. *Journal of Marketing*, 47(Fall), 18–31.

Arndt, J. (1980). 'Perspectives for a theory of marketing'. *Journal of Business Research*, 8, 389–402.

Arndt, J. (1985). 'On making marketing science more scientific: the role of observations, paradigms, metaphors and puzzle solving'. *Journal of Marketing*, 49, 11–23.

Arnold, M. and Fisher, J. (1996). 'Counterculture, criticisms, and crisis: assessing the effect of the sixties on marketing thought'. *Journal of Macromarketing*, 16(Spring), 118–133.

Arnould, E.J. and Thompson, C.J. (2005). 'Consumer Culture Theory (CCT): twenty years of research'. *Journal of Consumer Research*, 31(March), 868–882.

Bartels, R. (1976). *The History of Marketing Thought*, 2nd edition. Columbus, OH: Grid Inc.

Barthes, R. (1973). *Mythologies*. London: Paladin.

Baudrillard, J. (1975). *The Mirror of Production*. St Louis: Telos Press.

Baudrillard, J. (1983). 'The ecstasy of communication'. In H. Foster (ed.), *The Anti-aesthetic: Essays on Postmodern Culture*. Port Townsend, Washington, DC: Bay Press.

Baudrillard, J. (1990). *Fatal Strategies*. New York: Semiotext(e).

Baudrillard, J. (1993). 'Intellectuals, commitment and political power'. In M. Gane (ed.), *Baudrillard Live*. London: Routledge, pp. 72–80.

Bauman, Z. (1987). *Legislators and Interpreters: On Modernity, Post-modernity and Intellectuals*. Oxford: Polity Press.

Bauman, Z. (1994). *Postmodern Ethics*. Cambridge: Polity Press.

Belk, R. (1995). 'Studies in the new consumer behaviour'. In D. Miller (ed.), *Acknowledging Consumption*. London: Routledge, pp. 58–95.

Benton, R. (1987). 'The practical domain of marketing: the notion of a "free" enterprise economy as a guise for institutionalized marketing power'. *American Journal of Economics*, 46(4), 415–430.

Berman, M. (1983). *All That Is Solid Melts into Air: The Experience of Modernity*. London: Verso.

Bristor, J. and Fischer, E. (1993). 'Feminist thought: implications for consumer research'. *Journal of Consumer Research*, 19(March), 518–536.

Brook, P. (1968). *The Empty Space*. London: Penguin.

Brown, S. (1995). *Postmodern Marketing*. London: Routledge.

Brown, S. (1998). *Postmodern Marketing 2: Telling Tales*. London: International Thomson Press.

Brownlie, D. (2006). 'Emancipation, epiphany and resistance: on the underimagined and over overdetermined in critical marketing'. *Journal of Marketing Management*, 22(5/6), 505–528.

Brownlie, D. and Saren, M. (1997). 'Beyond the one-dimensional marketing manager: the discourse of theory, practice and relevance'. *International Journal of Research in Marketing*, 14, 147–161.

Brownlie, D., Saren, M., Wensley, R. and Whittington, R. (1993). *Rethinking Marketing: New Perspectives on the Discipline and the Profession*, Published Proceedings. Covertry: Warwick Business School.

Brownlie, D., Saren, M., Wensley, R. and Whittington, R. (1994). 'The new marketing myopia: critical perspectives on theory and research in marketing'. *European Journal of Marketing*, 28(3), 6–12.

Brownlie, D., Saren, M., Wensley, R. and Whittington, R. (1999). *Rethinking Marketing: Towards Critical Marketing Accountings*. London: Sage.

Burton, D. (2001). 'Critical marketing theory: the blueprint?' *European Journal of Marketing*, 35(5/6), 722–743.

Burton, D. (2002). 'Towards a critical multicultural marketing theory'. *Marketing Theory*, 2(2), 207–236.

Burton, D. (2005). 'Marketing theory matters'. *British Journal of Management*, 16(1), March, 5–18.

Catterall, M., Maclaren, P. and Stevens, L. (1999). 'Critical marketing in the classroom: possibilities and challenges'. *Marketing Intelligence and Planning*, 17(1), 344–353.

Catterall, M., Maclaren, P. and Stevens, L. (2002). 'Critical reflection in the marketing curriculum'. *Journal of Marketing Education*, 24(3), December, 184–192.

Cochoy, F. (1998). 'Another discipline for the market economy: marketing as a performative knowledge and know-how for capitalism'. In M. Callon (ed.), *The Laws of the Markets*. Oxford: Blackwell, pp. 194–221.

Connerton, P. (1976). *Critical Sociology*. Harmondsworth: Penguin.

Cooper, R. and Burrell, G. (1988). 'Modernism, postmodernism and organizational analysis: an introduction'. *Organization Studies*, 9(1), 91–112.

Davis, M. (1971). 'That's Interesting!', Philosophy of the Social Sciences, 1, p. 309–344.

Deetz, J. (1996). *In Small Things Forgotten: The Archaeology of Early American Life*. New York: Anchor Books.

Denzin, N. (2001). 'The seventh moment: qualitative inquiry and the practices of a more radical consumer research'. *Journal of Consumer Research*, 28(September), 324–330.

Deshpande, R. (1983). 'Paradigms lost: on theory and method in research in marketing'. *Journal of Marketing*, 47(Fall), 101–110.

Dholakia, N. and Arndt, J. (1985). *Changing the Course of Marketing: Alternative Paradigms for Widening Marketing Theory*. Greenwich, CT: JAI Press.

Dholakia, N., Firat, F. and Bagozzi, R. (1987). 'Rethinking marketing'. In F. Firat, N. Dholakia and R. Bagozzi (eds), *Philosophical and Radical Thought in Marketing*. Lexington, MA: DC Heath, pp. 375–384.

Durkheim, E. (1982). *The Rules of Sociological Method*. New York: The Free Press.

Eagleton, T. (1984). *The Function of Criticism*. London: Verso.

Eagleton, T. (1991). *Ideology: An Introduction*. London: Verso.

Firat, F (1987). 'The social Construction of Consumption Patterns: understanding Macro consumption Phenomena', in Philosophical and Radical thought in Marketing, ed. F. Firat et al., Lexington, MA: Lexington, 251–267.

Firat, A.F. (1992). 'Fragmentations in the postmodern'. In J.F. Sherry Jr. and B. Sternthal (eds), *Advances in Consumer Research*, Vol. 19. Provo, UT: Association for Consumer Research, pp. 203–206.

Firat, A.F. and Dholakia, N. (1998). *Consuming People: From Political Economy to Theaters of Consumption*. London: Routledge.

Firat, A.F. and Venkatesh, A. (1995). 'Liberatory postmodernism and the reenchantment of consumption'. *Journal of Consumer Research*, 22(December), 239–268.

Fournier, V. and Grey, C. (2000). 'At the critical moment: prospects for critical management studies'. *Human Relations*, 53(1), 7–32.

Frank, T. (1997). 'Alternative to what?' In T. Frank and M. Weiland (eds), *Commodify Your Dissent: Salvos from the Baffler*. London: W.W. Norton and Company Ltd, pp.145–161.

Friere, P. (1996). *Pedagogy of the Oppressed*. London: Penguin.

Fullerton, R. (1988). 'How modern is modern marketing? Marketing's evolution and the myth of the production era'. *Journal of Marketing*, 52, 108–125.

Gadamer, H.-G. (1989). *Truth and Method*. New York: Crossroad.

Geertz, C. (1973). *The Interpretation of Cultures*. New York: Basic Books.

Geertz, C. (1983). *Local Knowledge*. New York: Basic Books.

Giard, L. (1998). 'The nourishing arts'. In M. de Certeau, L. Giard and P. Mayol (eds), *The Practice of Everyday Life: Vol. 2. Living and Cooking*. Minnesota: Minnesota University Press, pp. 151–169.

Giddens, A. (1993). *New Rules of Sociological Method*, 2nd edition. Cambridge: Polity Press.

Goleman, D. (1985). *Vital Lies, Simple Truths*. New York: Simon and Schuster.

Grey, C. (1997). 'Towards a critique of managerialism: the contribution of Simone Weil'. *Journal of Management Studies*, 34(3), 591–611.

Grey, C. and Willmott, H. (2005). 'Introduction'. In C. Grey and H. Willmott (eds), *Critical Management Studies: A Reader*. Oxford: Oxford University Press, pp. 1–20.

Guillet de Monthoux, P. (2006). 'The oppression blues – or the aesthetics of a critical theorist'. *Consumption, Markets and Culture*, 9(2), 145–146.

Habermas, J. (1971). *Toward a Rational Society*. London: Heinemann.

Habermas, J. (1974). *Theory and Practice*. London: Heinemann.

Hakansson, H., Harrison, D. and Waluszewski, A. (2004). *Rethinking Marketing: Developing a New Understanding of Markets*. Chichester: John Wiley.

Hetrick, W. and Lozada, H. (1994). 'Construing the critical imagination: comments and necessary diversions'. *Journal of Consumer Research*, 21, 548–558.

Hewer, P. and Brownlie, D. (2006). 'Stoveside potterings and other transformations: on cooking representations of culinary culture'. In K. Ekstrom and H. Brembeck (eds), *European Advances in Consumer Research*, Vol. 7. Duluth, MN: Association for Consumer Research, pp. 623–634.

Holbrook, M. (1997). 'Looking back on looking backward: a retrospective review of Edward Bellamy's macromarketing classic'. *Journal of Macromarketing*, 17(Spring), 145–151.

Hollander, S. and Rassuli, K. (eds) (1993). *Marketing: Vol. 6. The International Library of Critical Writings in Business History*. Cheltenham: Edward Elgar Publishing.

Holt, D. (2002). 'Why do brands cause trouble? A dialectical theory of consumer culture and branding'. *Journal of Consumer Research*, 29(June), 70–90.

Hopper, T., Storey, J. and Willmott, H. (1987). 'Accounting for accounting: towards the development of a dialectical view'. *Accounting, Organizations and Society*, 12(5), 437–456.

Jameson, F (1991). 'Postmodernism: Or, The Cultural Logic of Late capitalism', Verso, London.

Knights, D. (1992). 'Changing spaces: the disruptive impact of a new epistemological location for the study of management'. *Academy of Management Review*, 17(3), 514–536.

Knights, D. and Willmott, H. (1997). 'The hype and hope of interdisciplinary management studies'. *British Journal of Management*, 8, 9–22.

Kozinets, R.V. (2002). 'Can consumers escape market? Emancipatory illuminations from burning man'. *Journal of Consumer Research*, 29(June), 20–38.

Law, J. (1994). *Organizing Modernity*. Oxford: Blackwell.

Levi-Strauss, C. (1970). *Introduction to a Science of Mythology: Vol. 1. The Raw and the Cooked*. London: Jonathan Cape.

Lilley, S. (1997). 'Stuck in the middle with you?' *British Journal of Management*, 8, 51–59.

Lyotard, J.-F. (1984). *The Postmodern Condition: A Report on Knowledge*. Manchester: Manchester University Press.

Marcuse, H. (1964). *One-Dimensional Man*, 2nd edition. London: Routledge.

Marx, K. and Engels, F. (1985). *The German Ideology*. London: Lawrence and Wishart.

McLaughlin, T. (1996). *Street Smarts and Critical Theory: Listening to the Vernacular*. London: University of Wisconsin Press.

McLaughlin, T. (1998). 'Theory outside the academy: streetsmarts and critical theory'. *Consumption, Markets and Culture*, 2(2), 201–232.

Miller, D. (1991). *Material Culture and Mass Consumption*. Oxford: Blackwell.

Mills, C.W. (1959). *The Sociological Imagination*. Oxford: Oxford University Press.

Mingers, J. (2000). 'What is it to be critical: teaching a critical approach to management undergraduates'. *Management Learning*, 31(2), 219–237.

Morgan, G. (1992). 'Marketing discourse and practice: towards a critical analysis'. In M. Alvesson and H. Willmott (eds), *Critical Management Studies*. London: Sage, pp. 136–158.

Morgan, G. (2003). 'Marketing and critique: prospects and problems'. In M. Alvesson and H. Willmott (eds), *Studying Management Critically*. London: Sage, pp. 111–131.

Murray, J. and Ozanne, J. (1991). 'The critical imagination: emancipatory interests in consumer research'. *Journal of Consumer Research*, 18, 129–144.

Murray, J., Ozanne, J. and Shapiro, J. (1994). 'Revitalizing the critical imagination: unleashing the crouched tiger'. *Journal of Consumer Research*, 21(December), 559–565.

Nash, C. (2000). 'Performativity in practice: some recent work in cultural geography'. *Progress in Human Geography*, 24(4), 653–664.

Ozanne, J. and Murray, J. (1995). 'Uniting critical theory and public policy to create the reflexively defiant consumer'. *American Behavioral Scientist*, 38(4), February, 516–525.

Parker, M. (1995). 'Critique in the name of what? Postmodernism and critical approaches to organization'. *Organization Studies*, 16(4), 553–564.

Parker, M. (2002). *Against Management: Organization in the Age of Managerialism*. Oxford: Blackwell.

Pierre, D.B.C. (2003). *Vernon God Little*. London: Faber and Faber.

Power, M. and Laughlin, R. (1992). 'Critical theory and accounting'. In M. Alvesson and H. Willmott (eds), *Critical Management Studies*. London: Sage, pp. 113–135.

Pulp (1995). *Common People*. Music: Pulp; Lyrics: Jarvis Cocker, Island Records.

Rorty, R. (1980). *Philosophy and the Mirror of Nature*. Oxford: Blackwell.

Sawchuck, K. (1994). 'Semiotics, cybernetics and the ecstasy of marketing communications'. In D. Kellner (ed.), *Baudrillard: A Critical Reader*. Oxford: Blackwell, pp. 89–116.

Solomon-Godeau, A. (1999). 'Living with contradictions: critical practices in the age of supply-side aesthetics'. In J. Evans and S. Hall (eds), *Visual Culture: The Reader*. London: Sage, pp. 224–243.

Thompson, C and M Troester (2002), 'Consumer Value Systems in the Age of Postmodern Fragmentation: The Case of the Natural Health Microculture', Journal of Consumer Research, 28, (March), 550–571.

Thompson, C. (1997). 'Interpreting consumers: a hermeneutical framework for deriving marketing insights from the texts of consumers' stories'. *Journal of Marketing Research*, XXXIV(November), 438–455.

Thompson, H. (1972). *Fear and Loathing in Las Vegas*. London: Paladin.

Thompson, P. (2005). 'Brands, boundaries and bandwagons: a critical reflection on critical management studies'. In C. Grey and H. Willmott (eds), *Critical Management Studies: A Reader*. Oxford: Oxford University Press, pp. 364–382.

Tinker, T. (2002). 'Disciplinary spin'. *Organization*, 9(3), 419–427.

Vargo, S. and Lusch, R. (2004). 'evolving to a new dominant logic for marketing'. *Journal of Marketing*, 68, January, 1–17.

Vink, N. (1992). 'Historical perspectives in marketing management: explicating experience'. *Journal of Marketing Management*, 8(3), 219–237.

Weil, S. (1963). *Gravity and Grace*. London: Routledge.

Werner, A. (1991). *Promotional Culture: Advertising, Ideology and Symbolic Expression*. London: Sage.

Williamson, J. (1978). *Decoding Advertisements: Ideology and Meaning in Advertising*. Trowbridge: Redwood Books.

Zephaniah, B. (1996). *Propa Propaganda*. Newcastle-upon-Tyne: Bloodaxe Books.

Zizek, S. (2005). *Interrogating the Real*. London: Continuum International Publishing Group.

5

Local Accounts: Authoring the Critical Marketing Thesis

Shona Bettany

The critical doctoral student in marketing has to tread a very uneasy path. In the critical thesis, the writer occupies an ambivalent location in relation to their disciplinary culture, as a critic of it, but at the same time negotiating their own acceptance and belonging to that culture through and beyond their doctoral research. Further, the ontologies that often underpin critical marketing doctorates contain a commitment to challenge the very foundations of the thesis genre and its assumed worlds of knowledge and knowledge making. At the same time there is a need to satisfy the requirements of this modernist genre, to produce a piece of research that scientifically makes an original contribution to a given field of knowledge.

Within this 'high tension zone' it is easy for the writer to fall into the security of one of the several critical positions. The implications of this are that these positions generate different kinds of authorial silence, the familiar silence of scientific authorship, the silence generated by adopting an elevated, outside position to the paradigm or the silences suggested by the 'death of the author' in contemporary poststructuralist/postmodern theorizing. Either way, the resulting work is in danger of performing a disembodiment of the writer that jars somewhat with the ideals of critical scholarship.

As academic critique, feminist scholarship challenges the masculine perspective underpinning these different kinds of disembodiment. As such, it has traditionally offered suggestions for negotiating this uneasy path in critical research. In this chapter, an 'experiential' account is given of the writer searching for discursive space to occupy as a critical doctoral author in marketing, drawing upon feminist theorizing of this 'author question'. This reconstructed tale attempts to provide suggestions as to how this question of the complexity of critical authorship for the doctoral student in marketing might be managed, notwithstanding an acceptance of partiality, of other untold and untellable stories, of silences and 'others', and its inevitable post hoc rationalization and reconstruction of events.

In the Beginning . . .

> *I have an authority problem. The day I was born, the midwife told my mother to settle down for the night, I wasn't going to be born for hours. Mother, who came from a long line of women with 'an authority problem', said, 'No, the baby is on its way.' The nurse re-examined her and said, now losing her patience somewhat, 'No, Mrs. Davidson, your baby will not be born tonight.' Mother kneeled up on the bed and I shot out onto the bed with a thumb in my mouth and a serious authority problem. It has lasted 40 years.*

This is a story that has been repeatedly told to me during my life. It is typical of those stories that are told to children as they grow up and with which they are endlessly fascinated as they begin to piece together 'who they are'. It located me within a working class tradition of female resistance to the positionings that are imposed on women from a community like mine, the unforgiving and often violent fishing communities in the North East of Scotland. It is one of the many stories which developed the notion much celebrated among the women in my family that *'the women in our family don't "know their place"*. This a dangerous position to be socialized into, whether in working class and impoverished 1960s Scotland, or in the relative comfort of a 21st-century university. One is likely to get ones fingers burned either way.

Like the story above, the doctoral thesis is a story that constructs and locates the doctoral student within the confines of what they are allowed to 'become' as an academic, using the language available from that location. The doctoral thesis, being the traditional route for a neophyte's socialization into an academic career within a specific discipline, is never just about the subject matter of the research, but about the 'subject matter' of the writer, what they are allowed 'to become' in negotiation with the conditions of possibility at hand. This issue of 'negotiated becoming' is true of all doctoral theses, but I think it is more pressing in the case of the critical doctoral thesis. As noted above, in the critical thesis, the writer occupies an ambivalent location in relation to their disciplinary culture, as a critic of it, but at the same time negotiating their own acceptance within that culture. The neophyte critical scholar is thus uniquely faced with managing the development of their ontological security as a scholar, while at the same time actively critiquing the location they are writing themselves into, and undermining the very process that will lead to their success! Through my experience of writing a critical thesis in marketing I understand the perils of this 'high tension zone' quite clearly and articulating the experience of working out how to be a critical scholar within this zone became central to the project. This chapter discusses the tensions, problems and some of the solutions that emerged during my own research, which might prove useful to the doctoral researcher with critical ambitions.

Question One: Who Am I?

Whatever your approach, the thesis is a book you write in order to be produced as an academic subject within your discipline and to be conferred the 'authority' that connotes. When authoring the critical thesis, you are producing yourself as an oppositional subject, as someone who is writing against the everyday mode of engagement. Therefore, the most important thing to work out during the critical thesis is who you are and/or who you want to be as a critic and the implications of this for your critical knowledge claims. I would add that to attend to your relations to the 'others' produced to enable your critical subjectivity is an important part of the exploration of those implications. In the feminist tradition, the critical position is not seen as something that can be picked up off the shelf and adopted, it is seen as a hard wrought, worked out position, carefully articulated through its potentials and limitations, and more importantly its implications and performances. The critical position is something which is not to be set in stone at the beginning of the research but is emergent with the research as this narrative recounts.

The 'Real World' Critic: 'The Personal Is Political'

I can remember the critical impulse towards marketing descending first as an undergraduate. I was being taught the rather utopian version of relationship marketing (RM) that was around in its early days, while at the same time, as a struggling student and single mother, I was being 'de-selected' by my bank. The same bank was co-incidentally running a very RM oriented advertising campaign and, as such, was being used as an example by the lecturer. At the time, RM was being discussed in terms of creating a better relationship, a 'win win' relationship with the consumer. Given my position at that time vis-à-vis my bank, this obviously generated a not inconsiderable level of anger in me that began to take the form of what might be called a 'critical impulse'. The thing that angered me most was that 'the consumer' in these formulations obviously didn't include me. As Adrienne Rich states, *'when someone with the authority of a teacher, say, describes the world and you are not in it, there is a moment of psychic disequilibrium, as if you looked in a mirror and saw nothing'* (Rich, 1993). For me, being overlooked has never gone down well. I was the first person in my family to go to university and although very 'starry eyed' about being there, I was already suffering from 'imposters syndrome' – or the belief that I didn't deserve the success or professional position I had achieved alongside a fear of being 'found out'. This encounter confirmed my suspicions that I was indeed 'out of place'. Rather than directing my anger at 'the teacher' (that was to come later) I focused my critical angst on the 'marketing world' outside the academy, specifically the banking system. Drawing on my scanty knowledge of feminism at that time, I mobilized my critical efforts around the famous 1960s feminist phrase *'the personal is political'*. As a sufferer of social injustice and inequality due to my status, my doctoral research began to take shape around the idea of critiquing the real world of marketing outside the academy in terms of addressing social justice and to enact change in the banking system. However, as I began to engage with the feminist canon in more depth I began to reflect upon this position and to feel the dilemmas in terms of my own critical position that this type of criticality implied.

As a critical doctoral student you might doing doctoral research that does not grate against the accepted mode of engagement with the discipline but is defined as critical through the subject matter it concerns itself with. Here, the 'other' of your critical self might be some aspect of the outside world of marketing. Of course, sound academic research with a social justice agenda is sorely needed in marketing and is a growing area of critique (Hastings and Saren, 2003). Moreover, in terms of mobilizing this type of critique, feminist critics still want to validate knowledge claims about, for example, domestic violence, gender inequalities and so on, as the basis for social transformation (Ramazanoglu and Holland, 2000). However, in my own research I felt uneasy about adopting this kind of critical position wholesale. Feminists have traditionally written against the Cartesian notion of the separation of the knower from the known as a power charged relationship upon which modern scientific project is based (Harding, 1991). They have criticized the concomitant instrumentality and control that this suggests. Traditional 'science' becomes a process whereby the acquiring of knowledge of 'something' (e.g. a group of disadvantaged consumers) hides the subjugation and exploitation of that 'something' in terms of the mastery and possession of a 'real world' by the knower to be appropriated and converted into what the knower needs. This creates a paradoxical critical position where the aim of the research is social justice but the primary beneficiary of that knowledge is often the knower in terms of career progression and academic cultural capital.

I had a transformatory agenda, but was also uneasy about how this kind of critical intervention positioned me as a neutral observer, theorist and critic of 'the real world of marketing', where I felt that I could act, through producing marketing knowledge, to expose and change the place where I felt I had been disenfranchised. Mobilizing critical, transformatory research from this position unproblematically creates a link between academic work and 'real world' change, while adopting a classic academic posture of the free floating intelligentsia, the objective and disembodied social scientist and commentator who is unreflexive about her own implications and benefits wrought through conducting such research. Topic based criticality, when conducted within the traditional modes of writing looks outwards unproblematically towards an external marketing reality beyond the textual constructions of the author. This I felt implicated me in academic silences that I couldn't equate with critical research. I felt that I wanted to transform and change through my research, but quickly became confused about this position. Not because I didn't think it was an important position to adopt, but because it seemed to be reinscribing the kinds of silences of academic authorship I felt uneasy with. For me, although work with critical and social change agendas is sorely required, it seemed necessary but not sufficient in order to enact a critical thesis. The thesis that was emerging from this kind of criticality seemed to me to be a 'thesis with a critical topic' but not a 'critical thesis'.

The 'Hero' Critic: 'The Saviour of Marketing'

My second 'critical impulse' arrived shortly after my doctoral research had begun. Through my exposure to working academics I began to read my situation in a slightly more nuanced way. I began to take notice of the way that the academics around me privileged the academic world rather than 'the real world'. Or rather I discovered that, despite the plethora of discussions about 'the real world' (i.e. outside) the discipline, the academic world was actually very 'real' indeed!! I noticed, and became involved with academics' concerns over what to research and what direction to take existing projects. This was mainly couched in terms related to the discipline rather than the 'outside world of marketing'. At the time I was reading feminist Marxist Dorothy Smith (1990). She argues that when (previously excluded) women engage with disciplinary knowledge for the first time a 'line of fault' often develops between their own lived experience and the knowledge frameworks presented to them. This prevents entry into that sphere without a more overt suspension of belief than many are prepared to accomplish. She argues that this then allows women from this unique outsider position to see the silences and omissions in the knowledge and the structures which hold them in place, conferring an epistemic privilege, or ability to have a better quality of vision than those others more implicated in the existing ideology. I began to read my lecture experience in terms of this. Perhaps I could 'see better' than the current academic researchers in RM, who seemed to be pursuing very different agendas, and therefore take up a critical position in terms of enlightenment of 'those who did not see'? This critical position was one with which I could direct my criticality at both the academic world and the world 'out there', enlightening academics who could use this new knowledge as a resource and route to work towards the changing of marketing practice.

Of course, there are huge problems with this critical position as well in terms of the kind of critic that it produces and the kind of relationship with 'the other' that it implies. There is an incredible hubris of conferring upon one-self the epistemic privilege of such a critical position (i.e. the ability to 'see' and 'know' better than the existing participants). Unfortunately, this *critical hero'* position, struggling against the unenlightened mainstream is all too eas-ily adopted and I found it very difficult to resist writing myself into the text as such. Paradoxically, the term 'critical' is a self-elevating concept for an author to use, it implies being self-defined as outside and above the norm and this, for just these reasons, is a very tenuous position to occupy unreflexively and still call oneself a critical academic. For me, elevating the author to a higher ground of epistemic privilege actually worked to silence, dominate and criti-cize those 'others' that share our disciplinary spaces.

Other critical academics have also struggled with the inescapable paradoxes of this position. Hackley (2001), for example, argues that the 'mainstream' use the guiding ideologies and rhetoric of scientism and the marketing concept to make claims and win power and legitimacy for their own point of view. He uses parody to discuss his own implication in this, highlighting that the 'shad-owy chorus' of the mainstream is important to his construction as a critical scholar as it is with all critical scholars. A similar critique to that often directed at 'the mainstream' was interestingly also often directed at critical marketing researchers during my own research, an ethnography of academics under-taking RM research in the UK, US and Finland. Critical marketers were seen as using the guiding ideologies and rhetoric of particular theories to make claims and win power and legitimacy for their own point of view. The prob-lem with this type of factionalism between mainstream and critical is that it is ultimately all reproducing a particularly masculine form of scholarship where all drawing of lines and sectors can be read as power and authority moves. As Haraway (1991, p. 186) aptly describes it, an *'academic battlefield, where blips of light called players disintegrate . . . each other in order to stay in the knowledge and power game'*. Unfortunately there is no escape from this. In the processes of pro-ducing ourselves as viable critical subjects we rely inescapably upon a 'non-critical' or 'differently critical' other. The danger here is to try to escape from or ignore the implications. Instead we need to challenge the tendency to base our critical subjectivity upon simplistic critical/mainstream formulations and to find ways to interfere with and destabilize this self-elevating and othering process.

The turning point for me in terms of this came while engaged in some research within which I could very much be said to have adopted the 'hero critic' position. I was developing a piece of research where a specific journal article would be subject to a critique and then the writer of that article would be shown this critique and asked to comment. What emerged from this piece of research was a systematic critique of a specific piece of research, with a con-trolled right of reply for the author and my further responses to their comments. This was then arranged into a quasi dialogue, with me as the final arbiter and author. Unsurprisingly, much disquiet emerged about this work from several sources and as such, it was felt that it could not proceed in that form. My engagement with one of the participants involved was to prove highly trans-formatory. Although she agreed with the tenor of most of what was written, she presented a picture in these exchanges of someone who was not free to write what she liked, who was bound by disciplinary, career and journal con-ventions. In terms of the idea of critique based on the politics of enlighten-ment and rescue of the 'hero scholar', she presented a picture *not* of someone who 'could not see', but of someone who could see very clearly the issues that were being raised, but could also see, and negotiate very well indeed, the conditions of possibility for speaking officially within those conventions. Through these exchanges I began to see the position I had taken through this research, vis-à-vis the research participants, as problematic. What I felt in these exchanges was not opposition but connection. Moreover, I began to feel unhappy with the dominating logic in my research which demanded a level of exposure from the academics in question which I would not have been happy with myself. In this case, I felt that instead of writing a critical thesis I was operating within a logic of simplifying, dominating and criticizing my discip-linary colleagues. I was performing the same separation and instrumentality that was troubling me in the previous manifestation.

Critic as 'Construction of the Text': 'What Difference Does It Make Who Is Speaking?'

During that period, I seemed to be looking for a way to escape from the '*Enlightenment dreams*' (Flax, 1992, p. 448), that were pulling me into these problematic positions. One solution that seemed to present itself to me at every turn at that time was the postmodernist critique emerging in marketing (Brown, 1995, 1998) and that had been present already for some time in femi-nist studies (Alcoff, 1988; Flax, 1987; Jardine, 1982; Nicholson, 1989). While involved with the ESRC critical marketing seminar series, from which this col-lection has been developed, I was struck by the number of doctoral students who were very confused as to what actually constitutes 'the critical'. Many students had defined criticality in terms of a specific ontological approach. Similarly, during my own research, many (not all) of the marketing academics I interviewed equated 'postmodernism' with 'critical'. In my interviews there seemed to be a mixture of admiration and dislike towards the postmodern emergence in marketing, together with an exhortation 'not to take it all too seriously'. Unfortunately, when you are trying to locate yourself as a particular kind of scholar within a specific discipline, you have to take (and reference) what you are given. The thing that the postmodern did 'do for me' was to allow me to articulate my third critical impulse around the discourses of mar-keting. During my readings of (particularly) Foucault, following up references from both marketing and feminist studies, I began to construct a new site of my 'disenfranchisement' and move away from the idea of either banks or my 'unenlightened' scholarly colleagues as my critical nemeses. I was reading my lecture experience now in terms of being produced as an 'unspeakable subject' within the discourses of RM.

The thing that struck me most strongly at the time was the difference between the way 'the postmodern' was being mobilized and discussed in marketing and the way this was happening in feminist studies. In feminist studies post-modernism has been used to challenge the notions of both a single epistemo-logical truth and the universal epistemic subject speaking from nowhere and to everyone. This challenge has been used politically to open up new spaces in discourse for multiple ways of knowing and to advance debates around identity and difference. In marketing, postmodernism seems to have emerged, unsurprisingly, as something quite different. Critical commentators such as Morgan (2003, p. 117) have argued that critical approaches to marketing have ostensibly targeted the *'positivism, performativity and scientism'* of the marketing discipline, as has the postmodern movement. However, although marketing's rendering of postmodernism has had a welcome broadening effect upon the marketing discipline, he argues, it has proved relatively impotent as a criti-cal force for change. He argues that the postmodern movement in marketing has been somewhat celebratory of consumer society and has focused its politi-cal energies towards issues of representation through a sustained critique of the positivist emphasis on research production in marketing. This critiquing of the positivist paradigm, he argues, actually elides into methodological plural-ism. Brown (1999, p. 51) is quoted as stating, *'postmodernism . . . [will] . . . let a thousand methodological flowers bloom'*, a statement which proved to be quite interesting in my personal story of critical development because I agree that postmodernism is, and has been, a liberatory development in terms of open-ing new disciplinary spaces for alternative ways of looking. However, the idea mentioned above that people often equate a specific ontology, like postmodern-ism, with critique in marketing is quite worrying if postmodernism has been pigeonholed by the marketing discipline as just another methodological choice. Feminist anthropologist Marilyn Strathern (cited in Rabinow 1986, p. 255) discusses the widespread advocacy of feminism as methodological pluralism, through recounting a story, with some annoyance, of a comment made by a senior male colleague in anthropology. The colleague praised feminism for enriching the discipline of anthropology, saying, *'let a thousand flowers bloom'*. Strathern recalls that although she agreed feminism had enriched anthropol-ogy, the comment made her feel uneasy. For Strathern, feminism *'proceeds from the initial and inassimilable fact of domination'*. The tolerance implied in this plur-alist approach paradoxically serves to assimilate feminist understandings into an improved *science* of anthropology contra the feminist political project in knowledge. It has already been argued that in marketing, critical approaches become assimilated into the dominant mode of research as merely new or dif-ferent methods (Desmond, 1995; Hackley, 2001; Kavanagh, 1994) and for this reason the idea that the use of alternative or unorthodox ontologies in market-ing provides an unproblematic route to criticality is problematic.

Added to this, I began to feel that in terms of the research 'other' these ontologies can be mobilized as the ultimate 'get out clause' for the epistemic subject looking for an alternative route to objectivity, instrumentality and control. I became uneasy with some of the easy silences generated through this type of critique and felt sometimes as I was writing I was literally disappearing 'up my own text'. Ahmed (1998, p. 125), drawing on Barthes,[1] and Foucault,[2] argues that postmodernism has (ironically) become narrativized through the death of the author. Of course, particularly in the case of Foucault, the benefits of politicizing the author question in discourse (in terms of the possible spaces of writing and of speakable and unspeakable subjects) that he enables were something I obviously didn't want to lose. However, like Ahmed, I still felt that the 'who' in terms of writing *did* matter. This is not in terms of a return to the fiction of the author as creative originator, and it is certainly not to say that every poststructuralist writer reproduces these silences. What it does say is that certain readings of these theoretical approaches, I felt, were allowing the writer to disappear in the folds of the theory in much the same way as the writer could disappear in the technologies of the scientific methodologies often being critiqued. Moreover, there was a paradoxical 'diagnostic' flavour to some of this writing, as the writer became the 'expert' diagnosing the 'problem with marketing' and marketing academics. The danger for me of this type of analysis is of the return to a fiction of a universal, transcendent epistemic subject, who could step back from their own messy involvements and critique a very neat construction of 'the field'. I felt very anchored into my own embodied engagement with marketing and that I was writing critically from a place and that place mattered. The specificity of my writing seemed to come from that location, as being 'placed outside', but not only that, as being the first person in my family to go to university, of being starry eyed about academia and having those naive illusions progressively shattered as I was drawn deeper into the castellated and boundaried culture of the marketing discipline. I was bouncing off the walls, grating along the interdisciplinary lines, split into multiple discursive and embodied locations. I felt inside and outside of several spaces at the same time. I could see the inescapability of all the critical positions above but came to the conclusion that there was never going to be an easy place for me to situate myself as a critic, there was no easy solution, no escape, and I had to learn to deal with these issues, to integrate them as an important part of my thesis.

Conclusion: 'Working It Out'

In the research that emerged, this entanglement of 'politics of location' formed a central part of the 'empirical' part of the study. That is, managing the thesis from these shifting and contradictory positions became explicitly part of my

---

[1] '...writing is the destruction of every voice, of every point of origin. Writing is that natural, composite, oblique space where our subject slips away...' (Barthes, 1977, p. 142).

[2] '... and behind all these questions we would hear hardly anything but the stirring of indifference: 'what difference does it make who is speaking?' (Foucault, 1980, p. 160).

'data'. Incorporating into the analysis my multiple and intersecting locations provided rich descriptions and analytical devices that would have been lost to one trying to perform an objective stance. This commitment to the interrogation of ones own author position within the text and attention to the entanglements of politics of location within doctoral research is, to me, the absolute crux and foundation of a critical approach to doctoral writing. Critical research should be *'the view from a body, always complex, contradictory . . . versus the view from above, from nowhere, from simplicity'* (Haraway, 1991, p. 195).

The research that emerged in the end was a critical feminist anthropology of the marketing discipline (focusing on RM). I felt that I could hold onto the idea of examining the marketing discipline in terms of its discursive constructions and boundaries, but in doing empirical research with marketing academics I allowed them to 'talk back' to the analysis. The 'data' then became the co-produced, co-emergent 'realities' that emerged from the many research encounters between the researcher and respondents. In these research encounters, researcher and respondent, both academics 'making marketing know ledge' worked to co-produce coherent selves within complex and multiple fields of power. As it turned out, the research became co-produced to the extent that at times it was unclear who was researcher and who was respondent.

One of the central planks behind 'working it out' was understanding the value of 'not knowing' and this was the starting point for my critical authorship, allowing myself to be an uncertain subject within my own writing. To be 'feeling my way' was how my thesis was narrated. There is a pull in thesis writing to privilege the *'production of one uniquely universally valid perfect reflection'* (Harding, 1998, p. 124) of what is being studied, whether this is 'marketing discourse' or some aspect of consumer behaviour. This is what might be called the 'golden apple' tendency, a thesis that resembles a golden apple plucked 'God like' from the tree of knowledge, presented for the consumption of the examiners. This is unsurprising given the weight of expectation of 'defence' built into the thesis process and the processes often encountered. The process I encountered as a doctoral student was fairly flexible, but still had the strange requirement to produce a literature review chapter and methodology chapter in my first year with the concomitant fiction that this was 'getting part of the thesis writing out of the way'! Certainly you have to engage with the literature, theory and methods, and writing is a good way to do this, but my methodology chapter certainly could not have been written until the end. As Kostkowska (2004) has recently argued, there is a tradition in feminist critical work of emphasizing 'process and questioning' rather than 'knowledge and findings'. Process and questioning centre on the local and particular of, not dislocation and abstraction from, the research encounter. Research like this is iterative and produces messy texts:

> texts that are aware of their own narrative apparatuses, that are sensitive to how reality is socially constructed, and that understand that writing is a way of 'framing' reality [the messy text] announces

its politics and ceaselessly interrogates the realities it invokes while folding the teller's story into the multivoiced history that is written.

Denzin (1996, p. 224)

Texts like this are unable to be chopped into pieces easily and 'got out of the way' before the engagement with 'the field'.

Of course, in order to successfully proceed you have to produce something which presents 'knowledge and findings', the modernist thesis genre demands this. There has to be a 'master narrative' in the thesis, which holds together enough to present an original contribution to a given field of knowledge. So how did I 'manage' this, while still critically subverting the kind of positions it implies? As I think has probably become apparent, for me, being critical hangs on the relation between the researcher and researched, however, this relation and its participants are ontologically figured. Attention to this relation became central to the task of organizing my thesis in such a way as to satisfy the thesis requirements and to subvert the process. An example of this is my review of different approaches to studying knowledge making in academic and scientific contexts. The review did not present each approach in terms of the logic of finding the best approach epistemologically to 'know' the field, as might be expected, but in terms of their implications for the researcher/respondent relationship and specifically how each approach would produce me as a critical subject. This allowed me to imagine several potential critical subjectivities which were explored to examine their implications and politics. This allowed me to present a literature review of a field thus satisfying the requirements of the genre, but also to disrupt the tendency to produce a dominant narrative and authorial voice that held together too obdurately.

My 'self' at the end of the process also 'folded back' and dialogued with other selves, and potential selves, that emerged during the research in the same way as the story of my critical selves is used here, not as a progress narrative with the implication that any one position is better than, or can replace the other, but as a discussion of the implications of all these inescapable positions on the research that emerges. In my methodology chapter, for example, three stories are woven together, the story of the original methodology I wrote as a first year student, the story of the 'encounter shock' of my engagement with the field and the story from the end, having worked out how to manage my research encounters methodologically. The stories fold into one another, as I dialogue between the researcher selves implied in them, highlighting the processual nature of the research and subverting the presentation of one dominant account and singular authorial voice. It is a messy chapter, but one that I think represents more clearly the 'reality' of the research process. Being reflexive like this is not an escape route from issues of representation, but subverts the hegemonic game of presenting an ostensibly critical thesis that simplistically reproduces the relations of ruling built into any scientific discourse.

'Working it out' doesn't mean 'solving it' but doing the best you can within a situation where finding the perfect solution is impossible. The performance of critical writing does not rely on easy solutions and positions that can be slipped into and occupied unreflexively, but, as I learned, is more like a series of question marks that hang over the writing and you as a writer. Being critical means constantly questioning what you are doing, who you are and what are the implications of this for yourself and the others that 'matter' within your work. This type of writing creates work which attends to 'the critical impulse' but also the kind of problematic subjectivities and relations this implies. It also writes in way that suggests how it might have been otherwise. Therefore it puts that critical subject under erasure; the inevitability of its problematic constructions is both recognized and destabilized in the writing process. Writing like this creates a critical thesis grounded in the embodied experience of 'the becoming' which should be seen as central to the critical thesis project, the 'becoming' of the critical marketing scholar.

References

Ahmed, S. (1998). *Differences that Matter: Feminist Theory and Postmodernism*. Cambridge: Cambridge University Press.

Alcoff, L. (1988). 'Cultural feminism versus post-structuralism: the identity crisis in feminist theory'. *Signs*, 13(3), 405–436.

Barthes, R. (1977). 'The death of the author'. In S. Heath (trans.). *Image–Music–Text*. London: Fontana.

Brown, S. (1995). *Postmodern Marketing*. London: Routledge.

Brown, S. (1998). *Postmodern Marketing 2: Telling Tales*. London: Thomson.

Brown, S. (1999). 'Marketing and literature: the anxiety of academic influence'. *Journal of Marketing*, 63(1), 1–15.

Desmond, J. (1995). 'Reclaiming the subject: de-commodifying marketing knowledge?' *Journal of Marketing Management*, 11, 721–746.

Denzin, N. (1996). *Interpretive Ethnography: Ethnographic Practices for the 21st Century*. London: Sage.

Flax, J. (1987). 'Postmodernism and gender relations in feminist theory'. *Signs*, 12(4), 33–42.

Flax J. (1992). 'The end of innocence'. In J. Butler and J.W. Scott (eds), *Feminists Theorize the Political*. London: Routledge.

Foucault, M. (1980). 'What is an author?' In J.V. Harari (ed.), *Textual Strategies: Perspectives in Post-Structuralist Criticism*. London: Menthuen.

Hackley, C. (2001). *Marketing and Social Construction: Exploring the Rhetorics of Managed Consumption*. London: Routledge.

Haraway, D. (1991). 'A cyborg manifesto: science, technology, and socialist-feminism in the late twentieth century'. In D. Haraway (ed.), *Simians, Cyborgs, and Women: The Reinvention of Nature*. New York: Routledge.

Harding, S. (1991). *Whose Science? Whose Knowledge?* New York: Cornell University Press.

Harding, S. (1998). *Is Science Multicultural? Postcolonialisms, Feminisms, and Epistemologies*. Bloomington: Indiana University Press.

Hastings, G. and Saren, M. (2003). 'The critical contribution of social marketing: theory and application'. *Marketing Theory*, 3, 305–322.

Jardine, A. (1982). 'Gynesis'. *Diacritics*, 12, 2(Summer), 54–64.

Kavanagh, D. (1994). 'Hunt vs Anderson: round 16'. *European Journal of Marketing*, 28(3), 26–41.

Kostkowska, J. (2004). 'To persistently not know something important'. *Feminist Theory*. London: Sage, pp. 185–203.

Morgan, G. (2003). 'Marketing and critique: prospects and problems'. In M. Alvesson and H. Willmott (eds), *Studying Management Critically*. London: Sage.

Nicholson, L. (ed.) (1989). *Feminism/Postmodernism*. London: Routledge.

Rabinow, P. (1986). 'Representations are social facts: modernity and post modernity in anthropology'. In J. Clifford and G.E. Marcus (eds), *Writing Culture: The Poetics and Politics of Ethnography*. Berkeley: University of California Press, pp. 234–261.

Ramazanoglu, C. and Holland, J. (2000). *Feminist Methodology: Challenges and Choices*. London: Sage.

Rich, A. (1993). 'Cartographies of silence'. *The Dream of a Common Language: Poems, 1974–1977*. New York: Norton.

Smith, D. (1990). *The Conceptual Practice of Power: A Feminist Sociology of Knowledge*. Boston: Northeastern University Press.

Part II

Critical Debates: Questioning Underlying Assumptions

6

Beyond Marketing Panaceas: In Praise of Societing

Olivier Badot, Ampelio Bucci and Bernard Cova

Introduction

For the past 20 years, there has been an energetic debate throughout the marketing scientific community concerning a possible change of paradigm (Dholakia and Arndt, 1985; Littler and Tynan, 2005; Sheth and Sisodia, 2006; Vargo and Lusch, 2004), in which a great majority of authors using a relatively top-down approach argue about the reasons of an evolution from one perspective to another. These authors, often distinguished academics, identify and discuss a change of paradigm and its resulting implications in developing certain positions with respect to the theory and practice of marketing, sometimes describing in detail the models, the methods and even the tools. In particular, this is the case in the transition from a transactional perspective to a relational perspective in marketing (Gronröos, 1997; Gummesson, 1997).

We propose here to nourish this debate by taking an opposite approach: using a bottom-up approach we will start from the production of 'marketing panaceas' (Brown, 1995) and alternative frameworks (Morris et al., 2002) – model, best practices and other miracle approaches – to which managers are exposed, in order to reconstruct the various structural pillars of the multitude of panaceas, and to ultimately highlight the major changes (or not) from a paradigmatic perspective. This approach seems more suitable to account for the fragmentation of marketing, its thought, its research topics including managerial implications, which is said to be characteristic of this fourth era of the marketing we have encountered since the 1980's (Webster Jr., 2005; Wilkie and Moore, 2003).

This chapter seeks to contribute to the general discussion of the evolution of the dominant logic in marketing through: (1) constructing an exhaustive list of all the panaceas appearing during the past 20 years; (2) seeking the underlying logics with each one of these panaceas, thereby permitting the structuring into groups panaceas according to the principal logics identified; and (3) discussing the validity of the word 'marketing' to encapsulate logics which no longer have the market as the central aspect.

A Panorama of Marketing Panaceas

As highlighted by Brown (1993a, 1993b), marketing panaceas form a vast practical literature intended to provide managers 'solutions to marketing's ills' (Brown, 1995, p. 50). These solutions are generally announced by their authors as being the base of a conceptual restorative of marketing and often in a very humble (!) way, as in 'new marketing'. 'Talk about a 'new marketing' has attracted considerable interest' (Palmer and Ponsonby, 2002, p. 177). Following in the footsteps of McKenna (1985) and Gummesson (1987), numerous authors have come forward – from Brookes (1988) to McDonald and Wilson (2002) – to announce the emergence of a new marketing redemptive based on a particular point of view: theirs! Some, such as Brookes, who one decade after having published a book entitled *New Marketing* (1988), published a second work on *New Marketing* (Little and Brookes, 1997), have gone on to become experts in the field of the new marketing. Certain authors become militant apostles of the cause of 'New Marketing' and design manifestos of 'New Marketing' (Grant, 1999). Others stylize their approach by using a prefix of Greek origin 'neo' to propose a 'Neo-marketing' (Badot and Cova, 1992; Moutinho et al., 2002; Zyman, 1999), a plural combination of various innovative approaches. The great majority of authors suggest through their text that they are the initiators of a form of new marketing and use a title rather like a brand on which they will be able to capitalize thereafter; for example, Schmitt (1999) with his work *Experiential Marketing*. In all cases, their new marketing panacea is supposed to challenge Kotlerian marketing ('old-school marketing') described by Smithee (1997) as in continuous crisis, if not already departed: it is the enemy which the panacea confronts to save companies and/or consumers, and it is also a way one calibrates oneself to show their difference and raison d'être. And it works! Towards the end of 2005, a chart made a tour of the world's web sites and blogs dedicated to marketing and consumption. It proliferated rapidly and is defended as a social cause by many actors on the Net, not only marketers, but also consumers and players such as programmers and developers. It was posted by Kathy Sierra, a Sun java instructor, on a blog in August 2005 (Figure 6.1) and points out how the *open source/cluetrain* world is causing traditional old-school kotlerian marketing to give way to a 'neo-marketing'.

Old-school marketing	Neo-marketing
Marketers/advertisers do it	*Everyone* does it
Focused on how the *company* kicks ass	Focused on how the *user* kicks ass
Marketers have the power	*Users* have the power
Advertising	Evangelizing
Tightly controlled 'brand message'	Brand hijacked by users
One-way broadcast	Two-way conversation
Company-created content	User-created content
He who out**spends**, wins	He who out**teaches**, wins
Mass markets	Selective, focused users
One-size-fits-all	Personalized, custom-tailored
Focus groups	User feedback and contributions … *betas*
Deception	Transparency
Bulls	Authenticity
Development often independent from marketing	Impossible to separate development and marketing
The story must be compelling, but can be fiction ('buy this and you'll have more sex')	The story must be compelling, and must be real ('buy this and you'll take better photos')
30-second spots are king	Word-of-mouth is king
Focus on branding	Focus on passionate users
Get the customer to believe in it	**YOU** believe in it

Figure 6.1 Neo-marketing versus old-school marketing according to Kathy Sierra (http://headrush.typepad.com/creating_passionate_users/, August 2005).

While the global movement of 'New Marketing' has previously been examined, most notably by Palmer and Ponsonby (2002) whose work studied the social construction of new marketing in such areas as one-to-one marketing, minimal work has been conducted into counting and categorizing these new marketing panaceas. Some work has been undertaken, but in a limited way and directed towards only one paradigmatic perspective (Brown, 1993a, b; Morris et al., 2002). Brown (1993a) chose eight marketing panaceas to highlight their common concerns – postmodernism according to him: an emphasis on dealing with the customer as an individual; a desire to retain existing customers rather than searching for new ones. Morris et al. (2002) analysed 13 marketing panaceas to determine their common entrepreneurial features: efficiency in marketing expenditures by leveraging resources, creative and alternative approaches for managing marketing variables, and an ability to affect change in the environment. In both cases, the marketing panaceas chosen were accurately selected to serve the re-conceptualization *a priori* of the authors.

In contrast, our approach is intended to be the inverse of the previous authors' deductive work. Using an inductive process, we examine existing marketing panaceas that exhibit broad representation in order to determine common threads among them, thus allowing us to carry out regroupings. In our research, only trans-sectoral and trans-segmentary panaceas are utilized. Indeed, it is our opinion, that these are the only ones that allow for universality in their approach, and thus consequently, can signal when a paradigm change in the discipline occurs. Thus, marketing panaceas dedicated to specific: sectors (aeronautical, arts and culture, banking and insurance, industry, construction, high-tech, luxury, fashion, NGO, policy, retail, sports, cities and territories, . . .); types of offers (products, services, projects, . . .); exchange and means of communication (blogs, the Internet, mobile phones, television, point of sale, . . .); specific segments, such as generational (youth, generation X or Y, seniors, . . .), geographical markets (Mediterranean, Pan-European, Global, . . .) or dedicated organizations grouped as a function of size (SME, MNCs, . . .) are not included in this research.

Furthermore, we retained only panaceas which integrated into their name the word 'marketing'. This led us to deliberately eliminate an extensive selection of B2B panaceas developed which do not use the term 'marketing', but rather terms such as 'selling' or 'management' to describe their approaches. These types of relational approaches include key partner management, key account management, client portfolio management, customer value management, as well as terms such as network management and supply chain management. Similarly, commercial approaches such as consultative selling, solution selling, value selling or enterprise selling (de Vincentis and Rackham, 1998) were omitted, as were contractual approaches such as full service contract or one stop shopping. Along the same lines, B2C approaches such as brand management or category management were not included.

In spite of these deletions, we easily arrived at more than 70 panaceas proposed in papers, articles or web sites (see Table 6.1). One can therefore understand the confusion of the marketing layman in the search of a valid and current approach to replace or improve on traditional kotlerian marketing. The landscape can be seen as a shapeless and shifting marketing panaceas in which all proclaim the title of 'New Marketing' by stressing marketing's 'new paradigm'. Panaceas can come from academics such as Philip Kotler (Kotler et al., 2002), industry consultants or practitioners in search of fame and recognition. It

Table 6.1   List of marketing panaceas 1985–2005.

Anti-marketing	Micro Marketing
Authenticity Marketing	Multilevel Marketing
Buzz Marketing	Multi-sensory Marketing
Cause-related Marketing	Network Marketing
Chrono-marketing	Neural Marketing
Co-marketing	Niche Marketing
Community Marketing	Non-business Marketing
Contextual Marketing	Nostalgia Marketing
Convergence Marketing	Olfactory Marketing
Counter Marketing	One-to-One Marketing
Creative Marketing	Permission Marketing
Cult Marketing	Radical Marketing
Customer Centric Marketing	Real-time Marketing
Database Marketing	Relationship Marketing
Eco-marketing	Retro-marketing
Emotion Marketing	Reverse Marketing
Empowerment Marketing	Scarcity Marketing
Entrepreneurial Marketing	Sensory Marketing
Environmental Marketing	Situational Marketing
Ethnic Marketing	Slow Marketing
Ethno-marketing	Social Marketing
Event Marketing	Societal Marketing
Expeditionary Marketing	Solution Marketing
Experience Marketing	Stakeholder Marketing
Exponential Marketing	Stealth Marketing
Family Marketing	Street Marketing
Geo-marketing	Sustainable Marketing
Grass Roots Marketing	Symbiotic Marketing
Green Marketing	Time-based Marketing
Guerilla Marketing	Total Relationship Marketing
Holistic Marketing	Trade Marketing
Interactive Marketing	Trend Marketing
Knowledge Marketing	Tribal Marketing
Life Event Marketing	Turbo Marketing
Loyalty Marketing	Undercover Marketing
Macro Marketing	Value Marketing
Maxi Marketing	Viral Marketing
Mega Marketing	Yield Marketing

should be noted that the majority of panaceas that have attained broader international recognition originate from America, whereas European or Asian initiatives have achieved more limited acknowledgement.

Though marketing has in the past adopted and adapted concepts from other disciplines, and has borrowed from other fields, for example metaphorical names such as guerrilla marketing, in reading this long list of panaceas, one can, like Smithee and Lee (2004), be initially struck by the strange couplings which it suggests. With the explosion of marketing panaceas over the past 20 years, this phenomenon seems to have taken an even greater hold and generates such odd names as tribal marketing or viral marketing. Smithee and Lee (2004) thus envisage a development of the use of the metaphor in marketing names: 'given the many successful outcomes of past interdisciplinary sorties in search of metaphor, much may be gained from focusing on virgin territories. Marketing has been slow to grasp the manifold opportunities that exist in fields as diverse as the medical sciences, the physical sciences and information sciences, to name just a few' (Smithee and Lee, 2004, p. 150) – and thus bet on the arrival of panaceas such as 'marketing by osmosis' or 'marketing transgenics'.

An Organization of Marketing Panaceas According to Their Logic

As specialists, rather than laymen, we attempt to interpret this group of panaceas by organizing them into categories concerned with the same underlying logic. With this intention each panacea was initially analysed according to the following checklist allowing it to be characterized by:

- history and raison d'être of the panacea according to its authors;
- central concepts;
- principal processes and/or tools;
- pre-requisites of implementation;
- type of strategy of offer;
- type of strategy of relation;
- assets and weaknesses.

Information which made it possible to feed each checklist comes from the articles, the works, the interviews or the web sites of their proponents.

Then, in an inductive way we sought to emphasize the family of subjacent logics most relevant to categorize the whole of the panaceas. After trying a number of different approaches between the panaceas and the categorization tests, it appeared to us that the most rigorous way to organize these panaceas was to consider the way in which their authors see or don't see the core object of marketing: *the market*. Indeed, marketing, even from its etymology, is centred on the market and, more precisely, on its actions on the market. Kotlerian marketing does not escape from it: the first key concept of marketing as described in the textbook *Marketing Management* is the market, and more specifically, its market-target, that is the segments on which the company will act. To a great extent, the majority of the marketing panaceas try to differentiate themselves from the kotlerian view of the market as a group of segments, to rest on alternative perspectives for the market which go beyond and/or beneath this view (Figure 6.2).

The first group of panaceas distinguishes itself from kotlerian marketing by focusing on the *market environment*, that is on the cultural, natural, political and social structures which encompass the market, and on the actors outside of the market who act on the market: Cause-Related Marketing, Eco-marketing, Environmental Marketing, Green Marketing, Holistic Marketing,

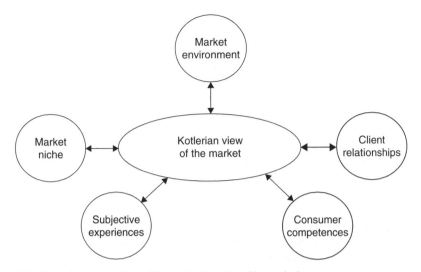

Figure 6.2 Alternative perspectives of the market introduced by marketing panaceas.

Macro Marketing, Maxi Marketing, Mega Marketing, Network Marketing, Non-Business Marketing, Social Marketing, Societal Marketing, Stakeholder Marketing, Sustainable Marketing, Symbiotic Marketing, Trend Marketing. The logic mobilized by this first group of panaceas is one of the embedding of the market in a broader unit which at the same time conditions and makes it possible (Hadjikhani and Thilenius, 2005).

A second group of panaceas positions itself differently from kotlerian marketing, by taking the perspective of the *market niches*, that is fragments of consumers of minimal size compared to the traditional segments, and integrating the regroupings – permanent like transitory – based on a common origin (ethnos group, territory) or a common passion (tribes, virus): Community Marketing, Ethnic Marketing, Ethno-marketing, Family Marketing, Geo-marketing, Micro Marketing, Niche Marketing, Street Marketing, Tribal Marketing, Viral Marketing. This group gave rise to a specific development, not always ethical, that relates to the mode of communication that is specific to certain niches considered to not respond to direct commercial messaging: Buzz Marketing, Exponential Marketing, Stealth Marketing, Undercover Marketing. The logic mobilized by this second group of panaceas is at the same time, one of hyper-fragmentation of the consumption of the postmodern type (Firat and Venkatesh, 1995), while also a recombining of consumption in a form borrowed from the archaic and preexistent social forms of the market: community, soil, tribe, . . . (Maffesoli, 1996).

A third group, which was a dominating factor in the 1990s, opened the way to a redefinition of the market through the form of *client relationships*: that is, of relations between the company and their customers (direct or indirect) designed to increase and recognize loyalty to a company, its brands, products and services. Contributions from industrial marketing, especially from the

IMP Group (Hakansson, 1982; Hakansson and Snehota, 1995), as well as from services marketing (Gronröos, 1997; Gummesson, 1997) support the panaceas concerned: Co-marketing, Customer Centric Marketing, Database Marketing, Interactive Marketing, Loyalty Marketing, Multilevel Marketing, One-to-One Marketing, Relationship Marketing, Total Relationship Marketing, Trade Marketing. The logic concerned with this third group of panaceas is one of moving from a market of mass (and segments) to one of a mass of markets: each specific client relationship being a market.

A fourth group of panaceas that has emerged strongly since the beginning of 2000 is one that is concerned with the *subjective experiences* of the customer: that is, what the customer experiences (emotions, feelings, . . .) with the offers coming from the market. The contributions of Consumer Culture Theory (CCT) (Arnould and Thompson, 2005) are noticeable in a number of panaceas: Cult Marketing, Emotion Marketing, Event Marketing, Experience Marketing, Life Event Marketing, Multi-sensory Marketing, Neural Marketing, Olfactory Marketing, Sensory Marketing, Situational Marketing. This group is so significant today that one can consider that it gave rise to the following subgroups:

- Panaceas organized around the temporality of the subjective experiences of customers: Chrono-marketing, Convergence Marketing, Contextual Marketing, Real-Time Marketing, Slow Marketing, Time-Based Marketing, Turbo Marketing, Yield Marketing.
- Panaceas organized around the authenticity of the subjective experiences of customers: Authenticity Marketing, Nostalgia Marketing, Retro-marketing, Scarcity Marketing.

Logic subjacent with this fourth group of panaceas is to take the individual consumer whose traditional role is as a purchaser and destructor of goods, and turn them into an active actor (customer agency) in their everyday life in which consumption and the market are integrated (Arnould and Thompson, 2005).

A fifth group of panaceas, for the moment the least significant, takes as its perspective the *competences of the customer*: that is, it does not focus on part of the market, nor on the relationship or customer experience as elements of the target-market, but rather on the competences of the customer as a basis of interaction, dialogue and especially of rebalancing: Anti-marketing, Counter Marketing, Empowerment Marketing, Grass Roots Marketing, Knowledge Marketing, Permission Marketing, Reverse Marketing, Solution Marketing, Value Marketing. Logic subjacent with this group of panaceas concerns an obliteration of the border between producer and consumer who thus together, become co-creators of solutions, meanings and values for the life of the consumer, as well as the activity of the company (Prahalad and Ramaswamy, 2004).

Finally, a restricted group of panaceas concerns itself not with a specific perspective of the market, but takes for a starting point the company, its resources and its means (limited): Creative Marketing, Entrepreneurial Marketing, Expeditionary Marketing, Guerrilla Marketing, Radical Marketing.

Beyond the Panaceas and Their Underlying Logics

What is astonishing in this reorganization of the panorama of marketing panaceas into five distinct logics (if we put aside the sixth one) is the fact that marketing whose etymology is tied to the word 'market' tries essentially to draw beyond (environment, social groups and social relations) and on this side (personal experiences and competences of the individuals) of the market to renew itself.

If one looks at all this from an external view of the discipline, as opposed to what Smithee and Lee (2004) proposed, one can even find it almost indecent to want at all costs to unite certain terms that are completely external to the market with the word marketing. That resembles a set of attempts to maintain marketing through an intravenous drip of fresh blood coming from fields external to the market: the metaphorical coupling of marketing with such a term suggests that marketing is able to seize some parts without inevitably marrying them to values that are subjacent to them (Cornelissen, 2003; O'Malley and Tynan, 1999). These attempts seem to go hand in hand with the marketization of goods and values which remained up to that point out of the commercial sphere (Boltanski and Chiapello, 2006): capitalism to regenerate itself must draw from outside the commercial sphere from what one can call the layers of authenticity of the company. The case of eco-marketing and the marketization of products derived from ecological agriculture is a good example of this operation in binomial marketing/capitalism. Unfortunately, as Boltanski and Chiapello (2006) showed, this led to an overriding result: a suspicion increasingly directed towards capitalism and marketing. Pairing marketing with an idea, a good, a value, . . ., but coming from beyond the market casts a certain doubt on the resulting marketing panacea.

Thus, there not only remains the issue of the change of the disciplines' dominant logic, but also one of its fields of investigation. A first reflection can lead researchers to drop the suffix 'ing' and to re-concentrate on the study of markets (Venkatesh and Penaloza, 2006). Indeed, Venkatesh and Penaloza (2006, p. 137) highlight 'the need to shift the disciplinary emphasis, not by disregarding the role of marketing, but by enlarging its scope to the market and in turn embedding such markets within the social and historical contexts. The discipline of marketing has centered over the past four decades on firm-level actions and managerial perspectives; in such an approach, either the larger context of the market was considered as given or it was assumed to be unchanged or unchangeable. This rather restricted approach has served and outlived its purpose and one consequence of continuing with it will result in ignoring the critical role of the broader institutional context called the market, whether it is local or global'. The market must thus be comprised as 'a set of institutions and actors located in a physical or virtual space where marketing-related transactions and activities take place' (Venkatesh and Penaloza, 2006, p. 136).

A second reflection, on the contrary, can result in dropping the word 'market' while keeping only the suffix 'ing'. Can we in effect, always speak about marketing when the action (-ing) required proceeds in the society and not only in the market. Perhaps instead, the neologism 'societing' proposed more than a dozen years ago appears more adaptable (Badot et al., 1993). What is societing? It is a term introduced by Latin researchers through the crossing of marketing and sociology (Badot et al., 1993), which generated a review by the same name (http://members.xoom.virgilio.it/societing/) and which means according to the authors either 'put in the society', for the marketers, or 'to make society', for the sociologists. This term regularly disappears then reappears in European literature on marketing and sociology (Cova, 1999; Cova and Cova, 2002; Earls, 2003; de Leonardis, 1999; Morace, 2002; Woolgar, 2004; Woolgar and Simakova, 2004). In societing, 'the company is not a simple economic actor who adapts to the market, but a social actor embedded in the societal context' (Badot et al., 1993, p. 51). This means for the company (Morace 2002) to put in the market, *and* also to put in society a product, a service, a brand, an experience, . . . In the same vein, actors not marketers, as Kathy Sierra notes, seek another word other than marketing to qualify their actions: 'There's still the problem of the word "marketing". We need a word that distinguishes the kinds of things we (developers/programmers, ministers, realtors, authors) do from old-school traditional marketing . . . My "neo-marketing" label is just lame . . . If framing it with a new word/phrase helps, perhaps that's a better approach than trying to give the word "marketing" a massive makeover' (http://headrush.typepad.com/creating_passionate_users/).

Rather than a shift of a paradigm to another type of transition, from the transaction to the relationship, from product to service, from product/service to experience, from product/service to solution, from creation to co-creation, from the individual to 'tribe', from market to network, from customer to stakeholder, . . ., what the adoption of the term societing will allow, is the taking into account all these swings in a responsible way: our sphere of activity is not any more the market, but the society with all the consequences that it comprises. One of the consequences in particular is not to consider this approach as paired with the development of capitalism, thereby avoiding the trap of over-marketing (Johansson, 2004).

But, this second reflection has a taste of deja vu if it is poorly understood: this occurs quite simply by 'broadening the concept of marketing' (Kotler and Levy, 1969) in a hidden way, by transforming it into societing. This turn would be played and the managerial perspective applied via kotlerian marketing to the market would extend now to the entire society: 'the broadening movement was an effort to free the marketing paradigm from the narrow confines of commercial marketing and to show its application to a far larger number of contexts in which exchange and relationship activities take place' (Kotler, 2005, p. 114). This idea has no place however. With the word societing, it is not a question of broadening the field of application of marketing techniques in a colonialist way applicable to all human activities, but on the contrary, it seeks to better account for all the actions undertaken by the company agents including brands, the consumers, the marketers, the stakeholders . . . While the study of marketing techniques privileges the perspective of marketing managers, the societing approach requires attention to the perspectives of marketers, as well as consumers and other operative agents. Taking this direction, the societing approach offers consumers the chance to play a greater role (Arnould and Thompson, 2005). They can, similar to companies or other agents introduce a meaning, an idea, etc. into society. It is what certain consumers and other actors suggest such as Kathy Sierra, when they call it a 'neo-marketing' of their wishes (see Figure 6.1).

We believe that the future of 'societing' is promising, with significant development to come from approaches centred on elements associated with the competences of the consumer. Whereas knowledge marketing is only in its first steps and is not yet a stabilized notion, the concept of customer empowerment seems to be the rallying cry of today's innovating thinkers. Recent experiences have clarified the difficulty that can exist for some companies in interacting with a type of consumer more qualified than ever due to the Internet. Consumers today appear more active, more participative, more resistant, more activist, more recreational, more social and community-minded than they ever have been before. The shared passion of certain consumers for a brand is translated through systems of group learning, bringing expertise and competences to bear; and therefore legitimate marketing provides the consumers more and more value. The presence of impassioned, linked and expert consumers, thus involves a rebalancing of the capacity in the relationship between the company and the consumer which societing must know to take into account. This will necessitate a genuine marketing revolution, and we hope for once not sully this word, as it is so often used for unimportant changes in marketing. Whereas, the idea of knowledge of the consumer is central to marketing, it is often considered in a restricted and manipulative manner as to know everything about the consumers in order to satisfy them, and thus secure their loyalty. Seldom, has the idea been proposed in marketing that the consumer has knowledge that can be interesting to the company. On the contrary, we believe that societing will push the company to take into account the 'Other', the consumer, not while leaning on him but while learning from him, his expertise and his experiences.

Conclusion

The extensive analysis of the marketing panaceas appearing over the past 20 years and the union against-nature between the market and of elements taken out of the market, result in us questioning the validity of the word marketing as the denomination of the human activities which we study. Whereas some propose to reform marketing by dropping the suffix 'ing' and to concentrate on the 'market' (Venkatesh and Penaloza, 2006), to the contrary we conclude that it is necessary to keep the suffix 'ing' and to get rid of the word market, as its logics of action no longer have the market as the focal aspect. We then propose the term 'societing' to indicate the study of the actions undertaken by the various actors such as consumers or companies on society.

Rather than broadening the concept of marketing, societing applies limits to it. It acts, in fact, as a catalyst for a company to give up the fundamentalism taken on by marketing management (Hetzel, 1995). There is generally a very simplistic vision of fundamentalism. One imagines it covered by a turban or one limits it to a monk. But, in fact, fundamentalism relates to all those which think they have the truth, and even to be the truth, and thus consequently regard the others as in error. Fundamentalism is a behaviour which is often thought as the right solution and never as the problem. Marketing management is fundamentalism. Conversely, societing is against the idea of fundamentalism. It is a movement to support the differences of others and perhaps, more import-antly, to start to learn from others whether consumers, stakeholders or other actors in society.

References

Arnould, E.J. and Thompson, C.J. (2005). 'Consumer Culture Theory (CCT): twenty years of research'. *Journal of Consumer Research*, 31(March), 868–882.

Badot, O. and Cova, B. (1992). *Le Néo-marketing*. Paris: ESF.

Badot, O., Bucci, A. and Cova, B. (1993). 'Societing: managerial response to European aestheticization'. *European Management Journal*, Special Issue EAP 20th Anniversary, 48–55.

Boltanski, L. and Chiapello, E. (2006). *The New Spirit of Capitalism*. London: Verso.

Brookes, R. (1988). *The New Marketing*. Aldershot, Hants: Gower.

Brown, S. (1993a). 'Postmodern Marketing?' *European Journal of Marketing*, 27(4), 19–34.

Brown, S. (1993b). 'Postmodern marketing: principles, practice and panaceas'. *Irish Marketing Review*, 6, 91–99.

Brown, S. (1995). *Postmodern Marketing*. London: Routledge.

Cornelissen, J.P. (2003). 'Metaphor as a method in the domain of marketing'. *Psychology and Marketing*, 20(3), 209–225.

Cova, B. (1999). 'From Marketing to Societing: *When the link is more important than the thing*'. In D. Brownlie, M. Saren, R. Wensley and R. Whittington (eds.), Rethinking Marketing. London: Sage, pp. 64–83.

Cova, B. and Cova, V. (2002). 'Tribal Marketing: *The Tribalisation of Society and its Impact on the Conduct of Marketing*'. European Journal of Marketing, 36(5/6), 595–620.

Dholakia, N. and Arndt, J. (eds) (1985). *Changing the Course of Marketing: Alternative Paradigms for Widening Marketing Theory, Research in Marketing*, Supplement 2. Greenwich, CT: JAI Press.

Earls, M. (2003). 'Advertising to the herd: how understanding our true nature challenges the ways we think about advertising and market research'. *International Journal of Market Research*, 45(3), 311–336.

Firat, A.F. and Venkatesh, A. (1995). 'Liberatory postmodernism and the reenchantment of consumption'. *Journal of Consumer Research*, 22(December), 239–267.

Grant, J. (1999). *The New Marketing Manifesto: The 12 Rules for Building Successful Brands in the 21st Century*. London: Orion Business.

Gronröos, C. (1997). 'From marketing mix to relationship marketing: towards a paradigmatic shift in marketing'. *Management Decision*, 35(3), 322–340.

Gummesson, E. (1987). 'The new marketing: developing long term interactive relationships'. *Long Range Planning*, 20(4), 10–20.

Gummesson, E. (1997). 'Relationship marketing as a paradigm shift: some conclusions from the 30R approach. *Management Decision*, 35(3), 267–273.

Hadjikhani, A. and Thilenius, P. (2005). *Non-Business Actors in a Business Network*. Amsterdam: Elsevier.

Hakansson, H. (ed.) (1982). *International Marketing and Purchasing of International Goods*. Chichester: John Wiley and Sons.

Hakansson, H. and Snehota, I. (1995). *Developing Relationships in Business Networks*. London: Routledge.

Hetzel, P. (1996). '*The Fall and Rise of Marketing Fundamentalism*'. In S. Brown, J. Bell and D. Carson (eds), Marketing Apocalypse – Eschatology, Escapology and the Illusion of the End. London: Routledge, pp. 171–186.

Johansson, J.K. (2004). *In Your Face, How American Marketing Excess Fuels Anti-Americanism*. Upper Saddle River, NJ: Pearson.

Kotler, P. (2005). 'The role played by the broadening of marketing movement in the history of marketing thought'. *Journal of Public Policy and Marketing*, 24(1), 114–116.

Kotler, P. and Levy, S. (1969). 'Broadening the concept of marketing'. *Journal of Marketing*, 33(1), 10–15.

Kotler, P., Jain, D.C. and Maesincee, S. (2002). *Marketing Moves: A New Approach to Profits, Growth and Renewal*. Harvard: HBS Press.

de Leonardis, O. (1999). 'Social markets, social quality, and the quality of social institutions'. *European Journal of Social Quality*, 1(1/2), 32–44.

Little, V. and Brookes, R. (1997). 'The new marketing: What does customer focus now mean?' *Marketing and Research Today: The Journal of the European Society for Opinion and Marketing Research*, 25(1), 96–105.

Littler, D. and Tynan, C. (2005). 'Where are we and where are we going?' *European Journal of Marketing*, 39(3/4), 261–271.

Maffesoli, M. (1996). *The Time of the Tribes*. London: Sage.

McDonald, M. and Wilson, H. (2002). *The New Marketing*. Oxford: Butterworth-Heinemann.

McKenna, R. (1985). *The Regis Touch*. New York: Addison Wesley.

Morace, F. (ed.) (2002). *European Asymmetries [Asimmetrie Europee]*. Milan: Scheiwiller.

Morris, M.H., Schindehutte, M. and LaForge, R.W. (2002). 'Entrepreneurial marketing: a construction integrating entrepreneurship and marketing perspectives'. *Journal of Marketing Theory and Practice*, Fall, 1–18.

Moutinho, L., Davies, F. and Hutcheson, G. (2002). 'Exploring key neo-marketing directions through the use of an academic "think tank"'. *European Journal of Marketing*, 36(4), 417–432.

O'Malley, L. and Tynan, C. (1999). 'Concept, metaphor or reality? The prognosis for relationships in consumer markets'. *Journal of Marketing Management*, 20(10), 571–579.

Palmer, A. and Ponsonby, S. (2002). 'The social construction of new marketing paradigms: the influence of personal perspectives'. *Journal of Marketing Management*, 18, 173–192.

Prahalad, C.K. and Ramaswamy, V. (2004). *The Future of Competition: Co-creating Unique Value with Customers*. Harvard: HBS Press.

Schmitt, B.H. (1999). *Experiential Marketing: How to Get Customers to SENSE, FEEL, THINK, ACT and RELATE to Your Company and Brands*. New York: The Free Press.

Sheth, J.N. and Sisodia, R.S. (eds) (2006). *Does Marketing Need Reform? Fresh Perspectives on the Future*. Armonk, NY: M.E. Sharpe.

Smithee, A. (1997). 'Kotler is dead!' *European Journal of Marketing*, 31(3/4), 317–325.

Smithee, A. and Lee, T. (2004). 'Future directions in marketing knowledge: a panoramic perspective from Hollywood'. *Journal of Business and Industrial Marketing*, 19(2), 149–154.

Vargo, S.L. and Lusch, R.F. (2004). 'Evolving to a new dominant logic for marketing'. *Journal of Marketing*, 68(January), 1–18.

Venkatesh, A. and Penaloza, L. (2006). 'From marketing to markets: a call for paradigm shift'. In J.N. Sheth and R.S. Sisodia (eds), *Does Marketing Need Reform? Fresh Perspectives on the Future*. Armonk, NY: M.E. Sharpe, pp. 134–150.

de Vincentis, J.R. and Rackham, N. (1998). 'Breadth of a salesman'. *The McKinsey Quarterly*, 4, 32–43.

Webster Jr., F.E. (2005). 'A perspective on the evolution of marketing management'. *Journal of Public Policy and Marketing*, 24(1), 121–126.

Wilkie, W.L. and Moore, E. (2003). 'Scholarly research in marketing: exploring the "4 eras" of thought development'. *Journal of Public Policy and Marketing*, 22(2), 116–146.

Woolgar, S. (2004). 'What happened to provocation in science and technology studies'. *History and Technology*, 20(4), 339–349.

Woolgar, S. and Simakova, E. (2004). 'Marketing marketing: an exploratory paper'. *Proceedings of the 4s-EASST Conference*, Paris, August.

Zyman, S. (1999). *The End of Marketing As We Know It*. New York: Collins.

7

Customer-Driven or Driving the Customer? Exploitation versus Exploration

Gilles Marion

Customer and market orientation are the cornerstones of marketing ideology. However, the crystallization of the marketing concept during the 1950s, and its continuous rediscovery since, has deterred neither ambiguity nor the dissenting voice of criticism. A multitude of interpretations have emerged that suggest that instead of being at the centre of a stable world we are continually moving between different meanings. In this chapter, the controversial ways in which researchers and gurus have interpreted market and customer orientation is represented as a mini-plot where researchers engage in heated debate. In an attempt to bring clarity to this issue of interpretation we contrast the notions of 'exploitation' and 'exploration' and bring them together in a parsimonious model which shows these concepts as 'interdefined'.

Introduction

Since the 1950s the notion of customer-focus has been established as the bed-rock of marketing's most taken-for-granted ideology (Deshpandé, 1999, p. 176). Many labels express this idea: 'the marketing concept', 'customer orientation', 'getting close to the customer', 'customer intimacy', 'being customer-led', 'customer centricity', etc. However, this abundance of nomenclatures does not necessarily serve to elucidate our understanding of the field. The first focus of this chapter will be to clarify these concepts through the review of the literature. I then intend to show how researchers frame (i.e. assign meaning to and interpret) their concepts and constructs. From here a parsimonious model will be proposed which interdefines them. By contrasting the notions of 'exploitation' with 'exploitation' I attempt to demonstrate that, in fact, getting close to the customer could be an impediment for entrepreneurial marketing.

The Market Concept: An Overview of Definitions

In the marketing textbooks it is often accepted as an article of faith that successful firms are customer-oriented. Of course the interface with customers is crucial for an organization's survival and prosperity, however the interpretation of this construct varies widely. Indeed, much marketing research has focused on defining concepts and clarifying language. This chapter thus begins by examining the usage of language within this field.

The Marketing Concept and the Organization

The marketing concept, the normative philosophy that underlies marketing management thought, was presented as 'the new concept of marketing' (Kotler, 1967, p. 6): 'It starts with the firm's existing and potential customers; it seeks profit through the creation of customer satisfaction; and it seeks to achieve this through an integrated corporate-wide marketing program.' Thus the link between the customer and the goals of the whole organization have been inextricably linked for almost 60 years and marketing management theory taught in Business Schools to the managers of tomorrow has rested on this conceptualization (Drucker, 1954; Keith, 1960; Levitt, 1960; McKitterick, 1957).

This concept is eminently compatible with free market economics and the idea of customer sovereignty. If a company is led by the marketing concept all else can be assumed to follow: 'A customer orientation is the logical basis for profit planning in a consumer-sovereign economy.' (Kotler, 1967, p. 11), 'The companies produce what the consumers want and in this way they maximize consumer satisfaction and earn their profits' (Kotler, 1983, p. 18). From the very earliest days this link between customer orientation and organizational goals has tended to be somewhat narrowly interpreted by some managers: 'Management today knows that the customer is king [. . .] it knows that the king requires that his needs be satisfied in the way he wants them satisfied and when he wants them satisfied' (Gustafson, 1957, p. 77).

However, this narrow interpretation neglects the fact that whilst the sovereign consumer may select the ends, it is the producer who selects the means by which the services will be rendered and who can also choose to withhold his service altogether. Kotler appears to take account of this as he modifies his assertions on the marketing concept over time, particularly his statements about the maximization of customer satisfaction: 'The purpose of the marketing concept is to help organisations achieve their goals [. . .] A company makes money by satisfying customer needs better than competitor can do' (Kotler, 1988, p. 22). One can interpret this as meaning that a company does not have to be excellent if its competitors are mediocre. Indeed, if we look at Kotler's statements today, we can see that the focus has changed with the balance of power now favouring the organisation rather than the customer: 'The purpose of marketing is not to *maximise* customer satisfaction, but to meet customer needs profitably' (Kotler et al., 2005, p. 17).

Thus whilst at first glance, the marketing concept seems to declare that the interests of firms and customers align when companies have taken the marketing concept to heart, on closer examination we can see that this fundamental concept can be quite vague regarding the balance between customer satisfaction and organizational goals. This leaves marketing managers with a delicate balancing act to perform between two competing priorities.

The Marketing Concept and the Market Place

In the 1990s under the label 'market orientation' three core themes or 'pillars' – customer orientation, coordinated marketing, profitability – underlying the definitions of the marketing concept began to be disputed. Kholi and Jaworski (1990, p. 3) asserted that profitability was not a component of a market orientation, rather a consequence and thus discarded this pillar from their definition. Hunt and Morgan (1995, p. 11) did not include inter-functional coordination because, though they believed it to be a factor that can contribute to the successful implementation of market orientation, they did not believe that such implementation factors should appear in a concept's definition. Thus they recommended discarding another pillar. The remaining and most decisive pillar was also fiercely debated as commentators began to make a distinction between customer orientation on the one hand and market orientation on the other.

Deshpandé et al. (1993, p. 27) 'see customer and market orientations as being synonymous [and] argue that a competitor orientation can be almost antithetical to a customer orientation when the focus is exclusively on the strengths of a competitor rather than on the unmet needs of the customer.

In contrast with this singular focus on customers, Kholi and Jaworski (1990) and Narver and Slater (1990), assert that a market orientation involves a dual focus on both customers and competitors. For them, the marketplace consists of consumers, retailers, wholesalers and competitor, as well as information agents such as consultants or trade associations, and regulatory institutions. In their view, therefore changes in the behaviour of all of those parties must be scanned and analysed by the marketer. This view of a market orientation is echoed by Porter's competitive analysis which encourages marketers not just to consider the immediate competition but also to be alert to potential competition from innovations and from suppliers and buyers vertically integrating (Porter, 1980).

The Marketing Concept and Customer Intimacy

The enduring trait of the supposed excellent firms in Peters and Waterman book (1982, pp. 156–199) was that they were close to their customers. However Shapiro, quite soon after the publication of *In Search of Excellence* voiced dissent (1988, p. 120): 'after years of research, I'm convinced that the term "market oriented" represents a set of processes touching on all aspects of the company. It's a great deal more than the cliché getting close to the customer'. Shapiro argues that this goal is meaningless because most companies sell to a variety of customers with varying and even conflicting desires and needs. The most important strategic decision is to choose the important customers: the key target accounts and market segments. Thus Shapiro defines market orientation as the degree to which the marketing concept is implemented. Moreover, 'after years of research' he 'found no meaningful difference between market-driven and customer orientation' (Shapiro, 1988, p. 120).

Customer intimacy (Treacy and Wiersema, 1993) yields fine-grained understanding of customers, insights which are used to fine-tune the firm's offer to its customers. Moreover, customer demand can be influenced by what is supplied and how it is supplied. Customer intimacy allows the supplier to anticipate changes in customer demand. The supplier may become close enough to influence the customer's course of action moving from being reactive to being proactive. The more extended the interaction with the customer, the more likely it is that some elements of strategy will be cooperative. Joint development of an offering is the most obvious example. Increasing involvement in the customer's business may help *lock in* the customer (Macdonald, 1995, p. 11). In this instance, the potential benefits of getting close to the customer is immediate and obvious. The notion is sufficiently succinct and fashionable to be embodied in many a mission statement. It could provide guidance and overarching direction for managers charged with implementation. It could also help to achieve a high level of organizational *buy-in* for a given marketing strategy (Noble and Mokwa, 1999, p. 63).

However, this process also has a down side: the firm may not only get close to customers, it may get too close. Increasing involvement in the customer's business may help lock in the customer, but it could also lead to increasing involvement of the customer in the supplier's business. The very integration that enlightens the supplier also allows the customer to become much more knowledgeable about the supplier's business and may well enable the customer to influence the supplier's business as much as the supplier influences the customer's. Manufacturers that get close to large retailers or advertising agencies that get close to large advertisers have not only to allow those customers to collect information about their activities, they have also to surrender some control over these activities.

Consequently developing close links with customers is not only beneficial it can also be detrimental (Danneels, 2003, p. 560). Getting close to the customer is not a flawed concept. Simply it should not be regarded as a taken-for-granted and easy course. It has consequences that can lead to being customer-compelled. The firm which takes customer intimacy seriously must consider the degree to which it can, should, and wishes to interact with this customer.

Being Customer-Compelled: The Role of Mental Representations

Day (1999, p. 5) warned against firms who are 'customer-compelled and try to respond to whatever their customers say they want, without exercising any discipline'. Why are firms reluctant to participate actively in potentially disruptive technologies or new business models? Because the mental representations that guide marketers give familiar customers disproportionate attention and because there is a path dependency behind all strategies.

Christensen and Bower (1996) found that companies catering to their current customers got stuck in developing incremental new products and missed the wave of disruptive technologies because resources were allocated to programs serving powerful, large, existing customers. Indeed it has become apparent since the 1970s that the religious adherence to customer orientation has detrimental effects in the new product arena (Bennett and Cooper, 1979, p. 77). The dangers of too much reliance on customer orientation lie in opting for customer satisfaction in the short run at the expense of superior products in the future. 'It may be useful to remember that the initial market estimate for computers in 1945 projected total world-wide sales for only ten units' (Hayes and Abernathy, 1980, p. 71). Customers may know what their needs are, but they define those needs in terms of existing products, processes and prices. 'It is risky to stay too focused on the immediate need of known and immediate customers when there is a disruption in technological capabilities or market behaviour' (Day, 1999, p. 13).

We see what we expect to see and changes build on what is already known. Customer understandings are mental representations that marketers used to make sense of their environment. Organizations and marketers create mental representations of their environment based on inferences about the effects of their actions: 'organizations receive cues from their environment as a result of their own actions upon that environment. These cues are then interpreted, and the interpretation form the basis of subsequent actions' (Danneels, 2003, p. 560). Marketers not only act on mental representation of their customers, but also their actions feed back into the mental representation on which they are based, and so on. This self-reinforcing process connects customer insight and action taken. Similarly, the market segmentation framework that marketers impose on the market and customer databases that cover only served customers contribute to this self-reinforcing process. Thus, if marketers see the world only through their current customers' eyes 'escaping the tyranny of the served markets' can become extremely difficult (Hamel and Prahalad, 1991, p. 83). In effect, organizations can become trapped with the mental representation of the marketing concept and thus move from the customer sovereignty to the tyrannical market.

Customer-Led and Market-Oriented

We have seen above that some companies are far too occupied with satisfying the immediate demands of their existent customers to concentrate resources on more fundamental change such as new products or new markets. Slater and Narver (1998) have heeded this critique. To guard against the hazards of being customer-led they strongly underline that a market orientation must include not only present customers but also potential customers: 'Market-oriented businesses are committed to understanding both the expressed and latent needs of their customers [. . .] A customer-led philosophy tends to be reactive and short term in its orientation, and focuses on customers' expressed desires and on measures of customer satisfaction' (Slater and Narver, 1998, pp. 1003–1005). The greater the proportion of activities of the firm are oriented to understand latent needs the greater its market orientation. They argue too that 'market orientation theory and evidence strongly indicates that a more well developed market orientation is associated with superior performance' (Slater and Narver, 1999, p. 1166). These assertions lead to three issues:

1 The notion of latent needs implies that marketers understand customer needs better than customers do themselves. This echoes a 30-year old statement from Drucker: 'The aim of marketing [. . .] is to know and understand the customer so well that the product or service fits [. . .] and sells itself' (Drucker, 1973, pp. 64–65). What is such an understanding? No more, and no less, than the mental representation that marketers use to make sense of their market. In fact the formulated side of marketing management has little to offer for the understanding of the relationships between the finite set of human needs described by the Maslow's pyramid of needs and the potentially infinite set of individual desires and preferences expressed through the market. Companies practising entrepreneurial marketing create products and markets rather than starting with a well-defined market and then managing markets, demand and customers. The discourse on needs, and particularly 'latent' needs, serves mainly as legitimization. To refer to a particular choice as need, rather than simply a preference, appears to offer some form of social justification for that choice and to claim some form of moral legitimation for it (Marion, 2006).

2 The 'market orientation' theory Slater and Narver refer to remains relatively undeveloped. In closing their commentary they make clear that much remains unknown about market orientation, and they note that 'the understanding of

what it means to be market-oriented and how a market orientation benefits the firm continues to evolve' (Slater and Narver, 1999, p. 1167).

3 In the empirical evidence that informs the debate (e.g. Deshpandé et al., 1993; Kholi et al., 1993; Narver and Slater, 1990) the measures employed focus on closeness to current customers and do not explicitly probe a company's exploration of potential customers. Moreover, most of the measures of firm performance have been based on managers' perceptions. Finally, while these scholars have not ignored and not denied the importance of innovation, they have developed measures that focus on serving and keeping customers. Thus many of the studies to date have been short term and are therefore unable to answer the question of the long-term importance of radical innovation.

Market-Driven versus Market-Driving

Confronted with the narrow interpretation of market orientation – as the adaptation of product offerings to existing customer preferences – the purpose of Jaworski et al. (2000) was to refine the notion. They suggest two approaches to market orientation: a market-driven and a market-driving approach. They noted, however, that the interpretation of market orientation has been mainly in terms of market-driven strategies based on firm's reaction to change in the marketplace. If every actor in the market follows a market-driven strategy and every firm adapts to competitors' strategic moves and stays aligned with customer requirements, there is no guarantee that a sustainable advantage can be achieved. Therefore, they contrast market-driven – as learning and reacting to the market as given – with market-driving as influencing the structure of the market and/or behaviour of market players in a direction that enhances the competitive position of the firm (Jaworski et al., 2000, p. 53).

However, any effort to develop a scale to measure market-driving as a construct has yet to be undertaken. Berthon et al. (1999, p. 45) suggest that two modes of operation can emerge from the association of a customer orientation and an innovation orientation: shaping and interacting. Shaping suggests that innovation defines human needs and hence determines the nature of customer demand by providing new products or services. Interacting suggests a dialogue between the market and innovation. Whatever those nuances 'The important point to stress is that one cannot reduce innovation orientation to market orientation, or vice versa' (Berthon et al., 2004, p. 1069).

Drucker's concept of a business as a whole embraced more than a customer orientation or the mere serving of customers. He also stressed customer *creation*. Yes it is the customer who determines what a business is, but the fact remains that 'Markets are not created by God, nature or economic forces [. . .] it is business action that creates the customer' (Drucker, 1954, p. 52). Berthon et al. (2004, p. 1067) make this point clear:

> there are aspects of business, which come before the customer, which enable the creation of the customer, and are concerned with

the creation of innovative products and services. In many instances, needs, wants, and even value co-arise when products are created.

To take an example, before George Eastman's invention few people had had the goal of taking photographs. Kodak devised the notion of 'amateur photography' and, at the same time, defined the object that would convince everybody to take photographs (Latour, 1987, p. 115). Breakthrough innovations do not only change markets they have far-reaching effects on the way society functions. New technologies which have changed markets and society are legion: the impact of the railroad in the 19th century, widespread automobile ownership in the 20th century, the influence of the microprocessor on countless consumer durables, etc. Products create their own demand by changing the way customers behave. This suggests that to achieve a superior business performance, firms need to actively influence the market rather than being only reactive to it.

It is not that innovation orientation completely ignores customers. Gatignon and Xuereb (1997) argue that a synthesis of technological and customer orientations is well suited to markets where uncertainty is high. It is just that firms following a technological orientation believe that existing customers may not know enough about radical new technologies to need them and want them. The firm's capacity to innovate is at the heart of market-driving. Innovativeness occurs in terms of the value proposition made to customers or in terms of the uniqueness of the business systems used in the creation, production and delivery of value: 'Market orientation without an entrepreneurial drive might focus the organisation efforts too narrowly and, at best, produce adaptive learning' (Slater and Narver, 1995, p. 71). The capacity to innovate depends on the propensity to take risk and the ability to manage risk through interactive organizational learning.

Discussion

I have been warned that the underlying philosophy of the marketing concept 'enunciated in generalities at the beginning, has come to mean different things to different people, so that diverse and often contradictory actions can be justified by the same precepts' (Sachs and Benson, 1978, p. 68). Nevertheless there is good news for the critical approach: changes in interpretation of the marketing concept and subsequent constructs have been induced by critical scrutiny. Yet the deconstruction of such labels has only been possible through a critical scrutiny, largely of the strategy literature. Hunt (1994, pp. 14–15) suggests an interpretation of this fact: the absence of original contributions to the strategy dialogue by the marketing literature can be explain by the 'norms that control assertion in marketing research [. . .] marketing reviewers react quite negatively when a manuscript offers a genuinely original contribution to knowledge'.

The bad news is that the gap between the conceptual subtleties of academic research and the content of most basic marketing textbooks is growing. During 50 years, countless cohorts of marketing students have absorbed the art and science of analysis, planning, implementation and control through the canonical text of marketing management either in its full version or in more diluted form that appears in clones (Brown, 2002, p. 314). What is important for this normative dominant logic is not to study and explain how marketing as a practice functions, but rather how marketing *should* function. Effective marketing can take many forms but what occupies most of the attention of the mainstream textbooks deals with the formulated and *exploitation* side of marketing, the easier part to learn which 'includes such things as refinement, choice, production, efficiency, selection, implementation, execution' (March, 1991, p. 71).

Exploration versus Exploitation

In spite of its pretentious claim to be universal, the marketing approach provided by most textbooks has little to offer that encourages the creative side of entrepreneurial marketing and exploration. This 'includes things captured by terms such as search, variations, risk taking, experimentation, play, flexibility, discovery, innovation' (March, 1991, p. 71). This bias is not really surprising because the search for new ideas or markets has less certain outcomes and longer time horizons than does further development of existing ones. Thus the rhetoric of customer-driven best practices, backed by traditional marketing management discourse, and reinforced by the typical focus of practitioners on short-term gains (improve sales this month, stock price this quarter, market share this week) is always more convincing than the rhetoric of entrepreneurial and risky next practices.

When describing the process of 'Creative Destruction', the essential fact about capitalist reality, Schumpeter (1942) identifies the exploration/exploitation distinction. He argues that the competition from the new product, the new technology, the new process or the new type of organization commands a decisive cost or quality advantage. This kind of competition is much more effective than competition within a rigid pattern of invariant conditions: 'In others words, the problem that is usually being visualized is how capitalism administers existing structures, whereas the relevant problem is how it creates and destroys them' (Schumpeter, 1942, p. 83).

If adaptive processes are likely to become effective in the short run they could be self-destructive in the long run. Organizations which are most able to adapt to a given market or a given competitive environment will prosper until there is a major discontinuity. Part of their learning is embedded in their mental representations about how things are to be done. Moreover, the certainty of today's incremental innovation can often destroy the potential of tomorrow's discontinuous innovation. The contradictions inherent in the multiple types of innovation create conflict and dissent between the units historically profitable, large and efficient, and the young entrepreneurial, risky and cash absorbing units. Because the power, resources and traditions tend to be anchored in the more traditional customer-driven units, these units try to ignore and even destroy the entrepreneurial units. While some suggest that organizations can operate in multiples mode simultaneously (Tushman and O'Reilly III, 1997) the problem is to integrate opposites.

Drucker defined two entrepreneurial functions: 'Because it is its purpose to create a customer, any business enterprise has two – and only those two – basic functions: marketing and innovation' (Drucker, 1954, p. 53). However, mainstream interpretations of Drucker have favoured the perspective of exploitation (getting, serving and keeping customer) and have discarded the *creation* of the customer that could result from exploration. Therefore, when Deshpandé, 1999, p. 167 asserts that 'the bedrock of marketing's most taken-for-granted ideology, [is] the marketing concept', the most important terms are not 'marketing concept' but 'taken-for-granted ideology'. The dominant logic of marketing interprets Drucker's thoughts in a way that simplifies them. It is a way to organize the set of beliefs and meanings that will inspire and legitimate the discipline and define its issues: what evidence has to be taken-for-granted and relevant and what has to be ignored. The 'customer-driven' approach seems plausible to the extent that exploitation practices can be pointed to as documentary evidence.

A Parsimonious Model to Interpret the Constructs

In the previous pages I looked to the controversial ways researchers and gurus interpret firm relationships to the marketplace. The literature has been presented as a mini-plot where researchers engage in heated debate. Interpretations are always stacked up, only to cancel each other out, while constructs that are proffered succeed, little by little, in pinning down a concrete meaning. Some argue that customer and market orientations are synonymous and that competitor orientation can be antithetical to customer orientation. Others assert that the single focus on customers introduces perceptual biases and therefore that market orientation is more than customer orientation. The cliché 'getting close to the customer' is critically discussed: while it allows the firm to better serve its customer it can be detrimental when it leads the firm to be customer-compelled. To guard against the hazards of being customer-led some argue that a market orientation should not only respond to customer's expressed wants but also understand their 'latent' needs because of the long-term importance of radical innovation. Some suggest two approaches to market orientation: market-driven and market-driving. Thus instead of being at the centre of a stable world we are continually moving between different meanings and interpretations.

Let us assume, for a while, that marketing is not a normative discipline but a descriptive one which may be normative – heroic speculation! To clarify the issue of interpretation I propose a parsimonious model (Figure 7.1) in order to show how these constructs are 'interdefined'. First I suggest that the meaning of 'customer-driven' and its variations (getting close to the customer, customer-compelled and customer-led) entails its opposite or contrary: 'customer-driving' (shaping customer behaviour, educating customers). 'Customer-driven' and 'customer-driving' are two opposite positions on the 'customer-focused' axis – a 'semantic axis' in which each of the two positions presupposes the other. Customer-focus is both a point of view from which to understand customer evolution and a continuum of possible actions for doing things with customers in limited or extended interaction. Customer-focus can lead to various degree of intimacy, to being customer-compelled as well as to shaping customer behaviour. These relationships usually exhibit a mixture of transaction-based elements.

Rather than rest at this simple binary opposition, I further propose an additional contradictory pair of constructs: that is 'market-driven' versus 'market-driving', two opposite positions on the 'market-focused' axis. Market-focused is both a point of view on how the marketplace and the industry structure will evolve and a continuum of possible actions for doing things within a networks of actors. It implies a competitive stance as well as a cooperative one in order to exploit the resources of networks of suppliers, distributors, consumer communities, professional associations, etc.

We are therefore left with four positions articulating a system of meaning. 'Market-driven' and 'customer-driven' are seen as complementary on the side of exploitation (to be market-driven is more than being customer-driven), while 'market-driving' and 'customer-driving' are seen as complementary on

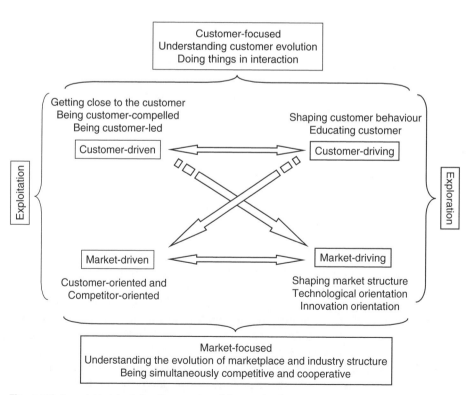

Figure 7.1 A model to interdefine the meaning of the constructs.

the side of exploration: customer-driving is only one way to drive the market. I have used a managerial perspective which permits me to construct such sentences as: 'market-focused management', 'customer-focused management', 'customer-driven management', 'market-driving management', etc. However, this is a descriptive system not a normative framework.

So, where does the idea of customer sovereignty fit in? Driving customers/markets seems to imply firm sovereignty while customer-/market-driven positions seems to imply customer sovereignty. This interpretation would be misleading. There is space in the system for customer agency in all four positions. Customer-driving does not imply that firms can act autonomously. A firm cannot drive customers legitimately without a deep-down understanding of the way in which customers- may contest or may participate in relationships. The potential customer (individual or organization) has always the choice to go to the marketplace or to exit and to engage in self-service and do-it-yourself activity. I argue that firms and marketers do not understand customer needs better than customers do themselves. Their understanding comes from their ability to interact with informed, empowered and active customers. A customer-driving organization believes that customers – and consumers – can choose the firms they want to have a relationship with (limited or extended) based on their own views of how value should be created for them and/or with them.

In the same vein a firm cannot drive a market legitimately without a strong guiding point of view (a vision) of how it wants to shape the market to its advantage. A market-driving organization does not simply respond adroitly to events and trends in the marketplace. Rather it breaks the rules of the game and conceives new ways to compete and to cooperate. Market-driving organizations, as well as customer-driving organizations, are change agents not content with protecting their position. Therefore marketing is fundamentally not only about exchange but also about change and cannot work legitimately without the active agency of the customer as a social actor.

Conclusion

The marketing discipline is full of gurus speaking with assurance of what is customer orientation or market orientation. Though all of the market orientation constructs include some measure of responsiveness to the customer, they are less consistent in their treatment of other factors such as competitor orientation or innovation orientation. I provide a parsimonious model to describe the relations between the various constructs coming from this stream of research. This way of organizing the language of the field could be absorbed by managers – and futures managers – into the mental representations that guide their actions. However, their challenge will be to unlearn third-rate ideas such as the customer as king, the passive audience, or the Maslovian 'theory' of needs. Predictably, the slowest adopters of a new mind-set will be fast moving consumer goods companies because the prevailing dominant logic both supports and is reinforced by their current marketing tools and strategy.

References

Bennett, R.C. and Cooper, R.G. (1979). 'The misuse of marketing: an American tragedy'. *Business Horizons*, 24(6), 51–61.

Berthon, P., Hulbert, J.M. and Pitt, L.F. (1999). 'To serve or create? Strategic orientations toward customers and innovation'. *California Management Review*, 42(1), 37–58.

Berthon, P., Hulbert, J.M. and Pitt, L.F. (2004). 'Innovation or customer orientation? An empirical investigation'. *European Journal of Marketing*, 38(9/10), 1065–1090.

Brown, S. (2002). 'Vote, vote, vote for Philip Kotler'. *European Journal of Marketing*, 36(3), 313–324.

Christensen, C. and Bower, J. (1996). 'Customer power, strategic investment, and the failure of leading firms'. *Strategic Management Journal*, 17(3), 197–218.

Danneels, (2003). 'Tight – loose coupling with customers: the enactment of customer orientation'. *Strategic Management Journal*, 24, 559–576.

Day, G.S. (1999). 'Misconceptions about market orientation'. *Journal of Market-Focused Management*, 4(1), 5–11.

Deshpandé, R. (1999). 'Foreseeing Marketing', *Journal of Marketing*, 63(Special issue), 164–167.

Deshpandé, R., Farley, J.U. and Webster Jr., F.E. (1993). 'Corporate culture, customer orientation, and innovativeness in Japanese firms: a quadrad analysis'. *Journal of Marketing*, 57(1), 23–37.

Drucker, P.F. (1954). *The Practice of Management*. New York: Harper and Brothers.

Drucker, P.F. (1973). *Management: Tasks, Responsibilities, Practices*. New York: Harper & Row.

Gatignon, H. and Xuereb, J.M. (1997). 'Strategic orientation of the firm and new product performance'. *Journal of Marketing Research*, 34(February), 77–90.

Gustafson, P. (1957). 'Selling tomorrow's market'. *Nation's Business*, 45(2), 76–88.

Hamel, G. and Prahalad, C.K. (1991). 'Corporate imagination and expeditionary marketing'. *Harvard Business Review*, 69(4), 81–92.

Hayes, R.H. and Abernathy, W.J. (1980). 'Managing our way to economic decline'. *Harvard Business Review*, 58(4), 67–77.

Hunt, S.D. (1994). 'On rethinking marketing: our discipline, our practice, our methods'. *European Journal of Marketing*, 28(3), 13–25.

Hunt, S.D. and Morgan, R.M. (1995). 'The comparative advantage theory of competition'. *Journal of Marketing*, 59(April), 1–15.

Jaworski, B. J., Kholi, A.K. and Sahay, A. (2000). 'Market-driven versus driving markets'. *Journal of the Academy of Marketing Science*, 28(1), 45–54.

Keith, R.J. (1960). 'The marketing revolution'. *Journal of Marketing*, 24(1), 35–38.

Kholi, A. K. and Jaworski, B. J. (1990). 'Market orientation: the construct, research propositions, and managerial implications'. *Journal of Marketing*, 54(2), 1–18.

Kholi, A. K., Jaworski, B. J. and Kumar, A. (1993). 'MARKOR: a measure of market orientation'. *Journal of Marketing Research*, 30(4), 467–477.

Kotler, P. (1967). *Marketing Management. Analysis, Planning, and Control.* Englewood Cliffs, NJ: Prentice Hall.

Kotler, P. (1983). *Principles of Marketing,* 2nd edition. Englewood Cliffs, NJ: Prentice Hall.

Kotler, P. (1988). *Marketing Management. Analysis, Planning, and Control,* 6th edition. Englewood Cliffs, NJ: Prentice Hall.

Kotler, P., Wong, V., Saunders, J. and Armstrong, G. (2005). *Principles of Marketing,* 4th European edition. Harlow: Pearson Education Ltd.

Latour, B. (1987). *Science in Action.* Cambridge Mass: Harvard University Press.

Levitt, T. (1960). 'Marketing Myopia'. *Harvard Business Review,* 38(4), 24–47.

Macdonald, S. (1995). 'Too close for comfort? The strategic implication of getting close to the customer'. *California Management Review,* 37(4), 8–28.

McKitterick, J.B. (1957). 'What is the marketing management concept'. In F.M. Bass (ed.), *The Frontiers of Marketing Though and Sciences.* Chicago, IL: American Marketing Association, pp. 71–82.

March, J. (1991). 'Exploration and exploitation in organizational learning'. *Organizational Science,* 2(1), 71–87.

Marion, G. (2006). 'Marketing ideology and criticism: legitimacy and legitimization'. *Marketing Theory,* 6(2), 245–262.

Narver, J.C. and Slater, S.F. (1990). 'The effects of a market orientation on business profitability'. *Journal of Marketing,* 54(4), 20–35.

Noble, C.H. and Mokwa, M.P. (1999). 'Implementing marketing strategies: developing and testing a managerial theory'. *Journal of Marketing,* 63(4), 57–73.

Peters, T. and Waterman, R. (1982). *In Search of Excellence: Lessons from America's Best Run Companies.* New York: Harper & Row.

Porter, M.E. (1980). *Competitive Advantage.* New York: The Free Press.

Sachs, W.S. and Benson, G. (1978). 'Is it not time to discard the marketing concept'? *Business Horizons,* 21(8), 68–74.

Schumpeter, J.A. (1942). *Capitalism, Socialism and Democracy.* New York: Harper.

Shapiro, B. (1988). 'What the hell is "market oriented"'. *Harvard Business Review,* 66(6), 119–125.

Slater, S.F. and Narver, J.C. (1995). 'Market orientation and the learning organization'. *Journal of Marketing,* 59(3), 63–74.

Slater, S.F. and Narver, J.C. (1998). 'Customer-led and market-oriented: let's not confuse the two'. *Strategic Management Journal,* 19(10), 1001–1006.

Slater, S.F. and Narver, J.C. (1999). 'Market-oriented is more than being customer-led'. *Strategic Management Journal,* 20(12), 1165–1168.

Treacy, M. and Wiersema, F. (1993). 'Customer intimacy and other value discipline'. *Harvard Business Review,* (January/February), 84–93.

Tushman, M.L. and O'Reilly III C.A. (1997). *Working Through innovation: A Practical Guide to Leading Organizational Change and Renewal.* Boston, MA: Harvard University School Press.

8

Advertising Literacy Revisited: Fat Children and Other Things

Brian M. Young

The first part of the title of this chapter, although clichéd, is hopefully not entirely devoid of meaning to the reader, although the latter part might only become clearer later. Over 20 years ago I used the phrase in another book chapter (Young, 1986) which was based on a conference in France on advertising to children. As far as I am aware I was the first person to invent the phrase and it has been picked up and used again and developed into a concept more powerful than my original formulation. For example Ritson and Elliott (1999) have taken it beyond a simple litany of skills and competencies that the average reader requires to appreciate the genre and have introduced considerations of interpretive communities who use advertising as just one resource in the their collective constructions of meaning. After 20 years though we now have a historical perspective to look again at how others have approached general issues and concerns in the area of advertising to kids and see just what has been achieved, where faults (but not blame) might lie, and how we can better go forward in the future. And with the even worse cliché 'whither advertising literacy?' hovering on my lips I shall get on with the job.

Children and advertising is a fairly regular visitor in the media and seldom fails to hit the headlines. At the time of writing the major concern is food advertising directed at children and the role such exposure might have in the current prevalence of obesity and overweight in children. In the past we have had issues as diverse as advertising of sugared products being a contributory factor in dental caries in children, whether advertising to children is unfair or deceptive as they can't understand it before a certain age, and the fairness of using celebrity endorsement as a rhetorical technique for marketing brands to kids. They appear with regular frequency and seem guaranteed to evoke passion in parents and others. Consequently politicians are not averse to using them to whip up interest and gain, in their own way, some visibility and approval from voters. To that extent the issue becomes a political football. But is there truth beneath the froth? Bandwagons and juggernauts roll on regardless and to that extent we live in and maybe have always lived a world driven by public relations (PR) but there surely is some reality under the rhetoric?

In order to find it however one has to dig quite deep. Those of us who work in academia will be very familiar with the international traffic in scientific communications and indeed teach our students the picky details of correct referencing, whatever the convention, as it is required so that researchers can find the right stuff. And as we also know that scientific knowledge does not exist in a vacuum. We have a duty to disseminate it and take into account the ethical and policy implications of such knowledge and research. We are (or should be) all good citizens now. But the sheer immensity of the data produced and its immediate availability through the web means that different levels of summary and digested material are made available to the interested reader. Take for example a recent Report by the Food Standards Agency (FSA) in the UK on food promotion to children (Hastings et al., 2003). For most people the first point of contact would be the various media discussions in press, radio, and television that emerged from the release of this Report. There were press releases that emerged at the launch of the report as well and the main issue that was addressed was the important question of childhood obesity and how advertising and marketing to children has an important role to play in it. The use of the ubiquitous metaphor of a 'ticking time bomb' is infectious as can be seen from a quote from the then chair of the FSA, Sir John Krebs:

> We already know that many children's diets contain more fat, sugar and salt than is recommended. We know that the level of obesity in children is rising and, in the words of the Chief Medical Officer, is a health time bomb that could explode.

The Report is in two volumes. The first volume contains an executive summary which states explicitly that they are going to look at the effect that this promotion has on children's 'food knowledge, preferences and behaviour' (op. cit., p. 1). Nothing about obesity there. Then there is a management summary followed by a review of the literature. The second volume consists of digests of articles that were consulted. So it is clear from the outset that the research brief which the authors fulfilled with a detailed and comprehensive piece of work was the role of food promotion to children in the context of their diet. But the goalposts have been shifted from executive summary to press release and space precludes me going into detail about how evidence which is hedged in the detailed analyses is transformed by firming up at more summary levels. The change from a study of the role of advertising in the diet of children to one which looks at what influence advertising has in obesity and overweight in children **is** important and cannot be justified as simply a result of summarizing and generalizing of the findings. It is well known now that advertising has a small role to play[1] in changing children's diet. But diet is not the end of the line in the obesity argument as diet is itself an input variable into another multifactorial mix of factors including genetic, physiological, socio-cultural, and activity (exercise) parameters. So the small link between advertising and diet will become even more reduced and attenuated before we reach the output – the fat child.[2]

As part of my own work I wanted to familiarize myself with the literature on obesity and overweight and how advertising and marketing to children might impact on this problem. Where best to go than the World Health Organization (WHO)? There seemed to be a relevant source (WHO, 2003) and it is to this we now turn. The question of evidence is considered systematically. Each chapter is structured with a particular theme and is divided into relevant sections and sub-sections. In general these reviews are extremely informative and up-to-date with extensive referencing – 139 citations in section 4 for example. So where does advertising to children fit in? Section 5.2 looks at obesity and excess weight gain. Although six citations are offered in support of 'heavy marketing of fast food outlets and energy-dense, micronutrient-poor foods and beverages' (p. 65) being a causative and probable risk factor that might promote weight gain and obesity, only four of these are individual research studies out of a total number of only 27 citations in this section as a whole. In contrast most of the other sections in the WHO Report have well over 100 citations. On this evidence, claims that although 'the heavy marketing of these food and beverages to young children causes obesity is not unequivocal . . . there is sufficient indirect evidence to warrant this practice being placed in the "probably" category and thus becoming a potential target for interventions' (p. 65) are made. The Report (section 5.1.2) uses four categories to classify evidence. As only two of these categories (*convincing evidence* and *probable evidence*) are entered in a summary table in the annex it is important to look at these in detail.

Convincing evidence is:

> Evidence . . . based on epidemiological studies showing consistent associations between exposure and disease, with little or no evidence to the contrary. The available evidence is based on a substantial

---

[1] The figures are derived from a small number of studies and are usually of the order of 2% of the variance accounted for being attributed to children's exposure to advertising.

[2] Interestingly a recent book on obesity (Gard and Wright, 2005) does not mention advertising or food promotion at all (see Young, 2005).

number of studies including prospective observational studies and where relevant, randomized, controlled trials of sufficient size, duration and quality showing consistent effects. The association should be biologically plausible.

Probable evidence has weaker criteria:

[It] is based on epidemiological studies showing fairly consistent associations between exposure and disease, but where there are perceived shortcomings in the available evidence or some evidence to the contrary, precluding a more definite judgement. Shortcomings in the evidence may be any of the following: insufficient duration of trials (or studies) available; inadequate sample sizes; incomplete follow-up. Laboratory evidence is usually supportive. Again the association should be biologically plausible.

Although the criteria for classification are based on medical and health considerations they are applicable to much evaluation of social science research on media influence or effects with perhaps 'disease' being replaced by 'dependent variable' and 'biologically plausible' replaced with 'theoretically predictable according to the model'.

So it should be possible to look at these four studies and see just what contribution they make to a judgement that heavy marketing of food and beverages to children 'probably' causes obesity. The first paper cited is by Robinson (1998) who examined the issue of whether television causes childhood obesity. He argued that cross-sectional studies have established a consistent and small correlation between adiposity and television viewing among children but this does not establish the direction of causality. In order for this to be established, precedence must be established as a necessary (although not sufficient) condition. In other words if television viewing is a true risk factor for childhood obesity then television viewing should predict future obesity. Of the two prospective studies cited by Robinson (Dietz and Gortmaker, 1985; Robinson et al., 1993), one made a weak but significant prediction and the other didn't. In order to establish that television viewing is a necessary and sufficient condition for childhood obesity one should have data derived from experimental studies where manipulation of the risk factor changes the outcome. At the moment then the best explanation is that the relationship between television viewing and body fatness is caused by both reduced energy expenditure from displacement of energy intake, and increased dietary intake. What is most interesting though is that none of these papers I have cited by Robinson (and the WHO cites one only) mention advertising and marketing of foods to children at all. They do talk about television viewing as does the WHO and television viewing together with sedentary life styles is mentioned in WHO (2003) quite frequently as linked risk factors. So we must conclude that this paper does not inform the debate whatsoever as it is irrelevant to the discussion. The second paper (#16) is Borzekowski and Robinson (2001). Poorer families, based on Head Start programme participation were recruited in California and 46 pre-schoolers (2–6 years) participated. Children in small groups either watched a videotape of a popular children's cartoon together with an educational segment and with no commercials in the tape at all; or the same videotape with several commercials of different branded products embedded in the programme content. Each small group of children was randomly assigned to either group. Shortly afterwards they were asked if they wanted one of two alternatives – both were similar in packaging but one had been shown to the child before in the experimental condition. Children in the experimental condition showed a significant shift (on most product categories) in favour if the item they had just seen in the videotape. Background information from parents showed little difference between groups in terms of exposure to media including TV ads. The authors do recognize that the extent to which one can generalize beyond the laboratory setting is limited by stating that 'we cannot be sure that the same effects would occur during viewing at home' (op. cit., p. 45) – such experiments have high internal validity but low external validity.

The third paper (#17) by Lewis and Hill (1998) has two parts. One is a survey in the UK of food advertising to children while the second study uses a sample of 103 children aged 10 years of age in the UK. They watched a popular TV programme with ads embedded in them and were assessed on body shape preferences and self-perceptions before and after viewing the videotape. Self-report measures of eating behaviour were also taken. BMI (body mass index) measures of children were obtained and the children were categorized on a percentile basis based on UK age-standardized norms. Each child watched both food and non-food adverts. The experiment was a well-designed analysis of variance with repeated measures on type of viewing. Results were by no means simple and the authors state that the effects were 'weak and complex' (p. 212) and that 'it would not be appropriate to speculate deeply either on the mechanism of these effects, or their likely long-term or behavioural consequences' (p. 212). They conclude that 'research in this area needs to progress' (p. 213). Finally, there is a paper (#18) by Taras and Gage (1995) that looked at the content of advertising to children over 5 weeks in January and February 1993 in the United States. So of the four papers, one is irrelevant and two look at the content analysis of advertising to children. One demonstrates short-term preference effects of advertising at the level of the brand with very young children and another produces a result that the authors tend to discount as weak and complex and suggest further research.

The point of this brief foray into the world of evidence is to show a simple truth which Buss (1975) called 'the sociology of psychological knowledge'. Knowledge is constructed and rhetoric and spin emerges during the process of transmission. That is if one starts at say the level of the press release and works backwards through press briefings, the executive summary of the report, the details of the report, and the abstracts on which the report is based, one gradually enters a world of hedged and qualified statements which of course are a pretty useless diet for consumption by hard-pressed executives or heads of committees. It's rare to get past the level of the executive summary and even in a communications or PR agency office full of researchers with access to the Internet the deepest level will probably be with the abstracts. So the box is never opened and what was actually *done* by the researchers is rarely if ever looked at. But if one does explore the citations that give academic gravitas to academic writing then often the evidence – as the above – shows is just not there.

I hope that these observations have left the reader with just a slight sceptical feeling about the literature on children and advertising. However before developing a vision of just what theory is required, it's necessary to establish an argument as to why this field lacks the rigour and theorizing that is present in other areas of advertising or developmental psychology. Certainly the demands of policy-makers and politicians have an influence but there are other areas of science and scholarship that have remained impervious to such pressure.[3] There are (at least) two reasons why the literature on advertising to children seems full of contradictory theories and findings. The first one is where the research comes from and who does it and the second is to do with the nature of children and childhood itself. I shall address these in turn.

A cursory glance at the literature will reveal that there are various authors publishing from different backgrounds. There is no single journal that covers the field[4] – and there may not even be an academic field in its own right – and the methods used are eclectic. So I can identify from memory researchers and scholars in marketing obviously, social marketing experts, health policy professionals, health psychologists, dieticians and nutritionists, dentists, medical doctors and professors, social psychologists, media psychologists, developmental psychologists, sociologists of childhood, consumer psychologists, consumer researchers, critical theorists, linguists, communication theorists, educationalists, experts in semiotics and cultural studies, and the list could go on. All of them have their own paradigms or acceptable styles of investigation and many of them will have different discourses each with their own metaphors, models, and ways of thinking. Each one of these people brings into the debate a preferred mode of practice and methodologies ranging from the free-wheeling procedures that hide within focus groups and qualitative analysis to the rigours of laboratory-based quantitative research. This is a conceptual as well as a linguistic Tower of Babel. I have been faced with a considerable problem when reviewing the field as so much of the material comes from different genres and backgrounds with different styles of approach. Indeed there is a case that there are different discourses surrounding the topic each discourse defining

---

[3] Although the role of genetics in behaviour has been treated atrociously in the popular press, that does not seem to influence the progress of this science and even the popularity of 'serious and popular' books on the subject (see Ridley, 2000).

[4] At the time of writing there is *Young Consumers* which was the *International Journal of Advertising and Marketing to Children* in a previous incarnation. But many academics in the field would seek other outlets for their work.

assumptions about and procedures for resolving issues in the area. So for example the discourse surrounding the FSA Report is scientific and quasi-medical with an emphasis on selecting research on the basis of a systematic evaluation of sources. This is obviously appropriate for the document to impact on public policy. If we turn to the main player – the ubiquitous child or kid – then we find that there is no consensus on the 'preferred' way of conceptualizing children and childhood. There are two dominant images[5] used in discussions about children and advertising. The child is the innocent and the 'kid' is the imp. Children are earnest, well behaved, in need of protection, innocent, and need to be taught. Kids are different. They are wild, self-contained, and adaptable. Put them into situations and they'll learn to cope. They're imps and they're growing older younger. These social representations of children have been with us for many years. In the UK context the history of children's TV was dominated by programmes such as *Blue Peter*; a long-running 'magazine' format with earnest demonstrations of how to help others and make interesting toys out of old toilet rolls. Children were being addressed. The kid burst onto the scene on so-called independent television (or ITV) a.k.a. commercially funded television and the trend-setting programme called *Tiswas* typified this approach in the 1980s. Kids screamed and laughed as adults had water and coloured 'gunge' poured on them and – in the tradition of pantomime – the humour although directed at children was full of ironic references for mums and dads too. It is enlightening to look at the publicity material that accompanies the many conferences where companies discuss how better to target children in the booming market of child-related merchandise. Only children weren't at the end of the marketer's metaphorical gun barrels. It was kids and the conferences were given snappy titles like *Kid Power '99* (and charged extortionate attendance fees for the privilege).

The variety of researchers from different backgrounds together with slippery and socially constructed concepts like childhood and children meant that contradictions and a lack of consensus in the literature have characterized much of the literature since the early 1970s. If we can't agree on which paradigms are best for scholarly inquiry and scientific research as well as which theoretical framework is best for describing the trajectory of development in children then a lack of agreement is predictable. I have discussed this before (Young, 1990) in the context of the child's understanding of the intent behind advertising. Given the importance of establishing a consensus on for example the age at which it can be said a child has a basic understanding of advertising in the context of advertising regulation then global companies, advertisers, health professionals, heads of government research departments, and various non-governmental organizations will want someone to act as an expert for them and want advice on the state of this art. The fact that such a state may not exist is conveniently ignored. To continue with the example of the age when children understand advertising: it is quite possible to set up hypotheses based on developmental theory that would suggest some children can understand

---

[5] For the history of images of children and childhood, see Aries (1973).

advertising at an early age if they are exposed to it and the culture within which they are immersed prioritizes such competencies as they are valuable and adaptive. Cross-cultural evidence for example shows that children in southern Africa are capable of acquiring sophisticated transaction skills when selling in the local market place and other work has shown that youngsters in the south Pacific can navigate and sail boats with great skill. It is also possible to argue from another theoretical position that development of children's understanding proceeds in a systematically driven way over the years so that children will not and cannot acquire a real understanding of advertising until late childhood. I hesitate to identify these two positions with well-known theorists in child development as the two I had in mind (Vygotsky and Piaget, respectively) are more complex than that but there are some psychologists who believe that development in children is primarily a matter of growth and maturation and others who claim that culture is the most important driver for change. Child psychology is not a unified science and the findings are contradictory, especially in advertising literacy and it is not difficult to find psychologists who are willing to argue a case that strengthens the case for more regulation of advertising to children whereas others will produce an equally well-evidenced case that children are more competent than that and advertising does them no harm.

In the remainder of this chapter I shall put forward my own preferred approach to defining advertising which I believe is more amenable to incorporating advertising literacy. Advertising is difficult to define in the context of the development of a psychological function like advertising literacy. Whereas the object of study under the lens of inquiry is well defined in, for example research on children's understanding of other people, or children's abilities to function with economic arrangements like money it is difficult to get a similar definition emerging when we look at advertising to children. Textbooks provide a variety of different definitions and if we take them and squeeze hard a few drops of mutually shared sense emerge. So advertising is a form of communication that is 'paid for', that is 'non-personal' (institutional rather than one-to-one) that has a general persuasive function, and so on. As textbooks are often for practitioners there is an emphasis on the various institutional arrangements that constitute the process of advertising and how advertising has an economic and commercial function. So the evolution of an understanding of advertising in the child can be seen to be part of what is often called economic or consumer socialization which deals with how the child acquires an understanding of the ways of that world and learns how to function within it. There is another approach and that is to look at it as a genre of communication with various functions that would define levels of understanding at different ages. So advertising entertains, informs, persuades, attracts attention, deals with commercially available goods and services, promotes, and uses rhetoric both visual and verbal. There may be more but these taken together constitute a set of family resemblances that are adequate to identify advertising. More important they define developmental streams where we can ask such questions as 'when do children see advertising as just entertainment and when do children understand visual rhetoric?'.[6]

There is a critical feature in that list that seems to have a special privilege. This is the fact that advertising is promotional. This feature is essential rather than instrumental. Advertising which is not promotional ceases to be advertising but advertising which doesn't entertain is just bad advertising.[7] Such blunt statements do not go down well with audiences primed for critical approaches so before you all reach for your counter-examples, let me elaborate. There have been several attempts by linguists and communication theorists to specify the various rules of communicative conduct that guide and govern our normal adult use of the various communicative systems at our disposal. The work of Grice (1975, 1978) is relevant here. Grice laid out what he called a cooperative principle that describes a basic tenet of cooperative conversation. This requires one to 'make your contribution such as is required, at the stage at which it occurs, by the accepted purpose or direction of the talk exchange in which you are engaged' (cited in Levinson, 1983, p. 101). What does this mean? Grice put forward several maxims that derived from this principle and they can be summarized by saying that participants in a cooperative exchange should communicate with sincerity, being relevant and clear while providing sufficient information. People, of course, often don't do this. So the power of Grice's approach lies in his prediction of what would happen if one of these rules was not obeyed. Imagine I asked you (what I thought was) a straight, sensible, pertinent question and got (what I thought was) an evasive, irrelevant reply back. At this apparent breach of rules of canonical communicative conduct I can make one of several inferences. One could be that you are deliberately being non-cooperative and do not wish to talk. Or, I could assume that the principle of cooperative communication is not being abandoned and that you are breaching the rule to some purpose. I then have to do some mental work in order to re-establish your communicative intent. Perhaps you are signalling to me that the topic is a sensitive one and should not be discussed now. Or you are trying to be sarcastic or humorous. The details of the inferences made, the extent to which these inferences are drawn and the conditions limiting them are not important in this context. What is important is that there are two stages in the process. One is the recognition of rule-breaking and the other consists of the details of the mental work done to reconstruct communicative intent. May (1981) was concerned with a particular communicative situation where one of the participants is Interested (as opposed to Disinterested) in that s(he) wished to generate a preferred response in the other. This would certainly include advertisers but would include many other people who

---

[6] The answer to the first is well known (pre-school children see advertising as just fun) whereas the answer to the latter is still to be found.

[7] I've ignored ironic advertising whether produced by the advertiser or constructed out of the 'raw' material of advertising by collective consumption but the approach in the next few pages using pragmatic rules is adequate to cope with that.

would be concerned with changing other people and were intentionally doing this.[8] Advertisers would come into this category as advertisers persuade people to buy brands, but other sources would also be included (such as advocates, exhorters, seducers, pleaders, and evangelists in various guises). May presents certain maxims for interpreting the messages of Interested participants, one of these being the so-called maxim of Best Face. The maxim of Best Face requires the reader to treat the case that is put as the strongest case that can be made. The type of approach exemplified by May is valuable as it places advertising with other kinds of communicative activities and establishes a firm characteristic of advertising. It should be possible to lay out various maxims on the lines of May (op. cit.) to account for the characteristics of communication by Interested parties. Advertising would then be placed in this category. If the maxim of Best Face is recognized more in the breach than in the observance, and that seems to be characteristic of Gricean rules, then other forms of inference occur. I am assuming now that the maxim of Best Face has some psychological validity. So, if the maxim of Best Face is violated this is recognized implicitly by the reader to the extent other forms of inference towards an interpretation are brought into play. If an ad is expected and the maxim of Best Face is brought to bear on the situation so that the case that is put is treated as the strongest case that can be made and it is apparent that the advertiser is understating the case, then the reader has some mental work to do.

So let's take an example. There are a couple of words in English which are used fairly frequently in advertising language – OLD and NEW. The latter probably occurs more than the former. But 'old' and 'new' have a simple semantics. They describe a change of state with old referring to the previous state and new referring to the changed state. There is no evaluation feature here apart from a mild cultural bias in favour of new being better than old although that is hard to find in certain parts of England. And yet new[9] always has dominant meaning of better in adspeak and old (when used about the brand) suggest patina (McCracken, 1991) – an accretion of value simply by being older. Wines, paintings, furniture are old in this sense. It seems that a more elegant and economic analysis of the semantics of advertising can be done by having a generic set of semantic features that is appropriate to most

---

[8] As I understand May's definition of 'interested' the communication should be intentional and in the communicator's interest. The former would necessarily exclude communicative accidents where for example some unintended communication causes behaviour that is in the communicator's interest such as 'accidentally' telling a story so that the tearful and grateful recipient who has 'seen the light' rewards the communicator. The preferences of the communicator can be altruistic so that the therapist communicates some information to the neurotic that is in the recipient's ultimate interests (some self-revelatory information) but has rather negative interpersonal effects (the neurotic starts to hate the therapist).

[9] New here referring to the brand which is generally accepted (Kumatoridani, 1982) to be the topic of advertising discourse with the rest of the ad being the comment.

genres and then impose a genre-specific rule that applies to all communication within that genre by restricting the selection of a certain features. May's principle is the one for promotional communication of which advertising is a good example.

So, in conclusion I hope I have argued a case for the reader that a sceptical eye is necessary when evaluating any claims that are made in the name of advertising to children. Different agendas, moving goalposts, shifting and changes discourses all contribute to a much of the misinformation and suspicion with evidence in the field. But we can move forward as long as a good theoretical analysis informs our research and I have outlined elements of a theory that I believe will provide such a foundation.

References

Aries, P. (1973). *Centuries of Childhood*. Harmondsworth: Penguin.

Borzekowski, D.L. and Robinson, T.N. (2001). 'The 30-second effect: an experiment revealing the impact of television commercials on food preferences of preschoolers'. *Journal of the American Dietetic Association*, 101, 42–46.

Buss, A.R. (1975). 'The emerging field of the sociology of psychological knowledge'. *American Psychologist*, 30(10), 988–1002.

Dietz, W.H. and Gortmaker, S.L. (1985). 'Do we fatten our children at the TV set? Television, viewing and obesity in children and adolescence'. *Pediatrics*, 75, 807–812.

Gard, M. and Wright, J. (2005). *The Obesity Epidemic: Science, Morality and Ideology*. London: Routledge.

Grice, H.P. (1975). 'Logic and conversation'. In P. Cole and J.L. Morgan (eds), *Syntax and Semantics 3: Speech Acts*. New York, NY: Academic Press, pp. 41–58.

Grice, H.P. (1978). 'Further notes on logic and conversation'. In P. Cole (ed.), *Syntax and Semantics 9: Pragmatics*. New York, NY: Academic Press, pp. 113–128.

Hastings, G., Stead, M., McDermott, L. et al. (2003). *Review of Research on the Effects of Food Promotion to Children*. Glasgow: Centre for Social Marketing, The University of Strathclyde.

Kumatoridani, T. (1982). *The Structure of Persuasive Discourse: A Cross-Cultural Analysis of the Language in American and Japanese Television Commercials*. PhD Thesis, Georgetown University, Washington, DC.

Levinson, S.C. (1983). *Pragmatics*. Cambridge: Cambridge University Press.

Lewis, M.K. and Hill, A.J. (1998). 'Food advertising on British children's television: a content analysis and experimental study with nine-year olds'. *International Journal of Obesity*, 22(3), 206–214.

May, J.D. (1981). 'Practical reasoning: extracting useful information from partial informants'. *Journal of Pragmatics*, 5, 45–59.

McCracken, G. (1991). *Culture and Consumption: New Approaches to the Symbolic Character of Consumer Goods and Activities*. Indiana: Indiana University Press.

Ridley, M. (2000). *Genome: The Autobiography of a Species*. London: Fourth Estate Ltd.

Ritson, M. and Elliott, R. (1999). 'The social uses of advertising: an ethnographic study of adolescent advertising audiences'. *Journal of Consumer Research*, 26, 260–277.

Robinson, T.N. (1998). 'Does television cause childhood obesity?' *Journal of the American Medical Association*, 279, 959–960.

Robinson, T.N., Hammer, L.D., Killen, J.D. et al. (1993). 'Does television viewing increase obesity and reduce physical activity? Cross-sectional and longitudinal analyses among adolescent girls'. *Pediatrics*, 91, 273–280.

Taras, H. and Gage, M. (1995). 'Advertised foods on children's television'. *Archives in Pediatric and Adolescent Medicine*, 149, 649–652.

World Health Organization (2003). *Diet, Nutrition and the Prevention of Chronic Diseases*. Geneva: WHO Technical Report Series 916.

Young, B.M. (1986). 'New approaches to old problems: the growth of advertising literacy'. In S. Ward and R. Brown (eds), *Commercial Television and European Children: An International Research Digest*. Aldershot, Hants: Gower. pp. 67–77, 82–83.

Young, B.M. (1990). *Television Advertising and Children*. Oxford: Oxford University Press.

Young, B.M. (2005). 'The obesity epidemic reviewed'. *Young Consumers*, 6(4), 20–25.

9

'Which Half?' Accounting for Ideology in Advertising

Liz McFall

It may be a bit of a stretch to apply Wanamaker's – or maybe Lord Lever's – maxim 'I know that half of the money I spend on advertising is wasted, the trouble is I don't know which half' to the problem of accounting for ideology in advertising but there are stronger reasons for doing so than might be supposed. The questions of effectiveness and ideology both signal a real accounting challenge, one that involves measuring qualities and values rather than quantities and costs. Invoking the 'which half' maxim is also meant to nudge attention back towards the internal dynamics and practices of the industry when for too many years to adopt a 'critical' perspective has meant to concentrate primarily on the externally visible texts and products of the industry.

This situation has arisen, in large part, through the definition of advertising as a site of special, ideological interest. Advertising occupies a 'special' location between the realms of culture and consumption and economy and production. This location has been rigorously mined in critical theory for its ideological significance in cementing and reproducing a given social and economic order. With such stakes in play it is little surprise that critical theory has eschewed the mundane practices, technologies and institutions that make up the industry in favour of developing analytical frameworks designed to crack the ideological code of the product itself. Yet these mundane details may still contain the best clues to how advertising works and why it looks the way that it does.

This chapter begins with a short overview of the way 'ideology' has been conceptualized in key critical accounts of advertising with the emphasis on establishing the elegance and totalizing reach of such accounts. It then moves on to argue that such accounts derive their cogency from rigid and particular approaches to the character and location of meaning. The more critical work on advertising loosened up to accommodate cross and intertextual accounts of meaning, to accommodate consumer's resistance, the symbolic dimension of material practices and institutional sites the less compelling the ideological account became. This chapter concludes by arguing that a more promising direction for future research is offered by reasserting the generative significance of internal advertising processes – such as the industry's advertising effectiveness awards schemes – in shaping the reality they purport to measure.

Ideology and Critical Accounts of Advertising

Any discussion of the role of ideology in critical accounts of advertising needs to pay due regard to Roland Barthes' discussion of the application of semiotic method to advertising images. His essay, *The Rhetoric of the Image*, was first published in 1964 but it set the tone for critical research, both conceptually and methodologically, well into the 1980s. To this end I want to take a closer look at Barthes' take on the ideological character of advertising before exploring how authors like Williamson (1978), Goldman (1992) and Wernick (1991) moved the debate forward. These accounts conceptualize the role of ideology in quite distinctive ways and there may be some nice distinctions between them that will be collapsed but I'm willing to risk this in order to show the persistence of certain ideas about the relationship between advertising, meaning and ideology in contemporary societies.

In his famous analysis of a *Panzani* foods advertisement depicting a string bag spilling out its contents, Barthes identifies three messages contained within the visual text. The first is the linguistic message which features the use of denotational and connotational elements to carry out the two main functions of *anchorage* and *relay*. Relay has a narrative action to carry the story forward but anchorage fixes meaning against the proliferation of multiple and undesirable meanings. It is at the level of anchorage 'that the morality and ideology of a society are above all invested' (1977, p. 40). The second 'non-coded-iconic' message presents in 'absolutely analogical' fashion objects which appear entirely natural. The function of this second message, in accordance with structuralist principles, is revealed through its relation to the third, 'coded-iconic message'. The 'non-coded-iconic message's' special function is to *naturalize* the coded message and it is here that the work of 'semantic artifice' really kicks in.

In the coded message there are a series of signs. Barthes isolates at least four including; a return from the market, 'Italianicity', total culinary service and the 'still life'. Barthes admits the presence, arising from the image's place in the magazine and the predominance of labels, of a further message revealing that the image is an advertisement. In a move consistent with structuralist semiotics' fixation with the text, Barthes reaches the rather odd conclusion that this *purely functional* information eludes signification, thus a first step to ruling the internal dynamics of advertising production outside of the construction of meaning is made.

There is nothing crude or simplistic in this account of meaning construction. Semiotics offers an elegant, nuanced and powerful account of the plural and active nature of the process of meaning making. Barthes, for instance, acknowledges that the number of readings will vary between different individuals. The image is a 'lexical unit' combining a range of different 'lexicons' or portions of language relating to specific bodies of practice or technique. Some individuals may lack certain lexicons but it is must be possible for one individual to have all lexicons referred to in a single advertisement. The tenability of the method depends on the possibility of a single individual, for example the analyst, 'owning' all the relevant lexical units to enable a complete, structural description. The plurality of possible readings is contained by the common domain of ideology which 'cannot but be single for a given society and history, no matter what signifiers of connotation it may use' (Barthes, 1977, p. 49).

This emphasis on the singular character of the ideological domain is remarkable as one of the primary sources of trouble for structuralist semiotic accounts from those who have struggled to square a univocal ideological explanation with the diversity of gender, ethnic, religious and cultural interests. Yet is also through invoking the ideological nature of meaning making that semiotics derives its power as a *total* explanation of social order. This is what Barthes means when he refers to the dialectical coordination of semiotics and ideology. Ideology does not just explain how semiotics as a formal process of signification relates to given interests, but semiotics explains how ideology works. For instance Barthes maintains that not all elements within the image are transformed into connotators – there always remains a certain denotation within the image which acts to naturalize, or in Barthes' words, 'to innocent the semantic artifice of connotation'. Coordination is the key here – ideology bridges between the structural layering of the text, multiple individual readings and the interests, generally construed as bourgeois, of a given society while at the same time the relations of signification enable ideology to be disseminated. Semiotically influenced approaches to advertising, thus, proffer not only a method, but a comprehensive social critique, what Barthes, with Marx in his sights, called a totalist explanation of social life. Barthes' vision of semiotics is quite in keeping with Marx's 'ruthless criticism of everything existing' that accounts for any phenomena in terms of the determinative action of the mode of production (Marx, 1978/1844, p. 12).

The most sustained and the most influential treatment in this vein is Judith Williamson's *Decoding Advertisements* (1978). In order to sell, she explains, adverts have to mean something and this involves connecting people and objects, making the two interchangeable. Adverts thereby 'sell us ourselves' in a society where the real origins of identity are obscured by the distortions imposed by consumption. These distortions conceal the true production/class basis of identity in false consumption-based distinctions fabricated by advertising. Williamson uses semiotic terminology to describe the transference of meaning to products through the currency of signs. This transference is crucial in advanced capitalist economies because of the need to differentiate basically similar products. To this end, bizarre juxtapositions of products and objects/meanings take on a natural status and this is construed, as in Barthes' formulation, as an ideological process. Adverts utilize a pre-existing referent system of meaning, because the product, prior to signification in the advert, has no meaning. Having captured meaning, the product becomes the signified, so Channel No. 5 equals Catherine Deneuve. This is a step towards the product itself as a signifier of meaning, having taken over the 'reality' from which its meaning was abducted. In this way products generate the feelings they represent, so *Clairol* equals happiness; or offer themselves as the currency for something else, so *Anne French* equals clear skin equals boyfriends. This process of meaning making is active and undertaken by the 'subject' as 'it is he or she who completes the circuit through which, once started . . . a current of 'meaning' flows continuously and apparently autonomously' (1978, p. 41).

In this way what Williamson labels the 'vicious circle' of meaning exchange between advertisements and subjects progresses through four discreet stages. In the first stage we create meaning through recognition of signifiers from the referent 'myth' system which we come to associate with the product. The crucial factor here is the implication of the subject in the exchange process and this provides the key to the ideological nature of the process. As for Barthes the subject's active involvement in the formal production of meaning ensures a simultaneously ideological moment in which constructed meanings appear natural. We make the exchange and complete the links set up in the advert, in doing so we 'become' the signified. In this second stage, subjects take on meanings from the product:

> Products whose only meaning derives from a re-hash of mythological elements already present in society, develop such an aura of significance that they tell something about their buyers and actually become adjectival in relation to them. . . . We are thus created not only as subjects but as particular kinds of subjects, by products in advertisements.
>
> Williamson (1978, p. 45)

For this to be successful, Williamson maintains, you must already recognize yourself as the kind of subject represented. Adverts address the subject as special, individual, and in this third stage, individuals recognize themselves, and are simultaneously constituted as, particular sorts of subject, at once individuals and part of a group. Finally, through the advertisement, we create ourselves. Having constituted subjects as members of a group, then as individuals, adverts, in their depiction of multiple aspects of the self, break the individual into a 'fragmented ego to be reunited by the product' (1978, p. 55). Williamson characterizes this appeal to a coherent, conscious self as an appeal, not to an inherent subject essence, but to an ideologically constructed consciousness. Fundamentally, ads act ideologically to reproduce subjects in a mould suited to the demands of capitalist economies. While the overt function of ads is to sell, their hidden function is to conserve society in a given form by resolving contradictions and reproducing consuming subjects.

These themes crop up in work by authors like Winship (1981), Dyer (1982) and Vestergaard and Schroder (1985) among others. Whatever their other differences such accounts share a baseline understanding of advertisements as ideological in utilizing a formal structure of signification that naturalizes or 'innocents' the specific, historical condition of contemporary capitalist economies. This view, with some shift of emphasis, also underpins the re-working of semiotic analysis advanced by Goldman (1992) and Goldman and Papson (1994, 1996). In *Reading Ads Socially* Goldman begins by identifying advertising as a key institution in 'producing and reproducing the material and ideological supremacy of commodity relations' a system he terms 'commodity hegemony' (1992, p. 2). This indicates a move away from the Althusserian model of interpellation towards a Gramscian framework. For Goldman, adverts contribute to a system of commodity hegemony because they reproduce a sense of commodity relations as a natural and inevitable part of the lives of different individuals.

Goldman's particular contribution to the method is the proposal of the mortise and the frame as structural elements. The mortise and frame function, to steer interpretation in a preferred direction. The term mortise refers to a joining device, a cavity that another part fits or passes through. The mortise formally structures the creation of meaning within the ad through 'routing' the connection between the image as signified and the product as signifier. Through the mortise, irrespective of the content of individual ads, 'an ideology and practice of commodity fetishism at a deep level of communicative competence' is reproduced (1992, p. 65). The emphasis here is slightly different from many other semiotic theorists in that greater significance is attached to the embeddedness of meaning within the system of advertisements and its extension beyond single texts to products as commodity-signs. Where Williamson's product is blank prior to signification in the advert, Goldman's product is a commodity-sign, carrying meaning from previous advertising and from the system of advertising. Here Goldman acknowledges his debt to an 'inter-textual' account of meaning but, as I hope to show later, there are limits to how far this revision is allowed to modify his application of semiotics.

Wernick's (1991) study departs further from earlier accounts by expressing the need for advertising critique to encompass more than the decoding of individual advertisements. An understanding of advertising's role, he argues, needs also take account of the broader promotional system spanning production, marketing and design. Through the notion of 'artificial semiosis', Wernick points to the emergence in the early 19th century, of the industrialized manufacture of meaning and myth, a process culminating in the production of dual character objects or commodity-signs. For Wernick, it is not the symbolic character of objects per se that is new, but the instrumentalized manner in which this character is instilled. In the industrial phase promotion becomes a strategic and integrated aspect of production and the resultant 'commodity-sign' an entirely new sort of product with a use-value inextricable from its manipulated image. Again, this is understood as an 'ideological' process in that advertisements act to unite commodities with attributed subject positions (Wernick, 1991, p. 31):

> The commodity they project as the object of desire is simultaneously presented as a cultural symbol charged with social significance; and the ego they seek to engage as the subject of desire is induced to adopt the socio-cultural identity attributed to those who already use the product.

There is not that much difference between this and Williamson's (1978) or Goldman's (1992) account of how advertising works through an Althusserian model of ideological interpellation. This is remarkable because at various points Wernick seeks to distance his analysis from more classically Marxist accounts of advertising's ideological action. Yet the distinctions between Wernick and accounts in the latter vein are finally rather subtle. As mentioned above, Wernick locates advertising within a much broader promotional system spanning production and design as part of his determination that advertising, however important, is only one part of an elaborate production system in which signification occurs at various stages. This doesn't, in the end, prevent Wernick from adopting a methodological approach based on decoding individual texts but it nevertheless marks a less restricted way of thinking about how and where signification occurs. Similarly in his acknowledgement of the difficulty of disentangling promotional symbolism from other cultural meanings, Wernick (1991, p. 32) notes:

> It is almost as difficult in the real world to make a rigorous distinction between the commodity and its manufactured symbolic aura as in the advertising text. What complicates the distinction is that products, even physical and practical ones, are inseparable from language (including visual language) and from patterns of use that are overlaid with ceremonial and cultural significance.

This difficulty is related to what Wernick calls the 'promotional intertext' that connects advertisements not only to their commodity-signs but to other ads and a shared cultural vocabulary which is both articulated and re-worked within advertising. Pushing these myriad semantic entanglements to one side, Wernick goes on to claim that the differences between generic cultural conventions attached to products and the specific brand identities that advertisers attempt to construct are nevertheless 'obvious'. This insistence upon the singularity of advertising's role in attaching meanings to commodities, leads Wernick (1991, p. 35) back to the key terms of structuralist accounts:

> By addressing individuals always as potential customers, and so attributing them a priori a social identity linked firmly to that role, advertising builds the standpoint of consumption into the design of its every text. . . . The consumerist address imprisons the subjectivity it projects into a totally commodified ontology. Being is reduced to having, desire to lack. . . . Production as human praxis – the satisfaction of human need through non-alienated self-activity – is obliterated as a thinkable thought.

Where Does It Mean? The Trouble with Ideology

Despite its power, reach and the elegant ambition of an explanation that has the world and its history in its purview, semiotics had by the end of the 1980s its fair share of critics. One of the most obvious criticisms of semiotics concerns the status of the analyst/interpreter, the figure Barthes' called the 'mythologist', the owner of all lexicons. For writers such as Leiss et al. (1990, p. 214) and Moeran (1996, p. 30), semiotics depends entirely on the impressionistic insights of analysts whose abilities to reach the 'deeper levels of meaning construction' varied significantly. Other authors have complained that the semiotician is set apart from the recipient of meaning, mysteriously equipped to stand outside the ideological universe that structures all other interpretations (Cook, 1992; Nava et al., 1997). For present purposes, however, the most interesting problem raised by the semiotic explanation of the ideological character of advertisements concerns the location of meaning. A deep paradox on this question runs through semiotic approaches to advertising because while the *theory* understands meaning as resident within the structural relations persisting across a system of representation on the whole the *method* tracks meaning within individual texts. The reason for this is clear: the structural analysis of texts as self-contained, competent entities for analysis presents a complex but manageable task, the analysis of relations which persist across a whole system of representation, however, is quite a different matter.

To make this point clearer it is worth referring briefly to Leymore's (1975) semiotic analysis of advertising systems. Leymore defines an advertising system as constituting all the advertisements of competitive brands. To this, she applies algebraic and statistical analysis of the relations between elements to enable her to draw conclusions like 'good : evil $\approx$ washing powders : not washing powders' (1975, p. 75). This relation demonstrates that the brand closest to the theme, washing powders equal good, is the one that achieves success in the market; a powder which deviates from the theme 'condemns itself to be identified with the signifier of the "not washing powders", which is evil' (1975, p. 75). Many of the conclusions that Leymore draws from her analysis

are similarly reductive and this is certainly a function of the difficulty of identifying meaning in systems. Leymore's algebraic method may enable her to
track oppositions and relations across an advertising system but in order to
make the task analytically manageable these relations have to be expressed in
very simple terms. It would simply not be practicable to conduct a comparative analysis of an 'advertising system' along the lines of Barthes' deconstruction of the *Panzani* ad.

Still, this is not the only problem with Leymore's approach. Equally trouble-
some is how the boundaries defining an advertising system should be drawn
temporally and in market terms. Semiotic analysis is synchronic, freezing the
object of analysis at a moment in time, but individual advertisements reference a whole universe of prior advertising they are not bounded within a
given 'season'. The competitive advertising market for many products is also
extremely fluid. Soap powder is an exceptionally well-defined market, other
markets are drawn not from common product characteristics but from common instances of use. Thus games consoles, mobile phones and mp3 players
compete in the same market as teenage Christmas gifts and therefore constitute an advertising 'system'. Markets are 'structures of mediation' constituted
through the application of specific commercial practices and technologies that
refer back, through market research for example, to the social practices of consumers (Slater, 2002).

Locating meaning in advertising systems offers no easy solutions to the
problem of attributing meaning *externally* to relations between elements within
a system but conducting analysis *internally* within individual representations.
This problem is exacerbated by the shift towards intertextual definitions of
meaning as 'plural, shattered, incapable of being tabulated' (Kristeva, 1984)
and located across different systems of signification. Goldman (1992) and
Goldman and Papson's (1994, 1996) accounts attempt to accommodate intertextuality whilst retaining a method of analysis focused primarily on individual texts. They accentuate the increasing prevalence since the 1980s, of rapid,
absurd and pastiche recombinations of sign values in the 'mature sign economy' of advertising. Opaque messages and techniques like parody and self-
mockery proliferate in a spiralling, self-referential generation of intertextual
'not-ads' (Goldman, 1992; Goldman and Papson, 1996). These shifts are part
of an acceleration of meaning prompted by a change in the form and structure
of commodity hegemony.

'Individuated meaning production' is accommodated within the logic
of contemporary commodity hegemony as the very openness of 'not-ads'
blocks counter hegemonic readings (1992, p. 198). The openness of interpretation wards off resistance at the same time as ensuring the crucial connection
between the commodity name and the advertising sign is made. This 'closed
circuit' between the commodity name and the reading is crucial to Goldman's
account because it maintains the link between ads, meaning and a given economic order, characterized as commodity hegemony. Despite the emphasis
on negotiation and intertextuality the account that he and later, Papson, provide remains close to the semiotic explanation expounded by Barthes and

Williamson. For the latter, readings are always drawn from a shared ideological universe while for the former; freedom of interpretation ultimately serves, rather than challenges, a hegemonic system.

This is an uneasy position. Advertisers 'steer meanings' but cannot guarantee interpretations that will either ratify 'preferred' meanings or produce 'aberrant' meanings (1992, p. 40). Yet the emphasis on the closed circuit between commodity and reading leaves little space for a truly oppositional reading – one that breaks the circuit – outside the ideological/hegemonic universe. This tension also characterizes Williamson and Barthes' accounts. Both stress the active involvement of the subject in the creation of meaning but as Williamson explains, this freedom is not quite what it seems. Freedom is illusory, a 'position given to you by the advertiser' (1978, p. 71). Subjects may be required to actively complete the circuit of meaning in ads but this process is largely predetermined, 'restricted to the carefully defined channels *provided* by the ad for its own decipherment' (1978, p. 72). This does not prevent Williamson and Goldman and Papson from claiming that people are wise to advertising and adept at resisting its messages in a move that is characteristic of the awkward fluctuation in semiotics between preferred and open, predetermined and active readings that are at once resisted and irresistible.

Goldman's 'intertextual' approach to meaning involves primarily an account of how advertising techniques like parody, pastiche and cross-referencing work without undermining a system of commodity hegemony. These are characteristics of advertising that had, in any case, already been recognized by writers like Williamson (1978, pp. 175–178) and Dyer (1982, pp. 185–187). But the notion of intertextuality is intended to summon up more than simply cross- and self-referentiality. It also involves recognition of the transposition of signifying practices across a range of different systems. This means that the regime of signification in advertising shapes, and is shaped by, other regimes like film and television, popular music and literature. While many semiotic theorists acknowledge in principle the play of influence across these regimes, in practice, advertising texts are treated as complete and self-contained systems of meaning. Even where, as in Goldman and Papson's (1996) analysis, more weight is given to cross-referentiality across signifying regimes, the relationship is unilinear with advertising always cast in the role of insatiable cultural appropriator, colonizer or 'cannibal'.

A further problem with the textual location of meaning, disregarded even by intertextual accounts, is the relationship between meaning systems and other dimensions of social life and practice. It is all very well to acknowledge how meaning is negotiated across texts but what of the role of practices? Referentiality across film, music and advertising may establish chains of meaning but material practices on both production and consumption sides also produce meaning. Representational work is inherent across the design of retailing, production and distribution systems as well as in shopping, leisure and working practices. Allowing for the symbolic character of practice only exacerbates the already unmanageable task of tracking the ideological content of advertising messages.

One of the most acute manifestations of the view that meaning resides in discrete systems of signification arises in the status attributed to the product in semiotic accounts of advertising. Advertising exists *prima facie* to instil meaning in products. In Williamson's account the *only* meaning of products is that instilled by the advert, the product is effectively a *tabula rasa* (1978, p. 45). The arbitrary connection between many products and appropriated meanings is taken as evidence that ads are free to harvest any attractive referent systems. This is a paradoxical treatment in a theoretical system that privileges the symbolic character of all objects. Advertising meanings somehow take precedence over any other meanings that may be associated with the brand, product or company outside of advertising. This is a singular version of the error which reduces the properties of products not just to their significations (cf. Callon and Muniesa, 2005; McFall, 2004) but to their advertising significations.

A related problem arises over the status of the producers of advertisements. The intentions, aims and strategies of advertising producers are left out of most critical accounts focused on the problematic of ideology, an omission which springs directly from the semiotic challenge to the idea of originary authorship. 'Obviously', Williamson argues, 'people invent and produce adverts, but apart from the fact that they are unknown and faceless, the ad in any case does not claim to speak from them, it is not their speech' (1978, p. 14). The absence of the author is consistent with the theoretical tenets of a method that refers back to a structuralist Marxist conception of social relations. If the consciousness of producers is derived from a common ideological universe the texts they produce necessarily transmit over-determined ideological meanings rendering their explicit intentions of little significance. The tenability of this position has been challenged on the basis that whilst producers clearly do not in any straightforward way dictate the meaning of advertisements, their specific modes of production are crucial to a robust assessment of advertising (Cronin, 2004; McFall, 2004; Miller, 1997; Moeran, 1996; Nixon, 1996, 2003; Slater, 2002). Micro-level production practices pale in semiotics next to the ideological role of advertising but the absence of an account of how advertisers actually conduct practice forces semiotic analysis into the business of endless philosophical abstractions about meaning.

Excessive abstraction, in fact, haunts the semiotic pursuit of meaning. The assumption that meaning is available for textual analysis to 'get at' raises difficult questions about the character and location of meaning which the emphasis on intertextuality does little to solve. Indeed accentuating the relations and references across different systems of signification only raises more questions about how 'systems' and the boundaries between them should be defined. An even more intransigent problem concerns the connection between meaning and concrete material practices. It is the significance of this relation that writers associated with the actor–network tradition like John Law (2002) are trying to get at in flagging their approach as a sort of 'semiotics of materiality'. Such problems with meaning and ideology also lay behind Foucault's determination to set aside what he considered the futility of semiotics as 'a task that nothing could limit' (Dean, 1994, p. 16). Foucault, of course, preferred to think in terms of discourses rather than ideologies as 'they need no interpretation, no one to assign them a meaning. If one reads texts in a particular way one perceives that they speak clearly to us and require no further supplementary sense or interpretation' (1980, p. 115). This encapsulates many of the criticisms that have been levelled at semiotics regarding the status of the interpreter and the location of meaning. Meaning, for Foucault, is the plural outcome of ongoing, active processes and therefore has no single, ideological core accessible only to the skilled analyst.

Accounting for Advertising

This final section of the chapter sets aside the question of ideology to focus instead on the generative significance of the internal processes of advertising. In particular the aim is to explore some of the reasons why a focus on mundane, production processes, including those designed to evaluate advertising effectiveness might reveal more than might be supposed about the form that advertising takes. This will involve a brief overview of ideas emanating from the sociology and anthropology of economic life that signal the different ways in which tools developed to measure aspects of an economic reality in turn shape that reality.

In *The Laws of the Market* (1998) Callon and his contributing authors make a sustained and persuasive argument that the task of economic sociology needs reframing to not simply assert the social context of economic practice but to explore the ways in which economics, broadly defined, formats or 'performs' the economy. The economy, here is conceptualized as the contingent outcome of a *process*, a 'mutual performance', in which the discipline(s) of economics, broadly defined to include economic sociology, business and organization studies and marketing, are implicated through their role in shaping the ways in which 'agencies' calculate. This, for Callon, opens up the sociology of economic life to an exploration of precisely how calculative agencies, in all their diverse forms, have emerged and been formatted (Callon, 1998, p. 510):

> It is not a matter of giving a soul back to a dehumanized agent, nor of rejecting the very idea of his existence. The objective may be to explore the diversity of calculative agencies, forms and distributions, and hence of organized markets. The market is no longer that cold, implacable and impersonal monster which imposes its laws and procedures while extending them ever further. It is a many-sided, diversified, evolving device which the social sciences as well as the actors themselves contribute to reconfigure.

Despite the clumsiness of the term, performance offers a way of 'rediscovering' the generative significance of advertising processes. This follows from the insistence in other sociologies of economic life that economic practices shape the reality they set out to measure. As Peter Miller drawing on the context of accounting practice explains, accountancy tools are 'largely improvised and adapted to the tasks and materials at hand' (1998, p. 190). No general principle defining what should and should not be measured exists, rather the relevant reality is constantly renegotiated and reconfigured in accounting. To practice or perform calculations accountants require tools and tools shape the meaning of the objects they are applied to. This is a point also made by Law (2002) in his account of the role of spreadsheets and the Thatcherite culture of 'enterprise' in creating a category of 'real costs' and by writers like Cochoy (1998, 2003) in relation to marketing practices and the formation of markets and marketing categories.

This work sits rather uneasily with critical accounts of the ideological potency of advertising. When Michael Schudson's *Advertising: The Uneasy Persuasion* first appeared in 1984 it was one of the first to take issue with overstated claims about the power of advertising. Advertisements, he suggested 'ordinarily work their wonders, to the extent that they work at all, on an inattentive public' (Michael Schudson, 1986, p. 3). In this, Schudson gave voice to a sentiment that industry practitioners had been citing in their defence for years, that within the industry itself considerable uncertainty exists about whether and exactly how advertising actually works. This lack of certainty is an ever-present undercurrent and surfaces frequently in the debate over whether creativity or effectiveness is the ultimate aim of advertising. When the Institute of Practitioners in Advertising (IPA) selected *Advertising Works* as the title for the publications series that accompanies their annual effectiveness award scheme it was at least partly in reference to this debate and the need to reassure clients. That such reassurance is even necessary doesn't accord all that well with structuralist or post-structuralist explanations of the ideological or hegemonic effects of advertising.

Ethnographic and historical accounts of advertising (Cronin, 2004; McFall, 2004; Miller, 1997; Moeran, 1996; Nixon, 1996, 2003) offer a glimpse of advertising as an inward-looking and self-referential culture. Advertising communities, like other interpretive communities, work with their eyes far more closely fixed on the competition than on the audience. The specific nature of everyday practices, technologies and institutions that make up these communities are potent forces shaping the nature of the product they create.

Systems like the IPA's *Advertising Works* effectiveness awards scheme can be viewed in this light as tools that ultimately shape the reality they purport to measure. Having achieved an effectiveness award, campaigns in the mould of *Carex's* 'washer or walker' or *Phones4u's* 'Scary Mary' or *Wonderbra's* 'Hello boys', go on to shape rules, practices and categories for future campaigns (Baker, 1995; Institute of Practitioners in Advertising, 2003). Advertising is a fast-moving, faddish and introspective business where techniques and innovations can rapidly take on the status of established knowledge shaping the form of future campaigns. The notion of performativity has some salience in this context in signposting the relationship between knowledges and practices in the ongoing constitution of markets. Advertising, both product and practice, is materially imprinted, or performed, by its own institutional practices and dynamics. This is no mere tautology but an acknowledgement of the plural ways in which the institution of advertising, its norms, practices and award schemes, self-generate or perform, the knowledges and practices which define it. An informed, critical account of advertising is one that takes seriously these norms, practices and institutions and resists the temptation to dismiss them in the pursuit of providing a broader, ideological explanation.

References

Baker, C. (1995). *Advertising Works 8*. Henley on Thames: NTC Publications Ltd.

Barthes, R. (1977). 'The rhetoric of the image'. *Image – Music – Text*. London: Fontana.

Callon, M. (ed.) (1998). *The Laws of the Market*. Oxford: Blackwell.

Callon, M. and Muniesa, F. (2005). 'Economic markets as calculative, collective devices'. *Organization Studies*, 26(8), 1229–1250.

Cochoy, F. (1998). 'Another discipline for the market economy: marketing as a performative knowledge and know-how for capitalism'. In M. Callon (ed.), *The Laws of the Market*. Oxford: Blackwell.

Cochoy, F. (2003). 'On the "captation" of publics: understanding the market thanks to Little Red Riding Hood'. *Workshop on Market(ing) Practice*. Stockholm School of Economics, Sketo, Sweden, June 14–16.

Cook, G. (1992). *The Discourse of Advertising*. London: Routledge.

Cronin, A. (2004). 'Regimes of mediation: advertising practitioners as cultural intermediaries?' *Consumption, Markets and Culture*, 7(4), 349–369.

Dean, M. (1994). *Critical and Effective Histories: Foucault's Methods and Historical Sociology*. London: Routledge.

Dyer, G. (1982). *Advertising as Communication*. London: Routledge.

Foucault, M. (1980). *Power/Knowledge*. Brighton: Harvester.

Goldman, R. (1992). *Reading Ads Socially*. London: Routledge.

Goldman, R. and Papson, S. (1994). 'Advertising in the age of hypersignification'. *Theory, Culture and Society*, 11, 23–53.

Goldman, R. and Papson, S. (1996). *Sign Wars: The Cluttered Landscape of Advertising*. New York: Guilford.

Institute of Practitioners in Advertising (2003). *AREA Advertising Works 5*, London: IPA.

Kristeva, J. (1984). *Revolution in Poetic Language*. New York: Columbia University Press.

Law, J. (2002). 'Economics as interference'. In P. du Gay and M. Pryke (eds), *Cultural Economy*. London: Sage.

Leiss, W., Kline, S. and Jhally, S. (1990/1986). *Social Communication in Advertising*. London: Routledge.

Leymore, V.L. (1975). *Hidden Myth: Structure and Symbolism in Advertising*. London: Heinemann.

McFall, L. (2004). *Advertising: A Cultural Economy*. London: Sage.

Marx, K. (1978/1844). 'For a ruthless criticism of everything existing'. In R.C.Tucker (ed.), *The Marx Engels Reader*. New York, London: Norton.

Miller, D. (1997). *Capitalism: An Ethnographic Approach*. London: Berg.

Miller, P. (1998). 'The margins of accounting'. In M. Callon (ed.), *The Laws of the Market*. Oxford: Blackwell.

Moeran, B. (1996). *A Japanese Advertising Agency*. Surrey: Curzon.

Nava, M., Blake, A., MacRury, I. and Richards, B. (eds) (1997). *Buy This Book: Studies in Advertising and Consumption*. London: Routledge.

Nixon, Sean (1996). *Hard Looks: Masculinities, spectatorship and contemporary consumption*. London, UCL Press Ltd.

Nixon, Sean (2003). *Advertising Cultures: gender, commerce, creativity*. London, Sage.

Schudson, Michael (1986). *Advertising, the uneasy persuasion: its dubious impact on American Society*. London, Routledge.

Slater, D. (2002). 'Capturing markets from the Economists'. In P. du Gay and M. Pryke (eds), *Cultural Economy*. London: Sage.

Vestergaard, T. and Schroder, K. (1985). *The Language of Advertising*. Oxford: Blackwell.

Wernick, A. (1991). *Promotional Culture: Advertising, Ideology and Symbolic Expression*. London: Sage.

Williamson, J. (1978). *Decoding Advertisements*. London: Marion Boyars.

Winship, J. (1981). 'Handling sex'. *Media, Culture and Society*, 3, 25–41.

10

Can Consumers Escape the Market?

Eric J. Arnould

Just as medieval society was balanced on God and the Devil, so
ours is balanced on consumption and its denunciation.
Baudrillard (1998/orig. 1970, p. 196)

Critiques from the right and left, from secular and a variety of religious perspectives inveigh against market capitalism and contemporary consumerism.
As Baudrillard's epigraph suggests this set of social practices is characteristic
of our age, and historical studies suggest that the choir of voices has increased
in amplitude as the scope of consumerism has expanded geographically
and culturally without for all of that altering its ritually evoked positions.
The chapter here simply interrogates (I dare not say deconstructs!) some of the
semantic and sociological dimensions of each of the component words of the
title in an effort to avoid the most highly ritualized form that this argument
tends otherwise to take. First, I review some positions on the notion of agency
and actorhood in consumer research, and suggest that agency is conceptually problematic. Second, I discuss the term consumers and propose that the
anti-consumption ideology that seems to underlie the overarching question
is in fact a class-based ideology, one that is consistent with a long history of
reformist ideology in the UK and the USA ultimately traceable to our common
Calvinist heritage. Third, I examine the idea of escape. Here we confront a

Romantic idea, the apotheosis of which is the utopian dream. Perhaps, hyper-reality and cyberspace constitute some interstitial spaces of escape. The dangers of escape are illustrated with an example. Next, I discuss that notion of the market entailed in the question. The term seems to cover a variety of distinct irritations ranging from the common market, to exchange, to consumption. Finally, some momentary escapes 'before the world is formed' are proposed.

Can or Should?

The verb that inaugurates this little interrogative sentence implies a physical or mental ability, a skill or capability as the dictionary tells us that enables an actor to do something. And unlike the verb 'may' it also implies that the actor acts under his or her own volition, or at least without the permission of another. Thus, it implies at the very least a folk theory of action or agency. As a semantic aside, the use of this verb in this interrogative sentence may in fact cover for the implicit belief that consumers not only can, but should escape the market, or at least today's globalized market capitalism. Some currents of contemporary pop social theory make this argument more explicitly (Halton, 2000; Klein, 2000; Ritzer, 1993), although the idea that humanity could exist outside of or prior to its objectification in material forms seems to fly in the face both of philosophy and anthropology (Miller, 1987; Strathern, 1979). In this chapter, however, I will deal with the question as asked and stick to 'can':

> Marx argued that producers or at least those who sold their labor to capitalists in order to make their living, should escape the market as a condition of reclaiming the full value of their labor and returning to a consumption regime that featured authentic use values over fetishized exchange values. And he argued that a socialist revolution that returned the means of production to the control of the working class was the precondition for this happy event (1998/orig. 1887).

Firat (2005) argues that globalization has rendered this prospect remote:

> Consumers of the world, a large majority of them, still lack the ability, the power to determine their own experiences and consumption patterns, despite the fact that they have, globally, more consumption choices. In effect, they are choosers among alternatives of consumption and modes of life that are determined largely without any effective input by consumers.

Where we to substitute the words 'workers' for 'consumers' we would be close to Marx's classic formulation of the dilemma.

Writing almost exactly 100 years after Marx, Jean Baudrillard argues that the problem of action is more acute still. He argued, 'differentiation may then take the form of the rejection of objects, the rejection of "consumption", and yet this still remains the very ultimate in consumption' (Baudrillard, 1998/orig. 1970, p. 90). What Baudrillard rejects here is ideas like eco-consumerism, green consumption, voluntary simplicity, down-sizing, going off the grid, and other such differentiating practices including religious fundamentalisms that may well be rationalized by actors in terms of a folk understanding in which such actions constitute action taken to escape from the market. And the reason, articulated at length in *The Consumer Society* is that the consumer economy that is heir to the production economy about which Marx wrote forecloses the possibility of escape, because all action is subordinate to the logic of the consumption of signs. Sign value has fully replaced use value. In other words, 'the solution to social contradiction is not equalization but differentiation. No revolution is possible at the level of a code' (Baudrillard, 1998/orig. 1970, p. 94). Baudrillard's vision is essentially conservative, but rejects consumers capability for action implied in the word 'can'.

Other proposals are no less pessimistic in implication. Bourdieu's (1977, 1984) theory of action and subsequent articulations in consumer research (Holt, 1998) argues that consumers invest in, exchange, and deploy various kinds of capital resources, of which one kind, cultural capital, is basically knowledge of various sign systems and consumption practices, subordinate to the logic of market capitalism. As in Baudrillard's theory how people consume defines and differentiates them as social categories and actors; what they consume is of less significance since this never amounts to more than differences at the level of quantity.

In consumer research on the subject of action, variants of rational choice theory more or less rule the roost. This work entails little critique of a presumed micro-economic man, but mainstream consumer research contents itself with examining the various causes and consequences of consumers' inability to process information in a manner that would produce optimum economic outcomes for them (Kahneman and Tversky, 2000; Kahneman et al., 1982). What this work shows is that people commonly make sub-optimal choices from a rationalist perspective, but nonetheless process information to make choices. However, no alternative to a market economy-dominated logic of action is generally imagined in this literature (but see McGraw et al., 2003), and indeed, there is a presumption that this mode of thinking is a human universal. This perspective seems immune even to trenchant criticism (e.g. Godelier, 1972; Mirowski, 2002).

On the other hand, Firat and Venkatesh (1995) offer an optimistic appraisal of the situation confronting the postmodern consumer who inhabits Baudrillard's world of signs. In postmodernity consumers enjoy more potential freedom of manoeuvre than was possible under the hegemony of modernism. They particularly see this in consumption that transcends the marketplace, and they claim, 'much consumption does take place outside the market system' (p. 258), although in truth the examples they cite are all annex to the market economy. Consumers' true ability to act comes about through the recognition that the postmodern consumer is 'a participant in an ongoing, never ending process of construction that includes a multiplicity of moments where things (most importantly as symbols) are consumed, produced, signified, represented, allocated, distributed and circulated' (p. 250; see also Miller 2005, p. 9). And further, '[p]ostmodernism is a call to make each willing consumer an equal participant in the determination of this production (construction) of self, as well as in all production . . .' (p. 260). The cyberworld may offer yet more freedom of action to the innovative consumer if one believes the claim that in cyberspace the consumer is freed from the constraints of social memory that hampers freedom of action in the socio-physical world (Venkatesh, 1998).

De Certeau (1984) and Maffesoli (1996) also offer optimistic assessments of consumers' capacity for extra-market action. De Certeau offers the possibility of 'detournement' or re-appropriation of market resources to ends not envisioned by marketers, and often through mundane or playful everyday practices, behaviours often seen in practice (Aubert-Gamet, 1997). In this view, consumers are gradually but inevitably eroding marketers' control through micro-emancipatory practices that decentre market-determined subjectivity and that accelerate fragmentation of the acting subject (Firat and Venkatesh, 1995, p. 255). Emancipation still requires what Ozanne and Murray (1995) call the reflexively defiant consumer. Consumer resistance is possible if one develops a reflexive distance from the marketing code (i.e. becomes code conscious), acknowledging its structuring effects rather than living within the code unwary (Miller, 2005, p. 9; Ozanne and Murray, 1995, pp. 522–523). Consumers can fend off the marketer-imposed code if they are able to disentangle the marketer's artifice from the value in use of marketer-supplied resources. One author even sees this prospect of small-scale emancipation in consumers' use of Wal-mart as a mythic resource for imagining small-town American utopia and engaging in a host of playful consumption practices (Badot, 2005).

Maffesoli's approach is optimistic but a bit different. He focuses not on the individual, but on sociability, or when '. . . the collective sensibility which arises from the aesthetic form results in an ethical connection' between acting subjects (Maffesoli, 1996, p. 18). This ethical connection, linked to the logic of the gift in the tradition of the French Anti-Utilitarian Social Movement (MAUSS) creates heteropia. In other words, 'communal sensibility favors a proximity centred ethos; that is, simply put a way of being that offers an alternative to both the production and distribution of goods (economic or symbolic)' (Maffesoli, 1996, p. 17). The emergence of quasi-cultic brand communities that have re-appropriated not only marketer-produced resources, but also marketing functions and grafted them onto a communitarian ethos might be read as evidence of the possibility for this type of extra-market action (Muniz and Schau, 2005).

Problems with Agency

In some consumer research, the various ideas referred to above may suggest that 'consumers have free reign in the play of signs to piece together a collage of meanings that express the [individual's] desired symbolic statements' (Murray, 2002, p. 428). Agency is opposed to the influence of '[sociocultural] classification systems that direct the meanings of things, reflect the social order and are central to its reproduction' (Murray, 2002, p. 428); that is, to the institutional ordering mechanisms discussed in much early sociology of consumption (Ewen, 2001/orig. 1976) and to power. In this line of thinking, numerous researchers employ agency or some synonym; for example, individual's sense of control (Kates, 2004, p. 456); autonomy (Thompson and Haytko, 1997, p. 16); free will (Belk et al., 2003, p. 331); ability to produce culture (Peñaloza, 2001, p. 393); produce producer's products (Kozinets et al., 2004, p. 671); transform brands into symbolic markers of cultural categories (Fournier, 1998, p. 367). Such uses are consonant generally either with the ideas advanced by De Certeau, Maffesoli or Firat and Venkatesh.

Unfortunately, the agency construct in consumption studies encounters fatal conceptual problems despite valiant attempts to rescue it from them (Emirbayer and Mische, 1998). First, as handled by Parsons and his descendents or Giddens and his circle, the notion of agency attributes (mostly post hoc) some form of innate capacity, ability, or intention to actors and their action (Fuchs, 2001; Loyal and Barnes, 2001). But this construct relies on a historical and particularly Western view of autonomous self (Meyer and Jepperson, 2000) that as Campbell (1987) and others have shown, is an artifact of the emergence of a Western market-driven economy, rooted in earlier developments in Western theology (Meyer and Jepperson, 2000) rather than ontologically separate therefrom. Thus, agency is really about the institutional authority to act, and thus agentic action is ultimately derived from actors' institutional roles.

A second problem with the agency construct presupposes the possibility of separating empirically 'free' from 'determined' behaviours (Loyal and Barnes, 2001). Unfortunately any action can be explicated with reference to elements of 'choice' or according to elements of 'causation' and it is neigh impossible to examine the antecedents of actions and find a feature of caused actions that is not possessed by chosen ones. In other words, according to these critics there is no difference in the characteristics of action that 'could have been otherwise' and those of action that 'could not have been otherwise'. In addition, the authors argue that sociological arguments are to be empirical, and 'whether or not it could have been otherwise, it was not otherwise, nothing empirical hangs on the might have been that was not'.

Third, in order for any entity to be adequately qualified to claim actorhood, it must possess 'the cultural construction of the capacity and authority to act for itself'. In other words, true actorhood necessitates authentic and legitimized functions and interests as well as 'behaving in terms of natural (scientifically expressible) laws' (Meyer and Jepperson, 2000). In other words, the concept of agency ignores the fact that agentic behaviours can hardly exist apart from cultural templates that authorize and guide action (e.g. on resistance; Thompson 2004, p. 172). Culture always shapes peoples' strategies for action, and live in a consumer culture, those strategies cannot be prior to this (Swidler, 1986).

In the end, the idea of consumer agency is little more than a fol perpetuates one kind of actorhood and evokes value-laden notic constraint, and transcendence of constraint via choice, constructed using cultural resources. In other words, if people act agentically they are agentic (Fuchs, 2001). From a sociological perspective agency may be thought of either as a residual category, consisting of that portion of variance unaccounted for by social structure in accounts of behaviour. Or agency may emerge as a variable at a particular scale of analysis. In Fuchs (2001) terms, agency increases in salience when the population is small, the sociological distance between phenomena is short, the relations between persons and/or things are intimate, and the observer is concerned with intentionality. At the end of the day, because it evokes the possibility of 'freedom', agency is a topic philosophical not a sociological problem (cf. illusion of freedom in Bourdieu, 1990; Loyal and Barnes, 2001).

Consumers

The next issue to consider is whether 'consumers' may escape the market. On this point, many sociological theorists are at the very least dubious. Consumers are thought to exist in a permanent state of longing deluded by empty commercial promises, that cannot satisfy these desires,

> The gap between the fantasy world of consumption day-dreams of perfect pleasure [Kristeva's comfort of the perfect mother] and the disappointments of reality is the basic motivation for Campbell's (1987) 'autonomous imaginative hedonism' which results in limitless wants and a permanent state of frustration.
>
> Elliott (1997, p. 292)

Indeed, in its extreme form, this work is overtly dystopian,

> The modern vision of the human of the future was a spindly creature with an enormous brain. Now we know that vision was wrong, because we are making the human of the future right now; 'it is' already well under way-that pathetic genderless creature, and we know in what remains of our Interneted souls that it will eventually be a pinheaded creature with huge, thick typing fingers.
>
> Halton (2000, p. 93)

to Ewen (2001/orig. 1976) and on to Schor (1998), there
try devoted to the proposition that consumers,
their degraded condition as pawns in a mar-
he *Overspent American*, Schor (1998) argues that
ponse to intense and apparently overwhelming
nbolic fantasies attached to many things we want
addition, television induces people try to imitate
d. In a rhetorical move typical of this work, Schor
d that people spent about $208 more a year for each

hour of TV they reported watching a week. However, she argues it is not the ads that encourage people to overspend so much, since people are conditioned to resist them. Consumers are more influenced by programmes that tend to show characters who lead affluent lifestyles they would never be able to afford in reality. Further, in implicit concord with Putnam's (2000) thesis of Americans' increasing disengagement from local community, consumers look to new reference groups: people on TV. Again she reports research that shows that the more TV people watch; the more likely they are to overestimate what the average American has.

The argument in this stream of work really depends on a kind of behaviourist model of psychological cause and effect, and paradoxically given the tenor of this work that consumers should do otherwise, that is act agentically in favour of a more 'ecologically sustainable' (Schor, 2005) or politically progressive way (Klein, 2000), this work implies that consumers are dupes, whose behaviour is decidedly deterministic. While progressive in intent, this work often makes a number of fundamental mistakes. First it often confuses causes with effects; the massive expenditure on advertising and marketing must be achieving its intended effects (Ewen, 2001/orig. 1976). And yet as marketers and consumer behaviour researchers know, commercial communication is at best a blunt rhetorical instrument; and there is abundant empirical evidence that consumers engage in all kinds of 'detournement', turning marketer provided resources to their own ends.

Second it often misinterprets aggregate data and offers spurious correlations. In a context of social and market fragmentation, interpreting aggregate data, for example annual expenditures in a government-defined product category, or hours per day spent on-line, in terms of general social tendencies is incautious. Thus, as suggested by Halton above, it is argued that all this mediated consumption must be bad for the self and society. Even anecdotal evidence raises doubts. A mother I know encourages her children to post and participate actively in Myspace.com, although the school they attend strongly discourages it because of the supposed 'dangers' of stalking and 'inappropriate' content. But this mom argues it enables her children to express themselves in ways they could not express themselves to her and provides her a valuable window on their worlds. Even closer to home, my 12-year-old daughter spends hours every week-end playing an on-line role-playing game. Is she an example of Halton's genderless thick-fingered pin-head? In fact, she plays the game with her older female cousin who lives in another state and who encouraged this joint, intensely social activity in order to establish a closer relationship with my daughter. Her cousin believes every teen-age girl needs a non-parental female role model to help her navigate the vicissitudes of the teen years. She believes this game playing will bring the two of them closer together in advance of prospective teen traumas. On a more broadly social level, an emergent literature suggests that active participation in contemporary media plays a more complex social and potentially liberatory political role than imagined in some of the sociological literature critical of consumption (Jong et al., 2005; Pickard, 2006; Simone, 2006; Strangelove, 2005).

A third problem with the portrayal of consumers in much of the critical sociology of consumption is an implicit class bias. Baudrillard (1998/orig. 1970, p. 91) argues,

> there is also a full-blow syndrome of anti-consumption, a very modern phenomenon . . . which is, at bottom, a metaconsumption and acts as a cultural indicator of class. This phenomenon . . . is a crucial one for the interpretation of our society, since one might be taken in by this formal reversal of signs and mistake what is merely a change in the form of the distance between classes as an effect of democratization. *It is on the basis of luxury that the lost simplicity is consumed.*
>
> Emphasis added

Baudrillard's critique of the critique of consumption is basically that the critics speak from a middle class subject position, and their arguments for voluntary simplicity (Elgin, 1993) or even involuntary simplicity (Schor, 2005) are steeped in a longstanding critique of materialism among middle and upper class North Americans (Vanderbilt, 1996), one often directed at the supposed consumer excesses of the working class (Scott, 2005). And as Baudrillard presciently discerned in 1970, voluntary simplicity indeed takes the form of luxury lifestyle consumption.

From a different standpoint, research in Consumer Culture Theory (Arnould and Thompson, 2005) increasingly critiques the essentialism implicated in the social science construct 'consumer'. For instance, is a person who employs free-floating firm provided resources to construct an avatar like on-line persona a consumer (Schau and Gilly, 2003)? Are those persons who remake and remanufacture firm provided resources not something other than consumers (Muniz and Schau, 2005)? More radically, if a person willingly transforms him- or herself through the acquisition of commercially available technological, biological, or biotechnological prostheses is she/he a consumer or a cyborg? (Schroeder, 1994; Warwick, 2003; Wood, 1998). And if the latter, what are the roots to cyborgization, and how should we rethink what consumer 'does' on this terrain (Mitchell, 2003)? Ironically, cyborgs with dramatically improved processing capabilities might actually start acting like the machines economists insist human beings are (Mirowski, 2002), and with what unintended consequences for business and social science then?

Escape

Next I turn to the question of escape. There is no doubt that the rich symbolic resources generated by market capitalism provides for all sorts of sign experimentation, 'even as the market makes its profits, it supplies some of the materials for alternative or oppositional symbolic work' (Willis, 1990). However, we have seen that Baudrillard argues that there is no escape at the level of the code. So perhaps it is worth reflecting on the idea of escape itself. And as soon as we do, we realize that this idea of escape is largely a product of modernity, and as argued extensively elsewhere is a specifically Romantic response to it (Brown et al., 1998; Campbell, 1987). Romantic consumption is a utopian gesture to reclaim personal authenticity (Arnould and Price, 2000) that appears in the Dionysian ecstasies of raves and anticonsumerist festivals (Kozinets, 2002), in the nostalgic consumption of retroscapes (Brown and Sherry Jr., 2003), in the prospective consumption of utopia (Kozinets, 2001; Maclaran and Brown, 2005), and in ecotourism (Arnould et al., 1998). Thus, the utopian spirit is very fully colonized by market logic.

Escaping the Market: A Dystopian Example of Globalization

Are there examples of communities that have escaped from the market? A case can be made, but the example is dystopian rather than utopian. In 1999, I had occasion to revisit the sites of research conducted in the 1970s in Zinder in rural Niger on contending consumer globalizations fuelled by global movements of religious pilgrims and economic migrants (Arnould, 1989; Arnould and Mohr, 2005). Zinder's agriculturally based economy has long been incorporated into global circuits of production and consumption, but by the turn of the millennium this was no longer the case. Structural adjustment programmes had done their work (Gervais, 1995; Green, 1998); its economy is thoroughly marginalized from these circuits. Zinder's sole remaining export of value consisted in sheep exported seasonally to Nigeria to celebrate the Muslim festival of Eid. Millet, sorghum, and cowpeas, for which there is no significant world market, are all that can be cultivated in this increasingly arid environment. Hence, Zinderois have virtually no economic resources; they have virtually no skills to sell on the world market, and nothing to buy; they have no control of the political-economic agenda. I was deeply moved by one old friend's frantic plea for the few cents needed to repair a bicycle tyre, his only means of livelihood. This level of desperation and evident deprivation of the means of consumption is consummate. My former field assistant remarked, 'One bad harvest and they are all dead men', a prediction partially confirmed by the disastrous 2005 agricultural season. This kind of escape is clearly not the kind envisioned by the critics of market capitalism.

Momentary Escapes: 'Before the World is Formed'

Is their no other escape from the market? The early Baudrillard recognized the possibility of momentary escape from the market if only in the interstices of social structure, in those moments of radical change, before the world is formed as he said. The guerilla semiotics of groups like Gorilla Girls or AdBusters! that destabilize taken-for-granted market logics are examples of what Baudrillard had in mind. Still we need not be entirely pessimistic about the possibility of escape from utilitarian market logic even if true escape from the global currents of market exchange has dystopic consequences, and the utopian idea of action and interpretation prior to the prevailing cultural mode of objectification, that is consumer culture, is illusory. Ilouz (1997) has shown contemporary Romantic love is in essence a consumption form; it is nonetheless true that agapic, storgic, and philiac love are experienced and practiced (Belk and Coon, 1993) in terms of a gift economy that offers escapes from market logic. Similarly, Miller (1998) has found elements not only of devotional love, but also religious sacrifice that likewise eludes market logic in mundane shopping and housekeeping. And the gift economy as shown by Mauss and modern commentators that took the form of a total social fact with a cultural logic of its own, like the market economy (Caillé, 2005/orig. 1994; Mauss, 1925; Sahlins, 1972) persistently influences contemporary gift exchange (Cheal, 1988; Hyde, 1983) and practices associated with inalienable wealth (Curasi et al., 2004; Godelier, 1999).

The Market

Market capitalism is attacked as the primary contemporary source of all kinds of social pathology. As already mentioned, these attacks fix advertising (Ewen, 2001/orig. 1976); brands (Klein, 2000); commercial electronic media (Halton, 2000), marketing research (Dávila, 2001), marketing formula (Rimke, 2000; Ritzer, 1993), and consumers and consumption itself (Schor, 1998) squarely in their sights. Falsity, materialism, kitsch, ecological collapse, routinization, global poverty, addiction, and obesity all flow from the expanding reach of market capitalism.

It is noteworthy that the form of these attacks has changed little since the 19th century when Marx worried about the fetishism of commodities displacing our concern with the exploitation of labour or Thoreau warned that market materialism subjected us to the vagaries of fashion and displaced our concerns from the true realm of spirituality (Keane, 2005), and first wave feminist social reformers worried about the immorality and social disorder entailed in working class consumerism (Scott, 2005). This repeated rehearsal of the demonization of the market is nicely summarized in Baudrillard's epitaph and makes one wonder whether the academic criticism of markets and consumption stems from critics position as objects of marketing or participants in a marketing system from which they seek an escape via a return to the master narratives of modernity (Bauman, 1994). In some cases it may indeed be a Calvinist expression of fear and regret concerning luxury and sex. Perhaps in some cases, it is no more than a jab at the Common Market!

In protest, one might invoke Bataille (1988/orig. 1967), who inspired by the potlatch of Northwest coastal Native Americans, insisted that wasteful consumption is the general necessary condition for a prosperous economy. Instead, we might agree with Ilouz (1997), who provides a balanced appreciation of late market capitalism following Simmel's (1978) insights in *The Philosophy of Money*. Ilouz (1997, pp. 1–2) says,

> . . . to the extent that it promotes the incorporation of all social groups into the market, it has created a powerful symbolic space unified by

> the twin spheres of consumption and mass media . . . it has frag-
> mented social classes into ever smaller communities of consump-
> tion of lifestyle groups. Capitalism makes possible the participation
> of everyone in the economic and symbolic sphere of consumption,
> yet sustain and reproduces itself through the concentration of wealth
> and the legitimation of social divisions.

Thus, global market capitalism does democratize the space of consumption, but at the cost of social fragmentation and a growing gap between rich and poor. But taking up the issue of a globalization of consumption and following recent research on materiality, I think it might be possible to argue that some authors have confused the problems of the market with another problem, that of objectification. Academic critics very often argue that the market promotes too much social division and too much consumption, but from the perspective of materiality, the problem is elsewhere. First,

> proper materialism is one that recognizes the irreducible relation of
> culture, which through production . . . creates persons in and through
> their materiality. Capitalism splits culture and person apart into com-
> modities separated from their intrinsic person-making capacities, and
> the illusion of pure humanism outside of materiality.
>
> Miller (2005, p. 17)

In other words, following a Hegelian logic (Miller, 1987) both society at a macro-level and persons at an individual level are created in and through the material forms that are projected into the world; in our culture, through marketed mediated consumption forms. Everything from Klingon language and clothing to on-line stock trades are created by humans, but created according to emergent strategies of action embedded in marketing culture. In turn, their existence produces us as 'Klingons' or on-line stock traders (Kozinets, 2001; McIntyre and Zwick, n.d.).

Second, all societies proceed through the creation of external forms, and all societies are threatened by such forms developing autonomous momentum that threatens people with estrangement, and in capitalism with alienation (Miller, 1987, p. 180). This is as true of pre-market peoples as those of us who live in late capitalism in which many appear to feel threatened by the apparatus of marketing, advertising, franchising, market research, and the like.

Third, because capitalism splits persons from commodities through the meditative apparatus of markets, when successful, consumer's post-acquisition behaviour in late capitalism constitutes in fact, a negation of the alienated commodity and its transformation into culturally meaningful objects (Kopytoff, 1985; Miller, 1987, pp. 191–193). As Douglas (1992) argued, goods are fundamentally means of communication through which the particular social position of individuals are experienced and communicated to others. Thus well-being is determined by the capacity for self-creation by a society or individual that is created through objects' appropriation (Miller, 2005, p. 20). So the enormous proliferation of lifestyle consumption communities from Goths to the cult of the Citroën DS (French, déese = English, goddess), from Star Trek fans to medieval re-enactors, may be viewed not as marketer-provoked social fragmentation, but consumption fuelled re-appropriation of differentiated selves.

It may be argued that the proliferation of objects may be implicated in the creation of particular social worlds and particular social identities that are generative of the sociality Maffesoli imagines in a global capitalist context. Consider, middle class Indonesians as described by Keane (2005, p. 1995),

> Middle-class men in Indonesian cities today have a rule-governed sartorial repertoire: a neotraditional outfit for weddings, safari suit for official meetings, long-sleeved batik shirt for receptions, shirt and tie for the office, sarong and *pici* for Friday prayers. These are coordinated with bodily habituses: the Javanese s*embah*, sitting on mats and eating with hands while in traditional clothes; firm handshake, direct eye contact, chairs and utensils in office attire; Islamic *salam* while in sarong. This cluster of habits expectations, and constrained possibilities [culture, in short] is the outcome of several generalizations of semiotic regimentation and stabilization.

Thus, the Indonesian subject does not have too many consumer goods; he is not a victim of consumer culture gone mad. Instead, he has an array of material possibilities that enable him to define himself effectively relative to the differentiated, globalized social order that he inhabits. Where he deprived of some of this array, his capacity to signal his availability to participate in contemporary Indonesian life would be constrained as would his capacity for self-definition. All these things are not superficial symbols of his sociality; they are constitutive of it.

For all of this, it is clearly true as the Nigerien counter-example shows that many groups are consumers to a far lesser extent than others, and their interests are therefore unduly underrepresented in global consumptionscapes (Appadurai, 1990), and this indeed results in a material culture constructed in the image of groups alien to the underrepresented. One may say that such groups are denied the means of consumption, and hence the means to realize themselves through material cultural forms. When people are unable to perceive the means of self-creation, or because objective conditions prevent us from self-creation through consumption, it is here that alienation and social pathology emerge, not from the engagement with the market or consumption or objects themselves (Miller, 1987, p. 189).

Conclusion

This chapter interrogated some of the sociological dimensions of the component words of the title in an effort to assess the meaningfulness of the question. First, I reviewed some positions on the consumers' freedom of action in consumer research, and suggested that agency is conceptually problematic. Second, I discussed the term consumers and propose that the anti-consumption ideology that seems to underlie the overarching question is in fact a class-based ideology, and an essentializing one at that. Third, I examine the idea of escape. Here I reminded readers that escape is a Romantic idea, a response to the modern machine age, the apotheosis of which is the utopian dream. The dangers of real escape were illustrated with an example from a part of the globe set adrift by the scaping processes of globalization (Appadurai, 1990). Next, I discussed the notion of the market entailed in the question and cycled around to more fundamental question of materiality and objectification that tend to get unhelpfully bundled with markets and marketing in some critical sociology. And curiously this discussion both accepts that estrangement is a part of the life experience of those deprived of the means of consumption, but it also ends on a hopeful response to the question posed at the outset. For following a number of anthropological commentators, I conclude that sometimes what 'consumer' does is as authentic an act of fully socialized self-realization as one may reasonably expect.

References

Appadurai, A. (1990). 'Disjuncture and difference in the global cultural economy'. *Public Culture*, 2(2), 1–24.

Arnould, E.J. (1989). 'Toward a broadened theory of preference formation and the diffusion of innovations: cases from Zinder Province, Niger Republic'. *Journal of Consumer Research*, 16(September), 239–267.

Arnould, E.J. and Mohr, J.J. (2005). 'Dynamic transformations of an indigenous market cluster: the leatherworking industry in Niger'. *Journal of the Academy of Marketing Science*, 33(Summer), 254–274.

Arnould, E.J. and Price, L.L. (2000). 'Authenticating acts and authoritative performances: questing for self and community'. In S. Ratneshwar, D.G. Mick and C.A. Huffman (eds), *The Why of Consumption: Contemporary Perspectives on Consumers Motives, Goals, and Desires*. New York and London: Routledge, pp. 140–163.

Arnould, E.J. and Thompson, C.J. (2005). 'Consumer culture theory (CCT): twenty years of research'. *Journal of Consumer Research*, 31(March), 868–883.

Arnould, E.J., Price, L.L. and Tierney, P. (1998). 'Communicative staging of the wilderness servicescape'. *Service Industries Journal*, 18(3), 90–115.

Aubert-Gamet, V. (1997). 'Twisting servicescapes: diversion of the physical environment in a re-appropriation process'. *International Journal of Service Industry Management*, 8(1), 26–41.

Badot, O. (2005). 'L'autre raison du succès de Wal-mart: une rhétorique de l'infra-ordinaire'. *Revue Française du Marketing*, 203(July), 97–118.

Baudrillard, J. (1998/orig. 1970). *The Consumer Society: Myths and Structures*. London and Thousand Oaks, CA: Sage.

Bataille, G. (1988/orig. 1967). *The Accursed Share: An Essay on General Economy*, trans. R. Hurley. New York: Zone Books.

Bauman, Z. (1994). 'Is There a Postmodern Sociology?' In S. Seidman (ed.), *The Postmodern Turn: New Perspectives on Social Theory*. Cambridge: Cambridge University Press, pp. 187–204.

Belk, R.W. and Coon, G.S. (1993). 'Gift giving as agapic love: an alternative to the exchange paradigm'. *Journal of Consumer Research*, 20(3), 393–418.

Belk, R.W., Ger, G. and Askegaard, S. (2003). 'The fire of desire: a multisited inquiry into consumer passion'. *Journal of Consumer Research*, 30(3), 326–351.

Bourdieu, P. (1977). *Outline of a Theory of Practice*. Cambridge: Cambridge University Press.

Bourdieu, P. (1984). *Distinction: A Social Critique of the Judgment of Taste*. Cambridge, MA: Harvard University Press.

Bourdieu, P. (1990). *The Logic of Practice*. Cambridge: Polity Press.

Brown, S. and Sherry Jr., J.F. (2003). *Time, Space, and the Market: Retroscapes Rising*. Armonk, NY: M.E. Sharpe.

Brown, S., Doherty, A.-M. and Clark, B. (1998). *Romancing the Market*. London and New York: Routledge.

Caillé, A. (2005/orig. 1994). *Don, Intérêt et Désintéressement: Bourdieu, Mauss, Platon et Quelques Autres*. Paris: Editions La Découverte/MAUSS.

Campbell, C. (1987). *The Romantic Ethic and the Spirit of Modern Consumerism*. New York: Blackwell.

Cheal, D. (1988). *The Gift Economy*. London and New York: Routledge.

Curasi, C., Price, L.L. and Arnould, E. (2004). 'How individuals' cherished possessions become families' inalienable wealth'. *Journal of Consumer Research*, 31(December), 609–622.

Dávila, A. (2001). *Latinos, Inc.: The Marketing and Making of a People*. Berkeley: University of California Press.

De Certeau, M. (1984). *The Practice of Everyday Life*. Berkeley: University of California Press.

Douglas, M. (1992). 'Why do people want goods?' In S. Hargreaves and A. Ross (eds), *Understanding the Enterprise Culture*. Edinburgh: Edinburgh University Press, pp. 19–31.

Elgin, D. (1993). *Voluntary Simplicity: Toward a Way of Life That Is Outwardly Simple, Inwardly Rich*. New York: William Morrow.

Elliott, R. (1997). 'Existential consumption and irrational desire'. *European Journal of Marketing*, 31(3/4), 285–296.

Emirbayer, M. and Mische, A. (1998). 'What is agency?' *American Journal of Sociology*, 103(4), 962–1023.

Ewen, S. (2001/orig. 1976), *Captains of Consciousness: Advertising and the Social Roots of the Consumer Culture*, 25th Anniversary edition. New York: Basic Books.

Firat, A. F. and Venkatash, A. (1995). 'Liberatory postmodernism and the reenchantment of consumption'. *Journal of Consumer Research*, 22(3), 239–267.

Firat, A.F. (2005). *'Meridian thinking in marketing. A comment on Cova'*. *Marketing Theory*, 5 (June), 215–219.

Fournier, S. (1998). 'Consumers and their brands: developing relationship theory in consumer research'. *Journal of Consumer Research*, 24(4), 343–373.

Fuchs, S. (2001). 'Beyond agency'. *Sociological Theory*, 19, 24–40.

Gervais, M. (1995). 'Structural adjustment in Niger: implementations, effects and determining political factors'. *Review of African Political Economy*, 22(March), 25–40.

Green, R.H. (1998). 'A cloth untrue: the evolution of structural adjustment in sub-Saharan Africa'. *Journal of International Affairs*, 52(Fall), 207–232.

Godelier, M. (1972). *Rationality and Irrationality in Economics*, trans. B. Pearce. New York: Monthly Review Press.

Godelier, M. (1999). *The Enigma of the Gift*. Cambridge: Polity Press.

Halton, E. (2000). 'Brain suck'. In M. Gottdiener (ed.), *New Forms of Consumption*. Lanham, MD: Rowman & Littlefield, pp. 93–109.

Holt, D.B. (1998). 'Does cultural capital structure American consumption?' *Journal of Consumer Research*, 25(June), 1–26.

Hyde, L. (1983). *The Gift: Imagination and the Erotic Life of Property*. New York: Random House.

Ilouz, E. (1997). *Consuming the Romantic Utopia*. Berkeley: University of California Press.

Jong, W., Shaw, M. and Stammers, N. (eds) (2005). *Global Activism, Global Media*. London: Pluto Press.

Kahneman, D. and Tversky, A. (eds) (2000). *Choices, Values, and Frames*. New York: Russell Sage Foundation.

Kahneman, D., Slovic, P. and Tversky, A. (eds) (1982). *Judgment Under Uncertainty: Heuristics and Biases*. New York: Cambridge University Press.

Kates, S.M. (2004). 'The dynamics of brand legitimacy: an interpretive study in the gay men's community'. *Journal of Consumer Research*, 31(2), 455–464.

Keane, W. (2005). 'Signs are not the garb of meaning: on the social analysis of material things'. In D. Miller (ed.), *Materiality*. Durham: Duke University Press, pp. 182–205.

Klein, N. (2000). *No Logo: Taking Aim at the Brand Bullies*. Toronto: Knopf.

Kopytoff, I. (1986). 'The cultural biography of things: commoditization as process'. In A. Appaduradi (ed), *The Social Life of Things*. Cambridge: Cambridge University Press, pp. 64–94.

Kozinets, R.V. (2001). 'Utopian enterprise: articulating the meaning of Star Trek's culture of consumption'. *Journal of Consumer Research*, 28 (June), 67–89.

Kozinets, R. V., Sherry Jr, J. F. Storm, D., Duhachek, A. (2004). Ludic Agency and Retail Spectacle,' *Journal of Consumer Research*, 31 (December), 658–673.

Kozinets, R.V. (2002). 'Can consumers escape the market? Emancipatory illuminations from Burning Man'. *Journal of Consumer Research*, 29 (June), 20–38.

Loyal, S. and Barnes, B. (2001). '"Agency" as a red herring in social theory'. *Philosophy of the Social Sciences*, 31(4), 507–524.

Maclaran, P. and Brown, S. (2005). 'The center cannot hold: consuming the utopian marketplace'. *Journal of Consumer Research*, 32(September), 311–324.

Maffesoli, M. (1996). *The Time of the Tribes: The Decline of Individualism in Mass Society*. London and Thousand Oaks, CA: Sage.

Marx, K. (1998/orig. 1887). *Capital: A Critique of Political Economy*, trans. S. Moore and E. Aveling, F. Engels (ed.). London: ElecBook (downloaded from http://

site.ebrary.com.ezproxy.library.arizona.edu/lib/arizona/Doc?id=2001687, 10 April 2006).

Mauss, M. (1925). *The Gift: Form and Functions of Exchange in Archaic Societies.* New York: W.W. Norton.

McGraw, A.P., Tetlock, P.E. and Kristel, O.V. (2003). 'The limits of fungibility: relational schemata and the value of things'. *Journal of Consumer Research,* 30(September), 219–229.

McIntyre, R. and Zwick, D. (n.d.). *The Birth of the Investing Self: Nasdaq, Neo-liberalism, and the (Dis)appearance of Global Responsibility.* Unpublished Manuscript, Schulich School of Business, York University, Toronto.

Meyer, J.W. and Jepperson, R.L. (2000). 'The "actors" of modern society: the cultural construction of social agency'. *Sociological Theory,* 181(March), 100–120.

Miller, D. (1987). *Material Culture and Mass Consumption.* Oxford: Basil Blackwell.

Miller, D. (1998). *A Theory of Shopping.* Ithaca, NY: Cornell University Press.

Miller, D. (2005). 'Materiality: an introduction'. In D. Miller (ed.), *Materiality.* Durham: Duke University Press, pp. 1–50.

Mirowski, P. (2002). *Machine Dreams: Economics Becomes a Cyborg Science.* Cambridge, MA: Cambridge University Press.

Mitchell, W.J. (2003). *Me++ The Cyborg, Self and the Networked City.* Cambridge, MA: MIT Press.

Muniz, A. and Schau, H. (2005). 'Religiosity in the abandoned Apple Newton brand community'. *Journal of Consumer Research,* 31(March), 737–748.

Murray, J.B. (2002). 'The politics of consumption: a re-inquiry on Thompson and Haytko's (1997) "Speaking of fashion"'. *Journal of Consumer Research,* 29(3), 427–440.

Ozanne, J. L. and Murray, J. B. (1995). 'Uniting critical theory and public policy to crerate the reflexively defiant consumer'. *The American Behavioral Scientist,* 38 (February), 516–526.

Packard, V.O. (1957). *The Hidden Persuaders.* New York: D. McKay Co.

Peñaloza, L. (2001). 'Consuming the American West: animating cultural meaning and memory at a stock show and rodeo'. *Journal of Consumer Research,* 28(3), 369–398.

Pickard, V.W. (2006). 'United yet autonomous: Indymedia and the struggle to sustain a radical democratic network'. *Media, Culture and Society,* 28(3), 315–336.

Putnam, R.D. (2000). *Bowling Alone: The Collapse and Revival of American Community.* New York: Simon & Schuster.

Rimke, H.M. (2000). 'Governing citizens through self-help literature'. *Cultural Studies,* 14(1), 61–78.

Ritzer, G. (1993). *The McDonaldization of Society.* Thousand Oaks, CA: Pine Forge Press.

Sahlins, M. (1972). *Stone Age Economics.* Chicago: Aldine.

Schau, H.J. and Gilly, M.C. (2003). 'We are what we post? Self-presentation in personal web space'. *Journal of Consumer Research,* 30(December), 385–404.

Schor, J.B. (1998). *The Overspent American: Upscaling, Downshifting, and the New Consumer.* New York: Basic Books.

Schor, J.B. (2005). 'Prices and quantities: unsustainable consumption and the global economy'. *Ecological Economics*, 55, 309–320.

Schroeder, R. (1994). 'Cyberculture, cyborg post-modernism and the sociology of virtual reality technologies'. *Futures*, 26(June), 519–529.

Scott, L.M. (2005). *Fresh Lipstick: Redressing Fashion and Feminism*. New York: Palgrave Macmillan.

Simmel, G. (1978). *The Philosophy of Money*, trans. T. Bottomore and D. Frisby. London and Boston: Routledge & Kegan Paul.

Simone, M. (2006). 'CODEPINK alert: mediated citizenship in the public sphere'. *Social Semiotics*, 16(2), 345–364.

Strangelove, M. (2005). *The Empire of Mind: Digital Piracy and the Anticapitalist Movement*. Toronto: University of Toronto Press.

Strathern, M. (1979). 'The self in self-decoration'. *Oceania*, 44, 241–257.

Swidler, A. (1986). 'Culture in action: symbols and strategies'. *American Sociological Review*, 51(2), 273–286.

Thompson, C.J. and Haytko, D.L. (1997). 'Speaking of fashion: consumers' uses of fashion discourses and the appropriation of countervailing cultural meanings'. *Journal of Consumer Research*, 24(1), 15–42.

Thompson, C.J. (2004). 'Marketplace mythology and discourses of power'. *Journal of Consumer Research*, 31 (June), 162–181.

Vanderbilt, T. (1996). 'It's a wonderful (simplified) life'. *The Nation*, 262(3), 20–22.

Venkatesh, A. (1998). 'Cybermarketscapes and consumer freedoms and identities'. *European Journal of Marketing*, 32(7/8), 664–687.

Warwick, K. (2003). 'Cyborg morals, cyborg values, cyborg ethics'. *Ethics and Information Technology*, 5(3), 131–137.

Willis, P. (1990). *Common Culture: Symbolic Work at Play in the Everyday Cultures of the Young*. Milton Keynes: Open University Press.

Wood, M. (1998). 'Agency and organization: toward a cyborg-consciousness'. *Human Relations*, 51(October), 1209–1227.

Part III

Effecting Change
Through Critique:
Social and
Environmental Issues

11

The Critical Role of Social Marketing

Ross Gordon, Gerard Hastings, Laura McDermott and Pierre Siquier

Criticism of conventional marketing is growing and well justified. However, to be effective any critique should not just find fault with the current situation, but identify ways forward – it should offer solutions. This chapter argues that *social marketing* does this by (a) suggesting a socially beneficial use for marketing techniques and ideas and (b) enabling the control and regulation of conventional marketing.

In the first section, we discuss the nature of marketing, its influence on human behaviour, and examine criticisms that have arisen both from within and outside of the discipline. We then introduce the idea of social marketing and explore its contribution to the critical marketing debate. Here we discuss the need to (i) critically examine the effects of commercial marketing on the health and welfare of society and (ii) apply these same tools and techniques to the resolution of social and health problems. In the third section of this chapter we argue that critical studies of commercial marketing can inform policy decision-making. However, before policy-makers can act, they require a sound evidence base on which all parties agree. We show – through three different case studies – how social marketing offers new insights to the task of building an evidence base for policy-makers.

We conclude by arguing that, if marketing is to survive the attacks which it finds itself under, and prosper as a serious and viable discipline it must change: commercial marketing has to be moderated and its powers adapted and utilized to affect positive behavioural outcomes for society. Social marketing provides a coherent framework for achieving these changes.

Introduction

Marketing has a bad name (Jobber, 2001). The discipline has been attacked internally and by external critics to the degree that as Alvesson incisively observes, 'Marketing is used almost as a pejorative term' (Alvesson, 1994).

Marketing is fundamentally about behaviour change; marketers are extremely good at getting us (the consumer) to do things. Yet not all behaviour change is desirable for society. Many societal problems – from alcohol fuelled anti-social teenagers to pollution-inducing gas-guzzling SUV drivers – are essentially matters of human behaviour. Moreover, many of these problems are perpetrated by marketers.

External Criticism

External criticism of the marketing discipline has emanated from a variety of sources such as Klein, Bakan, Monbiot and Chomsky. Klein attacks the corporate obsession with creating brands rather than producing tangible products. This creates a new wave of organizations whose 'work lay not in manufacturing but in marketing' (Klein, 2000). The explosion in marketing activity that fed the creation of massive global brands is described by Klein: 'they seize upon every corner of unmarketed landscape in search of the oxygen needed to inflate their brands. In the process, virtually nothing has been left unbranded' (Klein, 2000). The world is being rapidly commercialized to the point that 'advertising is now inescapable, whether on our TV or computer screens, huge outdoor billboards and electrical signs, wrapped around buses and subway cars, museums, concerts, galleries and sporting events' (Bakan, 2004). This focus on creating uberbrands has led to widespread corporate abuses that infringe labour and human rights (Klein, 2000). Marketers have left no stone unturned in attempting to find vehicles for marketing activity including sports, youth culture, cityscapes, and even controversial ventures involving children, schools and education (Klein, 2000).

Joel Bakan in the corporation is also critical of corporate abuses arguing that 'the corporation is a pathological institution, a dangerous possessor of the great power it wields over people and societies' (Bakan, 2004). The image Bakan constructs is of the corporation as a person, who relates to others only superficially via false identities of itself – identities created by marketing consultants. Corporations use branding strategies to 'create unique and attractive personalities for themselves' (Bakan, 2004) which enables them to create intellectual and emotional relationships with consumers, policy-makers, regulators employees and shareholders. This often irrational emotional connection which marketers aim to make with their target audience is demonstrated by Bakan through examples of 'pester power', where marketing strategies manipulate children to pester parents or their family members to purchase unrequired goods or services. Bakan describes a time when his son nagged him to buy Labatt beer during the Ice Hockey playoffs so he could get a replica Stanley Cup trophy that came with the promotion. Bakan argues that 'Labatt must have known that young children would be watching the playoffs with their parents ... and that most adults would not abandon their preferred brand of beer to obtain a Stanley Cup replica' (Bakan, 2004). Bakan is left with no doubt that 'part of the company's aim was to get my son to get me to buy its beer – which it did' (Bakan, 2004). The impact of the nag factor on consumer behaviour is considerable; an estimated 20–40% of all purchases would not have occurred unless a child nagged their parents or guardians (Bakan, 2004).

The effects of food advertising on children's behaviour have also been widely noted (Bakan, 2004; Monbiot, 2006). Attention has been drawn to the fact that British children are exposed to more adverts than any others in the European Union (EU), 'an average of 17 per hour on children's TV' (Monbiot, 1998). The resulting 'pestering' that is generated often causes tension in child–parent relationships and can lead to 'exasperated purchases of items against a parent's better judgement' (McDermott et al., 2006). Specific targeting of children by the marketing industry has even led to accusations of using schools 'as an advertising medium' (Monbiot, 2001). The criticism of food advertising to children has led to calls to increase regulatory controls in the UK, despite Ofcom's claims that stricter regulation would cost the industry too much. Yet the public health benefits of increased regulation could be as much as £990 million per year compared with Ofcom's estimated cost to the broadcasting industry of up to £290 million (Which, 2006).

Such criticisms lead to a questioning of the effectiveness of the current advertising regulations which are built around a system of co-regulation but in reality is largely self-regulated. Monbiot argues that 'both the ITC and ASA are weakly constituted and reluctant to use their limited powers' (Monbiot, 1998), whilst he accuses Ofcom of canoodling with the food industry (Monbiot, 2006). The penalties for misdemeanours are often weak: 'sanctions against advertisers who break codes of practice in Britain are ineffective' (Monbiot, 2001). Questions exist over the effectiveness of the regulatory system which governs not only food advertising (Hastings et al., 2003) but other forms of marketing such as alcohol marketing (Jackson et al., 2000).

Other marketing techniques criticized include viral campaigns – one example is organizations using false identities, email addresses and postings on web sites to attack green campaigners or scientists publishing findings on environmental harms. Companies have been accused of 'creating false citizens to try to change the way we think' (Monbiot, 2002). Monbiot balances his criticisms by questioning the wisdom of instances of false advertising by environmental groups such as Greenpeace and Friends of the Earth. Claims and counter claims over who maintains good ethical practice leads to the 'intractable problem ... of trying to separate good guys from bad guys' (Fahy, 2000). Yet the activities of environmental groups indulging in misinformation are small fry compared to the activities of organized industry, often supported by the media meaning 'the corporate interest and national interest often seems to be confused' (Monbiot, 1995). The 'politics of advertising' creates a situation in which 'the regulation of advertising in Britain ensures that we are allowed to hear only what is good about a product or activity, and expressly forbidden to hear what is bad' (Monbiot, 1999). Marketing is also used for political expedience with elections in Western Democracies fought using expensive and sophisticated marketing campaigns. 'Elections are run by the same guys who sell toothpaste' (Chomsky, 2005) and can also be used to forge an artificial image of political figures or systems in the nation's psyche (Chomsky, 2004).

Internal Criticism

Criticisms of marketing have also emerged from within the discipline itself. The managerialist ideology which dominates marketing thought and practice is inexorably linked with the system of (neo)-corporatism that has emerged as one of the dominant features in free market capitalist societies. Marketing – a core element of corporatism – is therefore subject to criticisms of corporate excesses. Michael Thomas (1999) describes the problem as corporatism out of control:

> We have unleashed a monster that no one can control, even that minority that profits from it. Unashamed self-interest is a vice, not a virtue. We must recognize that the usefulness of an activity is not necessarily measured by its profitability, and that what someone earns is not an indicator of their talents and abilities, still less their moral stature.

Marketing academics have formed an emerging stream of critical marketing scholarship, which claims that the basis of its contribution is in its capacity to encourage considered reflexivity within the marketing discipline through pedagogy and research which builds up a pervasive evidence base. This critical approach to marketing theory developed during the 1970s in the USA as a response to the changing social, economic and political landscape of the time (Burton, 2000). Academics and analysts began to question the 'positive' effects of marketing on society and whether it could provide any tangible benefits. Critical marketers have adopted various critical approaches such as sustainability (Fuller, 1999), ethics (Crane, 1997), feminism (Catterall et al., 1999), discourse analysis (Brownlie and Saren, 1997) and postmodernism (Firat and Venkatesh, 1993).

The dominant critical marketing position finds its roots in the work of Jurgen Habermas who conceptualized a critical theoretical approach. Habermasian critical theorists see the potential for the emancipation of the discipline through 'a re-invigoration of the Enlightenment project of creating a culture of reason' (Lowe et al., 2005) revealing the possibility of emancipation and rational-critical communication embedded in modern liberal institutions. This school of thought aims to challenge the dominant managerialist ideology in marketing with an alternative approach to marketing theory and practice, allowing citizens to be freed from the excesses of a mass consumerist society (Alvesson, 1994). This view has had a degree of impact on marketing theory and its ideas form much of the basis of the 'critical imagination' project (Murray and Ozanne, 1991). Although an alternative and more radical approach to critical marketing has been espoused (Hetrick and Lozanda, 1994) under the influence of other Frankfurt school theorists adopting a more pessimistic outlook, this has failed to make any profound impact within the marketing discipline.

Therefore, the contribution that critical thought can make to marketing theory is uncertain and its impact on marketing practice has been limited because of the gulf that exists between marketing academics and practitioners. Rather, the focus has been on criticizing current marketing processes and outcomes. However, critical theory should not just be about criticism for its own sake but should move towards solutions, 'a significant task of critical theory is to simultaneously critique contemporary society while envisioning new possibilities' (Burton, 2000). One of the identified weaknesses of critical theory has been the lack of potential solutions, 'many of these critiques can seem to consist of criticizing everything without offering solutions' (Catterall et al., 1999). Any solutions that are proposed are often too grandiose and unworkable (Monbiot, 1995, 1999, 2001).

This is where social marketing can help. The next section will describe social marketing and argue that it can help tackle the challenges and criticisms facing the marketing discipline in two ways:

1 By enabling the control and regulation of conventional marketing.
2 By providing a socially beneficial use for marketing techniques and ideas: the opportunity of behaviour change.

What is Social Marketing?

So what exactly is social marketing? Well, like generic marketing, social marketing is not a theory in itself. Instead, it is a framework that draws upon various other bodies of knowledge including sociology and psychology to develop an understanding of human behaviour and how it can be successfully influenced (Kotler and Zaltman, 1971). Varied definitions of social marketing exist, but one of the most useful was proposed by Lazer and Kelly (1973, p. ix) during the early days of the discipline:

> Social marketing is concerned with the application of marketing knowledge, concepts, and techniques to enhance social as well as economic ends. It is also concerned with analysis of the social consequence of marketing policies, decisions and activities.

This definition is especially useful because it conveys both sides of the social marketing 'coin'. On the one hand, social marketing encourages us to use our skills and insights as marketers to progress social good. On the other hand, it facilitates the control and regulation of conventional marketing through critical studies of its impact on the health and welfare of society.

Both dimensions are of equal importance as together they demonstrate the contribution that social marketing can make to the critical marketing debate. Though well known critics of commercial marketing highlight its deficiencies, they disappointingly stop short of offering any kind of solution. Social marketing can help here because it encourages active debate about the role that marketing should play in modern society. Marketing has often had an unwanted impact but it has also brought about great social benefits. In essence marketing is arguably amoral – so quite how it is used really becomes a question of ethics. Social marketing can help us get the balance right by ensuring that the potential for harm is monitored and controlled and that we also harness the power of marketing to improve our societal well-being.

By studying the impact of commercial marketing on human behaviour, social marketers can gain crucial insights that will enhance their abilities to use marketing for the greater good. The very power of commercial marketing and its influence on human behaviour has been documented in countless critical studies of its impact on society. Aside from all else, this simply underlines its potential to affect behaviour in other more socially desirable areas. Over the past 30 or so years, social marketers have systematically applied concepts from commercial marketing – concepts like consumer research, segmentation and targeting, the marketing 'mix', competitor analysis and, more recently, branding and stakeholder marketing – to topics as diverse as cancer prevention, domestic recycling and road safety.

Critical marketing also makes social marketers aware and able to take account of the competition. We, like our commercial counterparts, need to recognize legitimate sources of competition and the factors that may inhibit our target audience from adopting the very behaviours that we are promoting. Clearly the potential sources of competition to a social marketing campaign will be various – and will depend on the behaviour being promoted. One form of competition that we cannot ignore is the potential detrimental impact of commercial marketing in the very areas in which we are trying to change behaviour. Our ability to get children to eat a better diet will be vastly improved if we can move upstream and tackle some of the wider environmental factors that are making it difficult for them to consume the kinds of foods we would like them to. Encouraging policy-makers and legislators to ban junk food advertising to children, or retailers to stock healthy foods as opposed to confectionary at checkouts are just two examples of how we might achieve this. Good social marketing embraces this idea of going 'upstream' and tackling, not only the behaviour of individuals, but also that of professionals, organizations and policy-makers (Goldberg, 1995; Lefebvre, 1996).

Critical marketing is not necessarily something to be feared by the business community. Indeed it may offer numerous gains. Firms' efforts to successfully build brands and develop strong enduring relationships with their customers will prove considerably more challenging if key branches of marketing – like advertising and sales promotion – are continually being called into question. No one is better placed than we, as marketers ourselves, to use our understanding of the subject to advance not only the commercial bottom line, but also to identify marketing's worst excesses and guide policy-makers in their efforts to set reasonable limits. In areas like social welfare and public health, marketing could switch from reactively defending itself against accusations of being part of the problem, to proactively contributing to the solution.

The following section will demonstrate how critical studies of commercial marketing can inform policy decision-making thereby enabling regulation.

Enabling Regulation

Changes in the marketing environment can be achieved by enforcing regulation of marketing activities. However, policy-makers need a clear, rigorous and consensual evidence base before they can act. Not least because policy-relevant research findings can influence decisions 'involving millions of people and billions of dollars' (Franke, 2001). For evidence to be convincing a consensus among experts is crucial and corporations will not willingly accept restrictions on their activities if they feel that the evidence base does not support them. In short, when business and social interests clash, everyone – citizens, policy-makers and the business community – would benefit from a more rigorous, transparent and consensual way of measuring the impact of marketing on society.

Reaching consensus can be achieved in a number of ways. Various methods exist for appraising and synthesizing evidence. These methods include systematic review (SR), primary research and documentation analysis. Three examples of how these methods have applied to critical marketing research are now provided.

SR and Food Marketing to Young People

Like marketing, the medical community has too faced dilemmas in terms of reaching a consensus about the nature of evidence. Medicine has responded to this problem with the idea of 'evidence-based decision-making', with its emphasis on rigorous methods for reviewing existing research on a topic (Mulrow, 1994). The 'systematic review' (SR) is central to this new thinking (Boaz et al., 2002). Essentially, it is a method of literature review that is used to identify, assess and interpret all of the available evidence on a given topic. It usually relies only on the highest quality evidence and all of its procedures – from literature searching right through to study selection, appraisal and synthesis – are both rigorous and transparent. SR pretty much rules out any possibility for bias because it makes explicit the criteria for selection (Petticrew, 2001) thus overcoming reviewers' natural tendencies to favour certain studies over others. While the idea of reviewing secondary evidence itself is not new,

SR is pioneering because of its insistence on meeting agreed standards and adopting transparent and replicable procedures. For these reasons, SR offers built-in quality control that can allow policy-makers and legislators to proceed with confidence. Despite some challenges (e.g. dealing with different types of evidence), the principles of evidence-based decision-making and SR are increasingly being taken beyond medicine into fields as diverse as education, social welfare, criminal justice and health promotion, where policy options are also actively debated and the balance between professional and public interest has to be determined.

Recently, SR methods were applied for the first time to a marketing problem. A key site of particularly topical conflict in marketing is the debate concerning the promotion of food to children, and its possible contribution to rising levels of childhood obesity. To clarify the role of commercial food marketing in children's diets, in 2002 the UK Food Standards Agency (FSA) commissioned an SR on the extent and nature of food promotion to children, and any effect on their food knowledge, preferences and behaviour. Because of the controversy surrounding the topic it was crucial that the review was as rigorous and transparent as possible. A team of researchers from four leading UK universities was selected through peer review to conduct the SR. The research found that food promotion was having a detrimental impact on children, particularly in terms of their food preferences, purchase behaviour and consumption (Hastings et al., 2003).

As well as adhering to systematic procedures, the review was scrutinized by relentless peer review. Nearly 40 academic experts from a range of institutions and disciplines refereed some aspect the project. In addition, an independent advisory panel, with representatives from industry, public health and academia, provided regular guidance and scrutiny. The review also had to withstand critiques from commercial marketers. This included an alternative review of the evidence that was funded by an advertising trade organization (Young, 2003). Unlike the SR, this review relied on conventional literature review methods (i.e. it was not explicit about how sources had been identified and searched or what procedures were followed to appraise the quality of studies). It reached the opposite conclusion, finding that there was no evidence that food promotion influenced children. In an effort to reconcile these conflicting reviews, the FSA convened a meeting of senior academics who were asked to examine and compare the reviews and reach some kind of consensus. The expert panel questioned the grounds on which Young had selected and appraised studies and deemed the SR's procedures to be more reliable than the conventional review methods used by Young. In the end, the SR's findings were strongly endorsed by the panel (Food Standards Agency, 2003).

Because the review withstood all kinds of scrutiny, it was shown to be both comprehensive and rigorous. It is now widely regarded as the definitive piece of research on food promotion to children and its robustness has given policy-makers the confidence to proceed. The SR's findings were formally ratified by the FSA Board and have been accepted by the Ministry responsible for telecommunications (Department for Culture, Media and Sport). It has also directly informed government policy on the issue. The recent Public Health

White Paper states that 'there is a strong case for action to restrict further the advertising and promotion to children of those foods and drinks that are high in fat, salt and sugar' (Department of Health, 2004). The review has also informed Ofcom's (the government body responsible for regulating broadcast advertising in the UK) recent consultation on regulating food promotion to children (Ofcom, 2006). Further related policies have also been announced by the government (including bans on unhealthy vending machines in schools).

Primary Research and Alcohol Marketing to Young People

Similar requirements for a comprehensive evidence base are found in the area of alcohol marketing. The last decade has seen a 20% increase in alcohol consumption in the UK (ISD, 2004) and recent research indicates that alcohol consumption amongst young women has risen steeply to a point where there is now almost complete convergence with young men's alcohol consumption (Richards et al., 2004). Accompanying these trends has been a growth in binge drinking with young girls now reporting higher levels than their male counterparts (Currie et al., 2002). The UK now has one of the highest recorded rates of binge drinking and associated harm in the whole of Europe (Hibell et al., 1999). Alcohol consumption is associated with a broad range of social and health problems in the UK, at both personal and societal level (Klingemann and Gmel, 2001; World Health Organization (WHO), 2002).

Alcohol is currently a major topic given the considerable health and social impact generated by problem drinking (Prime Minister's Strategy Unit, 2004). This has led to significant interest in the factors which potentially influence drinking behaviour. One such factor that has been identified is alcohol marketing – but there is no consensus on its role, if any, in the problem. The alcohol industry has persistently argued that alcohol marketing has no effect on drinking behaviour but merely affects brands choice (Henry and Waterson, 1981). Meanwhile the health lobby generally take the view that alcohol marketing communications increase consumption of alcohol and are influential in the recruitment of new, often under age, drinkers.

The evidence on alcohol marketing and consumption comprises two types of evidence: (i) econometric studies that have used time series data to examine the relationship between aggregated alcohol consumption and supply variables such as advertising expenditure (Calfee and Scheraga, 1994; Duffy, 1990; Lee and Tremblay, 1992) and (ii) consumer studies examining the relationship between drinking behaviour and psychological effects such as recognition, appreciation and rewards derived from alcohol advertisements (Aitken et al., 1988). Though both types of studies have demonstrated links between alcohol advertising and behaviour, doubt remains over the strength and comprehensiveness of the evidence base, certainly in the minds of policy-makers:

> There is no clear case on the effect of advertising on behaviour. One recent study suggests that such an effect may exist, but is contradicted by others which find no such case. So the evidence is not sufficiently strong to suggest that measures such as a ban on

advertising or tightening existing restrictions about scheduling should be imposed by regulation.

Prime Minister's Strategy Unit (2004, p. 32)

This demonstrates the necessity of constructing a strong evidence base through primary research. Recent studies have suggested a causal link between alcohol marketing and drinking behaviour (Stacy et al., 2004; Snyder et al., 2006; Ellickson et al., 2006). Nevertheless there are undoubtedly gaps in the evidence base on the impact of alcohol marketing on drinking behaviour; there has been no longitudinal research carried out in the UK, no studies have looked at the impact of new media and viral marketing, there has been no attempt to examine the cumulative impact of marketing communications and branding, and no one has checked for any differential effect in terms of gender and inequality.

Research that commenced in 2006 at the Institute for Social Marketing (ISM) will aim to address some of the gaps in the evidence base and the lack of research carried out on the issue in the UK. The project, 'Assessing the Cumulative Impact of Alcohol Marketing Communications on Youth Drinking' will use a tried and tested research design adapted from the field of tobacco control research; with the inclusion of a longitudinal survey component and study cohort to provide an assessment of causal links between marketing communications and under-age drinking. The study will address the gaps in the evidence base as longitudinal research on the topic has not been carried out previously in the UK and previous studies have not assessed the cumulative impact of the whole marketing mix on youth drinking. The study along with similar research about to commence in New Zealand will add to the evidence base and allow for more informed policy decisions.

Documentation Analysis and the Marketing of Prescription-Only Medicines

In recent years, the marketing practices of the pharmaceutical industry have also been subject to scrutiny and criticism. One key area of concern is that inappropriate marketing may lead to the medicalization of society and an increase in the risk of drug-induced illness. In the UK, prescription-only (PO) medicines cannot be marketed directly to the public, and marketing to health professionals is self-regulated by the Association of the British Pharmaceutical Industry's (ABPI's) Code of Practice.

Very recently, and as part of its inquiry into the influence of the pharmaceutical industry, the House of Commons Health Select Committee commissioned a study of internal marketing documents that it had obtained from five UK pharmaceutical companies (Devlin et al., 2005). Each company was instructed to provide all promotional and product support material for specific brands or programmes. The Committee requested a range of documents, including: contact reports between clients and agencies, client briefs, creative briefs, media briefs, market research reports, details of public relations activity and any other documents relating to promotion and product support. A total of 49 boxes were obtained. It is impossible to know what proportion of the requested documents were sent, and if any were withheld. It is also possible that documents may have been lost or destroyed before the investigation. In addition, three of the five companies provided a very limited set of papers (e.g. one company provided 21 boxes of documents for two products, while another provided only three boxes to cover the same amount of activity). These problems meant that the research was limited to a small selection of marketing material, and that, if anything, was likely to understate any problems.

A qualitative analysis was undertaken on the documents to examine the provision of drug information and promotion, and assess the influence of the industry on prescribers, patients, consumers and the general public (House of Commons Health Committee, 2005). The aim of this analysis was to examine whether the marketing of PO medicines contravened the specifications outlined in the Code of Practice. Analysing such a large body of data qualitatively is best conducted using key themes (Silverman, 1995) and this process has been used previously to analyse industry documents in the areas of tobacco and food (Hastings and MacFadyen, 2000; McDermott and Angus, 2003). The documents were therefore analysed around four key themes taken from the Code of Practice:

1 Patients and the general public should not be targeted.
2 Promotion to health professionals should be objective and unambiguous.
3 Companies must take full responsibility for their public relations activity and the payment of 'reasonable' honoraria is permitted.
4 Promotional activity should be transparent.

The research highlighted considerable concerns about how the current ABPI Code of Practice is working. It has shown that, on occasions, the marketing of PO medicines transgresses the Code. Specifically, it is clear that:

- The general public and patients *are* seen as deliberate targets for marketing communications for PO medicines, and clever use is made of phenomena like channel and source effects and emotional drivers to maximize audience susceptibility. These campaigns are tied in to the performance of specific brands.
- Campaigns targeting health professionals use emotional drivers, irrational constructs and branding strategies that are far removed from the Code's requirement for communications to be 'accurate, balanced, fair, objective and unambiguous'.
- Public relations and paid 'key opinion leaders' are used to counter bad publicity (especially about product safety), and the treatment of these issues does not appear to be objective or balanced.
- Brand marketing is disguised and the need for new brands is artificially created prior to launch.

This examination clearly highlights huge contradictions between the Code of Practice and what is actually happening in reality. Documentation analysis is capable of revealing these kinds of discrepancies because it allows us to examine commercial marketing practice from an inside perspective. Clearly this provides us with much deeper and more reliable insights into marketers' activities; insights that would be lost if we were able only to rely on what we were told. Furthermore, this kind of research is capable of having a very direct bearing on both practice and policy as it highlights very specific cases where the Code of Practice just simply is not working. On the basis of this research, recommendations were made – not simply to strengthen the apparent weaknesses in the Code – but to radically overhaul the entire regulatory framework.

Documentation analysis has also been used extensively in the field of tobacco control to inform research and decision-making surrounding tobacco marketing, examining tobacco industry documents to assess how their products are marketed to consumers (Anderson et al., 2006; Cummings et al., 2002; Pollay, 2000).

In the following section we demonstrate how social marketing can provide solutions by effecting behaviour change in a variety of areas.

Changing Behaviour

Marketing is about changing behaviour and although much of the focus of marketing is geared towards consumption, and social marketing towards health behaviour change there are many very useful forms of behaviour change that society needs beyond mere consumption. Social marketing can be used to effect a wide range of behaviour changes in many different spheres; societal (e.g. introducing the Euro), political (e.g. promoting the EU), environmental (e.g. recycling) and health (e.g. smoking cessation, healthy eating). Very recently, a series of SRs demonstrated the ability of social marketing to improve diet, increase physical activity and tackle substance misuse (McDermott et al., in press; Stead et al., 2006).

Consideration of two case studies of social marketing influencing behaviour change can demonstrate this point; the Euro Introduction in France between 1997 and 2002 and the 'Help' programme, the anti-smoking campaign of the European Commission running between 2005 and 2008.

The Introduction of the Euro in France

The first example relates to the introduction of the Euro in France which occurred in 2002. A social marketing campaign was launched by the EU to ease the transition to the Euro by informing and improving people's attitudes towards the single currency in France which was ambivalent during the 1990s (Merriman, 2002). The main purpose of the campaign was to raise awareness amongst the French population of the impending changes and to effect behaviour change during the switch to the Euro in 2001–2002. Importantly the campaign sought to construct the correct social marketing mix much in the same way as the principals of commercial marketing, through the correct integration of, and coordination with all the relevant stakeholders such as The Finance

Ministry, Education Ministry, Central Bank, NGOs, Employers Organizations, Consumer Organizations and the Trade Unions.

Challenges facing the campaign included addressing the public perception of the European Union and Commission in France, public opinion surrounding currency change, discourse amongst consumer organizations and civil society around purchasing power, and reconciling the various messages emanating from the European institutions.

Phase 1 of the campaign was targeted at the population at large but was also segmented and targeted the private sector, school children, the elderly, disabled people and the poorest populations. The programme was aimed at the public at large through campaigns on TV and in the print media, at school children through information booklets and exercise books, the private sector through print media campaigns and information booklets and the elderly through posters and accounting booklets.

A key theme during the campaign and indeed with all social marketing interventions is the requirement to maintain message consistency. Often target audiences demonstrate apathy in terms of response to social communication messages, therefore a long-term view is required and messages need to maintain consistency over time. This can often be despite frequent pressures for change from a variety of political, commercial and societal sources.

Message consistency in the social marketing campaign for the introduction of the Euro into France was successfully maintained through the 6-year programme. This was achieved in the most part through the creative concept of Phase 2: the main campaign protagonist Lise. Lise was an adolescent girl who featured in campaign communications such as TV adverts, a Guide to the Euro, print media communications and on the web. The character was constructed to symbolize proximity, the future, simplicity and solidarity (see Figure 11.1).

The social marketing campaign designed to help with the transition to the Euro in France was a success with analysts commenting on a 'successful transition' . . . which 'was so much easier than that which occurred at the beginning of the Fifth Republic' (Merriman, 2002) with the successful introduction of the Euro demonstrating that 'a decade of social marketing by European governments could succeed' (Holden, 2001). This was despite forecasts of bleak and insurmountable problems by a variety of prominent economists (Dornbusch, 1996, Feldman, 1997, Friedman, 1997). During the lifecycle of the campaign representative population samples were asked 'your opinion about the Euro is . . .' The Opinion Barometer showed mostly positive opinions highest during the apex of Phase 1 and then again at Phase 2 demonstrating the impact of the campaign on public opinion, peaking at a high of 74% during February 2002 (see Figure 11.2).

The EC Help Anti-smoking Campaign

Tobacco is the largest single cause of preventable death, accounting for one in every seven fatalities, or over 650,000 deaths every year in the 25 Member States of the EU (ASPECT, 2004). As part of its tobacco control strategy, the European Commission has implemented an anti-smoking campaign across all 25 Member States (2005 Memo 05/68). The Help campaign builds upon previous EC anti-tobacco campaigns but is the first to be implemented in all 25 Member States.

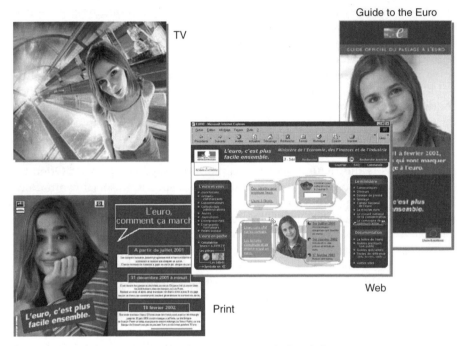

Figure 11.1 Campaign communications for the transition to the Euro in France.

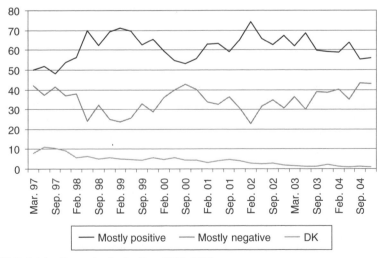

Figure 11.2 Opinion Barometer for the Euro 1997–2004.

Their combined population of over 450 million and the campaign's €72 million budget makes it one of the biggest ever social advertising campaigns.

The campaign aims to highlight the harmful effects of both active and passive smoking, encourage smokers to quit and promote a tobacco-free society. Its key component is a series of TV adverts featuring the same visual content but equivalent voiceover messages in the native language of each Member State. That said the campaign is much broader than just advertising. Support activities include a road-show which visited each of the 25 capitals prior to the first wave of advertising, PR activity, a web site that is, especially tailored to young people (www.help-eu.com), and links to existing smoking quit lines. The campaign has utilized several key principles of a social marketing approach including consumer research (comprising both extensive qualitative pre-testing of the campaign and quantitative post-test research across Europe), segmentation and targeting (by focusing on young adults and accounting for cultural difference between countries) and branding.

Stakeholder marketing is also a crucial component of the campaign. A diverse range of individuals and organizations have a vested interest in the campaign including the European Commission, the tobacco control community, the media, the respective health ministries in the Member States and the general public. Great efforts have been made to get these stakeholders 'onside' in order to maximize the impact of the campaign.

The research undertaken on the campaign to date shows that it is having a positive effect, especially on young people. Telephone interviews conducted with over 25 000 individuals across Europe revealed that over half (55%) of Europeans aged under 25 had been exposed to at least one of the three Help TV adverts.

The two cases examined here demonstrate that social marketing offers a framework for effecting behaviour change in a wide variety of fields, not just in health but in the political and wider societal spheres also. Furthermore social marketing behaviour change campaigns have been used and have proved successful in environmental as well as the more traditional health behaviour change uses.

Conclusion

Marketing is under threat from both external attacks and internal reservations and 'the dominance of marketing by the amoral scientism of the logical empiricists has led to material enslavement of modern societies' (Lowe et al., 2005, p. 198). The marketing discipline needs to be reclaimed, rescued and requires 'to promote a slowing down of frenetic consumption and to reduce the speed of global material greed and instant gratification' (Lowe et al., 2005, p. 198). If it is to survive as a serious and viable academic discipline it has to change: its use as a commercial tool has to be moderated and its powers brought to bear on more socially desirable goals; social marketing provides a coherent framework for achieving this.

References

Alvesson, M. (1994). 'Critical Theory and Consumer Marketing'. *Scandinavian Journal of Management*, 10(3), 291–313.

Anderson, S.J., Dewhirst, T. and Ling, P.M. (2006). 'Every document and picture tells a story: using internal corporate document reviews, semiotics, and content analysis to assess tobacco advertising'. *Tobacco Control*, 15, 254–261.

Aitken, P.P., Leather, D.S. and Scott, A.C. (1988). 'Ten-to sixteen-year-olds' perceptions of advertisements for alcoholic drinks'. *Alcohol and Alcoholism*, 23(6), 491–500.

ASPECT report (2004). 'Analysis of the Science and Policy for European Control of Tobacco,' European Commission.

Bakan, J. (2004). *The Corporation*. London: Constable.

Boaz, A., Ashby, D. and Young, K. (2002). 'Systematic reviews: what have they got to offer evidence based policy and practice?' *Working Paper 2*. ESRC UK Centre for Evidence Based Policy and Practice.

Brownlie, D. and Saren, M. (1997), 'Beyond the one-dimensional marketing manager: the discourse of theory, practice and relevance'. *International Journal of Research in Marketing*, 14, 147–161.

Burton, D. (2000). 'Critical Marketing Theory: the blueprint?' *European Journal of Marketing*, 35(5/6), 722–743.

Calfee, J. and Scheraga, C. (1994). 'The influence of advertising on alcohol consumption: a literature review and an econometric analysis of four European nations'. *International Journal of Advertising*, 13(4), 287–310.

Catterall, M., Maclaran, P. and Stevens, L. (1999). Marketing and Feminism: past, present and future. Accessed online at: http://www.mngt.waikato.ac.nz/ejrot/cmsconference/proceedings.htm

Chomsky, N. (2004). *The Apothesis of Ronald Reagan: Divinity Through Marketing*. Accessed online at: www.counterpunch.org

Chomsky, N. (2005). *Elections Run by Same Guys Who Sell Toothpaste*. Silver City, NM: International Relations Center.

Crane, A. (1997). 'The dynamics of marketing ethical products'. *Journal of Marketing Management*, 13, 6.

Cummings, K.M., Morley, C.P., Horan, J.K., Steger, C. and Leavell, N.R. (2002). 'Marketing to America's youth: evidence from corporate documents'. *Tobacco Control*, 11, 5–17.

Currie, C., Fairgrieve, J., Akhtar, P., Currie, D. (2002). *Scottish Schools Adolescent Lifestyle and Substance Misuse Survey*. National Report for the Scottish Executive, TSO.

Department of Health, HM Government, UK (2004). *Choosing Health: Making Healthier Choices Easier*. Public Health White Paper, Series No. CM 6374. London: The Stationery Office.

Devlin, E., Hasting, G. and Anderso, S. (2005). 'Dealing in drugs: an analysis of the pharmaceutical industry's marketing documents'. Appendix 33 (PI125) in *House of Commons Health Committee Report – The Influence of the Pharmaceutical Industry – 4th Report of Session 2004–05 Volume 2, 22nd March*.

London: The Stationery Office Ltd. http://www.publications.parliament.uk/pa/cm200405/cmselect/cmhealth/42/42ii.pdf

Dornbusch, R. (1996). 'Euro fantasies'. *Foreign Affairs*, September/October, 110–112.

Duffy, M. (1990). 'Advertising and alcoholic drink demand in the UK: some further Rotterdam model estimates'. *International Journal of Advertising*, 9, 247–257.

Fahy, J. (2000). 'Book review: No Logo'. *Journal of Marketing*, 64(3), 115–117.

Feldman, M. (1997). 'EMU and international conflict'. *Foreign Affairs* November/December, 60–73.

Firat, A.F. and Venkatesh, A. (1993). 'Postmodernity: the age of marketing'. *International Journal of Research in Marketing*, 10(3), 227–249.

Food Standards Agency (2003). *Outcome of an Academic Seminar to Review Recent Research on the Promotion of Foods to Children*, 31 October. London: Food Standards Agency.

Franke, G.R. (2001). 'Applications of meta-analysis for marketing and public policy: A review'. *Journal of Public Policy and Marketing*, 20, 2(Fall), 186.

Friedman, M. (1997). 'Why Europe Can't Afford the Euro'. *The Times* (London) (November 19).

Fuller, D.A. (1999). *Sustainable Marketing: Managerial–Ecological Issues*. London: Sage.

Goldberg, M.E. (1995), 'Social Marketing: are we fiddling while Rome burns?' *Journal of Consumer Psychology*, 4(4), 347–370.

Hastings, G. and MacFadyen, L.M. (2000). 'A day in the life of an advertising man: review of internal documents from the UK tobacco industry's principle advertising agencies'. *British Medical Journal*, 321, 366–371.

Hastings, G.B., Stead, M., McDermott, L., Forsyth, A., MacKintosh, A.M., Rayner, M., Godfrey, G., Carahar, M. and Angus, K. (2003). *Review of Research on the Effects of Food Promotion to Children – Final Report and Appendices. Prepared for the Food Standards Agency*. Published on Food Standards Agency website: www.foodstandards.gov.uk/news/newsarchive/promote

Henry, H.W. and Waterson, M.J. (1981). 'The case for advertising alcohol and tobacco products'. In D.S. Leather, G.B. Hastings and J.K. Davis (eds), *Health Education and the Media*. Oxford: Pergamon Press, pp. 115–127.

Hetrick, W.P. and Lozada, H.R. (1994) 'Constructing the Critical Imagination: Comments and Necessary Diversions', *Journal of Consumer Research*, 21 (December): 548–58.

Hibell, B., Andersson, B., Ahlström, S., Balakireva, O., Bjarnason, T., Kokkevi, A. and Morgan, M. (1999). *The 1999 European School Survey Project on Alcohol and Other Drugs (ESPAD) Report*.

House of Commons Health Committee (2005). *The Influence of the Pharmaceutical Industry – Fourth Report of Session 2005–05*, Vol. 1. London: The Stationery Office.

Holden, A. (2001). 'Who is watching the weakened Euro: U.S. international marketers hope someone in Europe will act'. *Academy of Collegiate Marketing Educators*. New Orleans: Louisiana (February 28–March 3).

ISD (2004). Alcohol briefing (unpublished report).

Jackson, M., Hastings, G., Wheeler, C., Eadie, D. and MacKintosh, A. (2000). Marketing alcohol to young people: implications for industry regulation and research policy. *Addiction* 95, S597–S608.

Jobber, D. (2001). *Principles and Practices of Marketing*. Maidenhead: McGraw Hill.

Klein, N. (2000). *No Logo: Taking Aim at the Brand Bullies*. London: Flamingo.

Klingemann, H. and Gmel, G. (2001). *Mapping the Social Consequences of Alcohol*. Dordrecht: Kluwer.

Kotler, P. and Zaltman, G. (1971). 'Social marketing: an approach to planned social change'. *Journal of Marketing*, 35, 3–12.

Lazer, W. and Kelley, E.J. (1973). *Social Marketing: Perspectives and Viewpoints*. Homewood: Richard D. Irwin.

Lee, B. and Tremblay, V.J. (1992). 'Advertising and the US market demand for beer'. *Applied Economics*, 24, 69–76.

Lefebvre, R.C. (1996). '25 years of Social Marketing: looking back to the future'. *Social Marketing Quarterly*, Special Issue, 51–58.

Lowe, S., Carr, A., Thomas, M. and Watkins-Mathys, L. (2005). 'The fourth hermeneutic in marketing theory'. *Marketing Theory*, 5(2), 185–203.

McDermott, L., Angus, K. (2003). Preliminary analysis of food industry advertising documents, Memorandum to the House of Commons Health Select Committee. November 2003. Available online: http://www.publications.parliament.uk/pa/cm200304/cmselect/cmhealth/23/23we62.htm

McDermott, L., O'Sullivan, T., Stead, M. and Hastings, G. (2006). Food advertising, pester power and its effects. *International Journal of Advertising*, **25**(4): 513–539.

McDermott, L., Stead, M., Hastings, G., Kent, R. and Banerjee, S. (under review). 'Social marketing interventions for changing nutrition behaviour: a systematic review', Submitted to *Preventive Medicine*.

McDermott et al. (under review). At the time of writing this paper is under review with *Preventive Medicine*.

Merriman, J. (2002). 'Some observations on the transition to the Euro in France'. *Conference on the Transition to the Euro*, University of Notre Dame.

Monbiot, G. (1995). 'Greens must be whiter than white'. *Guardian*, 5th October, archive accessed online at: www.monbiot.com

Monbiot, G. (1998). 'Pester power'. *Guardian*, December 4th, archive accessed online at: www.monbiot.com

Monbiot, G. (1999) 'No Politics Please', *Guardian*, August 26th, archive accessed online at www.monbiot.com

Monbiot, G. (2001). *Captive State: The Corporate Takeover of Britain*. London: Pan.

Monbiot, G. (2002). 'The fake persuaders'. *Guardian*, 14th May, archive accessed online at: www.monbiot.com

Monbiot, G. (2006). 'Feeding crime'. *Guardian*, 2nd May 2006, archive accessed online at: www.monbiot.com

Mulrow, C.D. (1994). 'Systematic reviews: rationale for systematic reviews'. *British Medical Journal*, 309, 597–599.

Murray, Jeff B., and Julie L. Ozanne, (1991). "The Critical Imagination: Emancipatory Interest in Consumer Research," *Journal of Consumer Research*," 18 (September), 129–144.

Ofcom (2006). 'Television advertising of food and drink products to children – Options for new restrictions'. Available at http://www.ofcom.org.uk/consult/condocs/foodads

Petticrew, M. (2001). 'Systematic reviews from astronomy to zoology: myths and misconceptions'. *British Medical Journal*, 332, 98–101.

Prime Minister's Strategy Unit (2004). *The alcohol harm reduction strategy for England*. London: The Stationery Office.

Pollay, R.W. (2000). 'Targeting youth and concerned smokers: evidence from Canadian tobacco industry documents'. *Tobacco Control*, 9, 136–147.

Richards, L., Fox, K., Roberts, C., Fletcher, L. and Goddard, E. (2004). *Living in Britain 31, Results from the 2002 General Household Survey*. London: ONS.

Silverman, D. (ed.) (1995). *Interpreting Qualitative Data*. London: Sage.

Snyder, L.B., Milici, F., Sun, X.H., Strizhakova, Y. and Slater, M. (2004). "*The Effects of Alcohol Advertising on Drinking Among Youth*," Archives of Pediatrics and Adolescent Medicine 160(2006): 18–24.

Stacy, A.W., Zogg, J.B., Unger, J.B. and Dent, C.W. (2004). 'Exposure to televised alcohol ads and subsequent adolescent alcohol'. *Use American Journal of Health Behaviour*, 28(6), 498–509.

Stead, M., Gordon, R., Angus, K. and McDermott, L. (2006). 'Effectiveness of social marketing interventions in bringing about individual, environmental and policy-level changes', paper submitted to *Health Education* (copy available from authors).

Thomas, M.J. (1999). 'Thoughts on building a just and stakeholding society'. *20th Anniversary Conference*, Alliance of Universities for Democracy, Budapest (Hungary), 7 November.

Which? (2006). 'Failing children: Ofcom's proposals on food advertising to children'. Accessed online at: http://www.which.net/campaigns/food/kidsfood/0604ofcomproposals.pdf

World Health Organization (2002). *The World Health Report 2002: Reducing Risks, Promoting Healthy Life*. Geneva: WHO.

Young, B. (2003). *Advertising and Food Choice in Children: A Review of the Literature*. London: The Advertising Association.

12

Making Sense of Consumer Disadvantage

Kathy Hamilton

Within new consumer behaviour research the emphasis on how consumption relates to the rest of human existence has created more legitimacy for macro- and non-managerial marketing topics (Belk, 1995). However, interest in societal consequences of marketing does not appear to extend the same degree of legitimacy to all consumer populations. Disadvantaged consumer groups often remain excluded or at least underrepresented in this research stream. As Henderson (1998, p. 157) notes, people in the non-dominant social system are traditionally 'underresearched and underserved'. From a critical marketing perspective, lack of interest in disadvantaged consumers is wrong. Critics suggest that the imbalance of marketing exchanges create inequities and unethical practices in the relationship between marketers and disadvantaged consumers (Alwitt and Donley, 1996). Criticism is also aimed at marketing's obsession with targeting the most wealthy and profitable consumers as a cause of social inequality (Curtis, 2000).

Recent calls for transformative consumer research have highlighted the need for further interest in this area (Association for Consumer Research, 2005). Transformative consumer research is research that has the potential to make a positive difference in the lives of consumers and as such is likely to be accompanied by increased interest in disadvantaged and vulnerable consumer groups. Researching such diverse consumer populations can result in insights into human behaviour that have the potential to enhance quality of life (Henderson, 1998; Moore and Miller, 1999). A less ambitious but still important aim is to provide such consumers with 'a voice'. Reinharz (1992) cites demystification as one of a number of transformative research strategies where the aim is to investigate and challenge common myths and stereotypes that persist about such groups.

This chapter focuses on those consumers who, for various reasons, are excluded from enjoying the benefits of a consumer society. The plethora of terms associated with consumer disadvantage can make it a confusing construct. In response, the chapter begins with an attempt to define what is meant by consumer disadvantage. The sources of disadvantage are then discussed. This is followed by a review of literature on various groups of disadvantaged consumers and finally future research areas are identified.

Defining Consumer Disadvantage and Related Constructs

Woodliffe (2004) highlights the need for further research interest on consumer disadvantage, particularly relating to its conceptualization and identifying and understanding its dimensions. Although the notion of the disadvantaged consumer has attracted some attention from retail geographers, marketers and consumer researchers, it has not been well defined. In order to contribute to transformative consumer research, it is important to understand the construct of consumer disadvantage. A better understanding of consumer disadvantage is also important in order for future studies to operationalize the term. Lack of interest in disadvantaged consumers means that the differences or similarities between terms such as consumer disadvantage, consumer vulnerability and consumer detriment remain obscure. The paucity of academic interest necessitates the help of regulators and various consumer-focused organizations to define the field of study. Definitions overlap and terms are defined in different ways by different authors. This section aims to make sense of this uncertainty.

The National Consumer Council (2003, p. 1) define consumer disadvantage as 'The extreme difficulties consumers experience in sustaining adequate consumption of a range of goods and services socially defined as necessary for meeting basic physical and social needs.' This definition raises a number of issues. First, adequate consumption is 'socially defined', meaning that the consumption activities of the general public rather than experts or analysts define what constitutes appropriate or acceptable consumer behaviour. Secondly, the importance placed on public perceptions indicates that consumer disadvantage is a relative concept, that is, consumers are disadvantaged if they encounter difficulties in meeting societal norms of consumption. Consequently, those defined as disadvantaged will differ according to the society to which they belong. Thirdly, this definition incorporates both physical and social needs. This is in line with the results of the Poverty and Social Exclusion Survey of

Britain (PSE) which indicate that the interpretation of necessities is no longer restricted to basic needs, but also includes social customs, obligations and activities (Gordon et al., 2000).

Bromley and Thomas (1993) suggest that there are two underlying dimensions of consumer disadvantage, first, poor mobility in terms of restricted access to shopping opportunities and secondly, social disadvantage, meaning the range of factors that reduce purchasing power and physically restricting disabilities that restrict shopping opportunities. In relation to access to goods and services, a defining feature of consumer disadvantage is poor mobility associated with carlessness (Bromley and Thomas, 1993). This creates disadvantage if goods and services are not available close to consumers' homes. For example, in the food retailing industry there has been interest in the concept of food deserts, that is, populated areas with little or no food retail provision (Cummins and Macintyre, 1999; Curtis, 2000). Further, in the financial sector, the geographical redistribution of financial infrastructure away from lower-income communities has resulted in geographical pockets of financial exclusion, economic decline, poverty and deprivation, as low-income households often do not have access to financial institutions and savings incentives (Beverly and Sherraden, 1999; Kempson et al., 2000; Leyshon and Thrift, 1995). Bromley and Thomas' (1993) second point suggests that poor consumers and physically disabled consumers may be particularly susceptible to consumer disadvantage. Research on each of these groups will be reviewed later in the chapter.

Several authors have attempted to define vulnerable consumers. In the following definition offered by Andreasen and Manning (1990, p. 13), a strong link is established between consumer disadvantage and consumer vulnerability. They suggest that vulnerable consumers are 'those who are at a disadvantage in exchange relationships where that disadvantage is attributable to characteristics that are largely not controllable by them at the time of the transaction'. Using this definition disadvantaged consumers can also be described as vulnerable consumers in that as consumer disadvantage increases, so too will consumer vulnerability. This definition provides further information about the source of vulnerability, implying that vulnerability is not attributable to the consumer's own faults. Baker et al. (2005) state that there are a variety of factors that are beyond consumers' control that contribute to vulnerability such as stigmatization, the distribution of resources, physical elements, logistical elements and other environmental conditions such as economic, social and political violence or upheaval. While vulnerability is created by factors outside the consumer's control, consumer disadvantage is not restricted to outside influences but may also derive from the personal characteristics of the consumer (e.g. Andreasen, 1975).

In a legal context, Morgan et al. (1995, p. 267) suggest that the term 'vulnerable consumers' is generally used by contemporary courts to describe 'small groups of consumers who have idiosyncratic reactions to products that are otherwise harmless when used by most people'. This is a narrow perspective, focusing only on product use. It thus neglects aspects of access and exchange restrictions that are integral to the definition of consumer disadvantage. The reference to 'small groups' also contrasts with statistics highlighting the extent of various forms of consumer disadvantage. In the USA, 12.7% of the population, some 37 million people, are said to be living in poverty (US Census Bureau, 2004). In the UK, the General Consumer Council (2001) estimate that between 13 and 14 million people live in poverty. It is estimated that there are 36 million people with chronic disabilities in the USA (Mueller, 1990) and 8.5 million in the UK (Kleinman, 2002).

Baker et al. (2005, p. 134) offer an alternative and more comprehensive definition of consumer vulnerability:

> Consumer vulnerability is a state of powerlessness that arises from an imbalance in marketplace interactions or from the consumption of marketing messages and products. It occurs when control is not in an individual's hands, creating a dependence on external factors (e.g. marketers) to create fairness in the marketplace. The actual vulnerability arises from the interaction of individual states, individual characteristics, and external conditions within a context where consumption goals may be hindered and the experience affects personal and social perceptions of self.

This definition highlights how the exchange relationships between vulnerable consumers and marketers results in a power imbalance in favour of marketers. Previous research has suggested that marketers do not use their power to create fairness in the marketplace. For example, Goss (1995) highlights how marketers use technology such as geodemographic information systems to gather information about customers and consequently increase their marketing power. This allows marketers to be more precise with their target marketing strategies and further alienate unwanted consumers. This definition also tells us something of the negative outcomes that can result from consumer vulnerability such as reduced self-esteem.

The definition of consumer vulnerability appears to be broader than the definition of consumer disadvantage. Baker et al. (2005) suggest that previous consumer vulnerability research includes investigations of groups based on the visible characteristics of individuals such as ethnicity, race and age; states of body such as disabilities; and states of mind such as grief. Research on states of mind demonstrates that all consumers have the potential to be vulnerable because everyone at some time will be affected by grief. As such, disadvantaged consumers are by definition vulnerable consumers but vulnerable consumers are not necessarily disadvantaged consumers. A further illustration of this relates to children. Research has suggested that children may be vulnerable to the persuasion attempts of advertising (Laczniak et al., 1995). However, this does not mean that all children encounter disadvantage in the marketplace.

Baker et al. (2005) suggest that the difference between consumer disadvantage and consumer vulnerability relates to the issue of personal characteristics. They suggest that consumers are vulnerable due to factors outside their control but consumers are disadvantaged due to personal characteristics. As such, consumer disadvantage refers to certain consumer groups while consumer vulnerability refers to barriers that limit control and freedom of choice. However, this distinction does not coincide with previous research. For example, Ringold (2005, p. 202) suggests that consumer vulnerability can arise from both personal characteristics as well as the marketplace barriers. She suggests vulnerable consumers cannot navigate the marketplace because they 'fail to understand their own preferences and/or lack the knowledge, skills or freedom (i.e. personal prerogatives and marketplace options) to act on them'. Equally, both the National Consumer Council's (2003) definition of consumer disadvantage (see above) and Andreasen's (1975) model of the sources of consumer disadvantage (to be discussed in the next section) demonstrate that consumer disadvantage is not only attributable to personal attributes.

Although not as commonly used, two other interrelated concepts are consumer deprivation and consumer detriment. Consumer deprivation is 'a state of observable and demonstrable disadvantage relative to the local community or the wider society or nation to which an individual, family or group belong' (Townsend 1987, p. 125). This primarily relates to consumer disadvantage caused by poverty. Research conducted for the Office of Fair Trading (OFT) (2006) suggests that consumer detriment arises when a consumer suffers as a result of dealings with an organization and where the suffering is at least partly attributable to the organization (accidentally or deliberately) treating the customer unfairly. This research suggests consumer detriment can be represented by financial loss, stress, inconvenience, fear or upset and disappointment. It advances previous research by the OFT that considered consumer detriment from an economic perspective, by acknowledging the psychological problems associated with consumer detriment. While consumer detriment refers to disadvantage resulting from dealings with a specific organization, consumer disadvantage is the broader concept that encompasses all detriment encountered in relation to accessing necessary goods and services.

To summarize, consumer disadvantage, consumer vulnerability, consumer deprivation and consumer detriment are overlapping and interrelated concepts that have been defined in different ways by different authors. As both consumer deprivation and consumer detriment are encompassed in consumer disadvantage, the main area for distinction is between consumer disadvantage and consumer vulnerability. It appears that there are two main areas for distinction. First, consumer vulnerability is not normally attributed to faults of the consumer but rather to barriers in the marketplace. Consumer disadvantage can be caused by both individual characteristics of consumers and barriers in the marketplace. The second distinction relates to scope. While all consumers are likely to encounter vulnerability at some point in their lives, not all consumers will be affected by consumer disadvantage.

Sources of Consumer Disadvantage

Andreasen (1975) suggests three basic hypotheses about the sources of consumer disadvantage that result in barriers to effective consumption. First, the disadvantaged consumer hypothesis argues that the problems of disadvantaged consumers are primarily attributable to their own personal characteristics including values, attitudes and goals. Secondly, the market structure hypothesis claims that the problem is the places where the disadvantaged consumers shop and finally, the exploitation hypothesis argues that the problem is the exploitative practices of the merchants with whom disadvantaged consumers come in contact. These three hypotheses are not mutually exclusive.

However, Andreasen's (1975) sources of consumer disadvantage are dated and no longer reflect and demonstrate the multiple sources of disadvantage in today's society. In relation to individual characteristics, Andreasen (1975) implies that disadvantage can be blamed on the actions of individual consumers. However, this neglects the fact that disadvantage can also emanate from personal forces outside the control of the individual such as disability, race or gender.

Although Andreasen (1975) demonstrates that consumer disadvantage can be attributed to marketers, the transition to a consumer society (Miles, 2001) has greatly increased the extent of marketer-induced disadvantage. Market place forces that increase consumer disadvantage include factors relating to the structural context in which consumers live. It is argued that we live in a consumer society that is 'directed largely by the accumulation and consumption of material goods' (O'Shaughnessy and O'Shaughnessy, 2002, p. 525). As Arnould and Thompson (2005) suggest, a central feature of the consumer culture are desire-inducing marketing symbols. The various techniques employed by marketers to increase awareness of social comparison and the need to keep up, create a strong social pressure to consume (Szmigin, 2003) and contribute to the exclusion and shame for those for whom this is not possible (Bowring, 2000).

The pressures to conform are also augmented by the increased emphasis placed on consumption as an expression of identity (Belk, 1988). Baudrillard (1998) advocates the sign value of consumption suggesting that it should be defined as a system of communication and exchange. Disadvantaged consumers who encounter difficulties in accessing goods and services are denied this opportunity of identity creation as they cannot participate in the consumption experiences needed to 'buy' their identities. Through various marketing communication messages, marketers promote a consumption lifestyle that advocates the abundance of consumption opportunities and constructs an ideology of free choice. However, free choice is dependent on the ability to access consumer goods and services, denying disadvantaged consumers many of the advantages and enhancement associated with this style of consumption.

Who are Disadvantaged Consumers?

Much of the research on consumer disadvantage focuses on one group of consumers rather than taking a holistic view (Woodliffe, 2004). Some of the consumer groups identified as disadvantaged consumers will now be discussed with reference to the relevant literature.

Poor or Low-Income Consumers

Poor or low-income consumers are individuals whose financial resources or income results in them being unable to obtain the goods and services needed for an 'adequate' and 'socially acceptable' standard of living (Darley and Johnson, 1985). The poor, who are limited in their ability to respond to the temptations of the marketplace, have been marginalized from mainstream society and described as 'unwanted', 'abnormal', 'non-consumers' and 'flawed consumers' (Bauman, 1998). This marginalization is accentuated by marketers disinterest in poorer consumers (Curtis, 2000). Poor consumers face a number of exchange restrictions that lead to consumer disadvantage in the marketplace such as limited product availability (Hill and Stephens, 1997).

Since the publication of *The Poor Pay More* (Caplovitz, 1967), it has generally been accepted that the poor suffer price discrimination in the marketplace. Early research concluded that poor consumers in the UK face a consumer detriment factor of 11%, meaning that poor families have to spend 11% extra to get equivalent goods and services to average families (Aird, 1977). Many studies have investigated the price of food for low-income consumers (Bell and Burlin, 1993; Chung and Myers, 1999; Coe, 1971; Cummins and Macintyre, 1999; General Consumer Council, 2001; Goodman, 1968). Evidence has confirmed that supermarket prices are often higher in poor neighbourhoods, resulting in the poor paying more for grocery products because the stores that charge the lowest prices are not located in their neighbourhoods (Chung and Myers, 1999).

Another potential reason for the inflated prices offered to low-income consumers may be the dubious and unethical practices of marketers. Andreasen (1975, p. 180) suggests that exploitative merchants use an endless range of techniques to encourage poor consumers to purchase products that they cannot afford and to pay more than they need to. For example, the 'free' gimmick, where the gimmick is not free but the cost is incorporated into the price of the tie-in item, or the 'fear-sell' tactic, where consumers are convinced there will be dire consequences unless the product or service is acquired, is often used to encourage poor consumers to purchase insurance services. More recent research in the USA suggests that direct price discrimination occurs when some shops in low-income areas increase prices to coincide with the issue of welfare and various government support cheques (Bell and Burlin, 1993). Furthermore, in the UK, the Citizens' Organizing Foundation have criticized a number of major supermarket chains, including Tesco and Sainsbury's, for charging higher prices in poor areas than in rich areas (Monbiot, 2000).

Poor consumers often show great skills in exploiting their environment to exert some control within their lives and adapt to the financial realities with which they are faced (Alwitt and Donley, 1996; Hill and Stephens, 1997). In their model of impoverished consumer behaviour, Hill and Stephens (1997) categorize coping strategies as either emotional or behavioural. Emotional coping strategies include distancing or fantasizing about a better future (Hill and Stephens, 1997). Kempson et al. (1994) found that low-income consumers adopt a number of behavioural coping strategies including maximizing income, managing the family budget, obtaining financial help from others and making use of consumer credit.

Low Literate Consumers

Adkins and Ozanne (2005a, p. 94) define consumer literacy as 'the ability to find and manipulate text and numbers to accomplish consumption-related tasks within a specific marketing context in which other skills and knowledge are also employed'.

Low-literate consumers may face economic, physical and psychological harm in meeting their consumer needs and may view the marketplace as a 'threatening place' (Adkins and Ozanne, 2005b, p. 155). Low literate consumers experience consumer disadvantage because lack of literacy skills limits their ability to process information in the marketplace (Viswanathan and Harris, 1999). The evaluation of alternatives for low literate consumers may require considerable cognitive effort even for tasks that others regard as straightforward (Wallendorf, 2001). Indeed, Viswanathan and Harris (2001) found that low literate consumers make little attempt to evaluate alternatives; rather they focus on perceptual processes such as locating a product or reading price information. Similarly, Jae and DelVecchio (2004) found that low literate consumers encounter disadvantage when making product choices because they tend to choose products based on peripheral cues (e.g. package colour) rather than central cues. This results in substandard product choices as peripheral cues can drive choice for poorer quality products.

Adkins and Ozanne (2005a) found that low literate consumers coped with their situations with varying degrees of success thus influencing the extent to which they experience consumer disadvantage. Some low literate consumers are disempowered in the marketplace and find exchange transactions stressful. They make mistakes such as buying the wrong product or failing to properly cook prepackaged food. These low literate consumers constrain their buying thus limiting their choice of goods and services, and frequently do not get their needs met. On the other hand, Adkins and Ozanne (2005a) found that some low literate consumers may employ a range of coping strategies to fight against the stigma of illiteracy, thus challenging the stereotype of the low literate consumer being vulnerable.

Disabled Consumers

Disabled consumers refer to those who are 'limited in significant ways that impair their daily activities and consumer behaviour' (Baker et al., 2001, p. 215). Kaufman (1995) suggests that marketers and consumer researchers have not adequately considered the needs of disabled consumers. Indeed, rather than considering disabled consumers as a viable target market, the disabled consider is only viewed as important in terms of creating a barrier-free shopping environment to meet the demands of disability discrimination legislation (Burnett, 1996). Reedy (1993) suggests that disabled consumers can be divided into four groups, namely mobility impairments, hearing impairments, visual impairments and speech impairments. Although research is limited, mobility-impaired and visually impaired consumers have received some attention by consumer researchers.

The challenges faced by the mobility-impaired spend much less time shopping consumers restricts aspects of typical consumer behaviour, for example, access may be restricted in terms of transportation access or access in certain store environments. Kaufman-Scarborough (1999) found that mobility-disabled consumers encounter a number of obstacles in the marketplace, for example, inaccessible displays and difficulty trying on clothes in fitting rooms. The embarrassment cause by access difficulties may also limit the choice of goods and services for mobility-disabled consumers. To illustrate, Burnett (1996) found that mobility-impaired consumers are more likely to shop for necessities in grocery stores rather than speciality or department stores. Additionally, in comparison to non-disabled consumers, the mobility-impaired spend much less time shopping.

Baker (2006) found that visually impaired consumers want to experience consumer normalcy, that is, live like other consumers and be acceptable to both themselves and others in consumption contexts. Baker et al.'s (2001) research demonstrates that such consumers attempt to cope and adapt to their situations to maintain some degree of independence in the marketplace. They use a variety of alternative sources to help them gather information such as memories of past experiences, listening to advertisements on the TV or radio, selecting products by feel and smell or enlisting the help of a personal shopper.

Minorities

Ethnic minorities may encounter consumer disadvantage in the form of retail redlining. This occurs when firms do not serve certain neighbourhoods if they are composed primarily of ethnic-minority households regardless of their ability to pay for the goods and services (D'Rozario and Williams, 2005). One example of this is provided by Crockett and Wallendorf (2004) who discuss the plight of Milwaukee's largely black and Hispanic neighbourhoods who face consumer disadvantage in the form of restricted access to goods and services in areas such as banking and financial services, housing, clothing and pharmacies. It is suggested that an uneven distribution of stores results in the highest priced retailers with the worst food selection being located in Black Milwaukee.

Penaloza (1995) highlights a number of factors that make Mexican immigrants vulnerable to consumer disadvantage in the USA. These include difficulties with reading or speaking English and difficulties with a new currency. Many immigrants also hold the belief that the US market system exhibits qualities of fairness, leaving them open to disadvantage in market exchanges. For example, immigrants may be offered Spanish food and music at a premium price.

Research has also been critical of advertising that contributes to stereotypes of minority consumers (Bristor et al., 1995; Taylor et al., 2005). Bristor et al. (1995) found that television advertisements involving African Americans indicate a subtle ideology of white superiority as portrayals of African Americans remain narrow and they are often assigned token roles with limited exposure time. Similarly, Taylor et al.'s (2005) investigation of Asian Americans in magazine advertisements also suggests that stereotypes persist and Asian Americans are seldom portrayed in family or social settings.

Further Research

Although there has been some research interest in different groups of disadvantaged consumers, there remains much potential for future research inquiry. As disadvantaged consumers are not often the subject of interest within marketing and consumer research, further investigation aimed at questioning myths and stereotypes is needed (Hamilton and Catterall, 2005).

Research suggests that consumers who are disadvantaged in terms of poverty (Hill and Stephens, 1997), illiteracy (Adkins and Ozanne, 2005a) and disability (Baker et al., 2001) employ coping strategies in attempts to minimize disadvantage. This suggests that disadvantaged consumers attempt to exert some control over their lives. Future studies on coping strategies could focus on control in terms of consumer empowerment. Knowledge of coping strategies employed by disadvantaged consumers could also be used to develop consumer education programmes. In line with the aim of transformative consumer research, studies such as this are needed as they can result in real benefits for consumers.

None of the definitions suggest that consumer disadvantage is a permanent state; rather it is a dynamic concept. For example, the average length of time in poverty ranges from 4 months (O'Boyle, 1998) to just over 4 years (Alwitt and Donley, 1996). However, research to date has focused on the experiences and hardships people endure while living in poverty with little attention given to the actual transition process. Future studies on the effects of income reductions could adopt before and after or continuous approaches, for example, identifying families approaching retirement or families in communities facing significant job losses or redundancies from the closure or downsizing of employer companies. The ways in which families escape from poverty, how they adapt to an increase in income and the reconstruction of identity after the transition from poverty all offer potential as future research topics. In terms of consumer literacy, studies could span before and after literacy programmes.

At present disadvantaged consumers are, in many instances, neglected consumers. Fischer (2000) suggests that it is debatable whether consumers marginalized by the market are better or worse off in not attracting the attention of marketers. For example, companies are criticized for targeting sin products, such as alcohol and cigarettes at disadvantaged consumers. As companies are increasingly expected to fulfil social responsibility aims, perhaps marketers should not be permitted to deliberately neglect and abdicate responsibility for meeting the needs of disadvantaged consumers. The important issue here is that disadvantaged consumers (especially the poor) are only targeted with necessity products, so as they are not placed under more pressure to consume what they cannot afford. Information on the consumer loyalty, lifetime value and bad debts of disadvantaged groups such as the poor or ethnic minorities may go some way to dispel the assumption that disadvantaged consumers are risky and unprofitable.

In line with this, studies of businesses that have profitably targeted disadvantaged consumers may encourage businesses to be more creative and innovative ·in relation to target marketing and the development and promotion of products/services aimed at disadvantaged consumers (see Curtis, 2000). Marketing and consumer researchers are often encouraged to conduct research in line with business interests and profit goals, one possible reason for the neglect of disadvantaged consumers. However, Prahalad's (2006), *The Fortune at the Bottom of Pyramid* provides excellent examples of how marketers can meet the needs of poor consumers and simultaneously make a profit.

As well as research on disadvantaged consumer groups, future research could focus on other parties involved in exchanges with disadvantaged consumers. For example, studies could consider the marketers' perspective in terms of how they view transactions with disadvantaged consumers. It may also be interesting to consider the relationship between disadvantaged and non-disadvantaged consumers. To illustrate, research on the societal perceptions of disadvantaged consumers would provide a deeper understanding of the stigmatization process.

Conclusion

Research suggests that some groups of consumers face real disadvantages in the marketplace. Indeed some consumers may be doubly disadvantaged, for example, there may be overlap between low literate consumers and low-income consumers (Adkins and Ozanne, 2005a) or between disabled consumers and low-income consumers (Burnett, 1996). This chapter has attempted to clarify the definition and scope of consumer disadvantage with the aim of encouraging future research in this area. Research on disadvantaged consumers has the potential to offer benefits to the consumers under study perhaps by affecting public policy. There may also be wider implications as research in this area may also contribute to knowledge on non-disadvantaged consumers. This suggests that it is time to raise the profile of disadvantaged groups.

References

Adkins, N.R. and Ozanne, J.L. (2005a). 'The low literate consumer'. *Journal of Consumer Research*, 32(1), 93–105.

Adkins, N.R. and Ozanne, J.L. (2005b). 'Critical consumer education: empowering the low-literate consumer'. *Journal of Macromarketing*, 25(2), 153–162.

Aird, A. (1977). 'Goods and services'. In F. Williams (ed.), *Why the Poor Pay More*. London: Macmillan Press for the National Consumer Council.

Alwitt, L.F. and Donley, T.D. (1996). *The Low-Income Consumer, Adjusting the Balance of Exchange*. Thousand Oaks, CA: Sage.

Andreasen, A.R. (1975). *The Disadvantaged Consumer*. New York: The Free Press.

Andreasen, A.R. and Manning, J. (1990). 'The dissatisfaction and complaining behavior of vulnerable consumers'. *Journal of Consumer Satisfaction, Dissatisfaction and Complaining Behavior*, 3, 12–20.

Arnould, E.J. and Thompson, C.J. (2005). 'Consumer culture theory (CCT): twenty years of research'. *Journal of Consumer Research*, 31(4), 868–882.

Association for Consumer Research (2005). 'For consumers: steps towards transformative consumer research'. Call for Papers. San Antonio, TX: Association for Consumer Research.

Baker, S.M. (2006). 'Consumer normalcy: understanding the value of shopping through narratives of consumers with visual impairments'. *Journal of Retailing*, 82(1), 37–50.

Baker, S.M., Stephens, D.L. and Hill, R.P. (2001). 'Marketplace experiences of consumers with visual impairments: beyond the Americans with disabilities act'. *Journal of Public Policy and Marketing*, 20(2), 215–224.

Baker, S.M., Gentry, J.W. and Rittenburg, T.L. (2005). 'Building understanding in the domain of consumer vulnerability'. *Journal of Macromarketing*, 25(2), 128–139.

Baudrillard, J. (1998). *The Consumer Society*. London: Sage.

Bauman, Z. (1998). *Work, Consumerism and the New Poor*. Buckingham: Open University Press.

Belk, R.W. (1988). 'Possessions and the extended self'. *Journal of Consumer Research*, 15(2), 139–168.

Belk, R.W. (1995). 'Studies in the new consumer behaviour'. In D. Miller (ed.), *Acknowledging Consumption*. London: Routledge, pp. 58–95.

Bell, J. and Burlin, B.M. (1993). 'In urban areas: many of the poor still pay more for food'. *Journal of Public Policy and Marketing*, 12(2), 268–271.

Beverly, S.G. and Sherraden, M. (1999). 'Institutional determinants of saving: implications for low-income households and public policy'. *Journal of Socio-Economics*, 28, 457–473.

Bowring, F. (2000). 'Social exclusion: limitations of the debate'. *Critical Social Policy*, 20(3), 307–330.

Bristor, J.M., Lee, R.G. and Hunt, M.R. (1995). 'Race and ideology: African-American images in television advertising'. *Journal of Public Policy and Marketing*, 14(1), 48–59.

Bromley, R.D.F. and Thomas, C. (1993). 'The retail revolution, the carless shopper and disadvantage'. *Transactions of the Institute of British Geographers*, 18(2), 222–236.

Burnett, J.J. (1996). 'What services marketers need to know about the mobility-disabled consumer'. *The Journal of Services Marketing*, 10(3), 3–20.

Caplovitz, D. (1967). *The Poor Pay More, Consumer Practices of Low-Income Families*. New York: The Free Press.

Chung, C. and Myers, S.L. (1999). 'Do the poor pay more for food? An analysis of grocery store availability and food price disparities'. *The Journal of Consumer Affairs*, 33(2), 276–296.

Coe, B.D. (1971). 'Private versus national preference among lower and middle income consumers'. *Journal of Retailing*, 47(3), 61–72.

Crockett, D. and Wallendorf, M. (2004). 'The role of normative political ideology in consumer behavior'. *Journal of Consumer Research*, 31(3), 511–528.

Cummins, S. and Macintyre, S. (1999). 'The location of food stores in urban areas: a case study in Glasgow'. *British Food Journal*, 101(7), 545–553.

Curtis, J. (2000). 'Low income, low priority'. *Marketing*, 26(October), 36–37.

Darley, W.K. and Johnson, D.M. (1985). 'A contemporary analysis of the low income consumer: an international perspective'. In C.T. Tan and J.N. Sheth (eds), *Historical Perspectives in Consumer Research: National and International Perspectives*. Provo, UT: Association for Consumer Research, pp. 206–210.

D'Rozario, D. and Williams, J.D. (2005). 'Retail redlining: definition, theory, typology, and measurement'. *Journal of Macromarketing*, 25(2), 175–186.

Fischer, E. (2000). 'A postmodern analysis of the implications of the discourse of mass customisation for marginalised and prized consumers'. In M. Catterall, P. Maclaran and L. Stevens (eds), *Marketing and Feminism*. London: Routledge, pp. 220–238.

General Consumer Council (2001). 'Hungry for change – community action to tackle food poverty'. *The Price of Being Poor*, Paper 1. Northern Ireland: General Consumer Council.

Goodman, C.S. (1968). 'Do the poor pay more?' *Journal of Marketing*, 32 (January), 18–24.

Gordon, D., Adelman, L., Ashworth, K., Bradshaw, J., Levitas, R., Middleton, S., Pantazis, C., Patsios, D., Payne, S., Townsend, P. and Williams, J. (2000). *Poverty and Social Exclusion in Britain*. York: Joseph Rowntree Foundation.

Goss, J. (1995). 'Marketing the new marketing: the strategic discourse of geodemographic information systems'. In J. Pickles (ed.), *Ground Truth*. New York: The Guilford Press, pp. 130–170.

Hamilton, K. and Catterall, M. (2005). 'Towards a better understanding of the low-income consumer'. In G. Menon and A.R. Rao (eds), *Advances in Consumer Research*, Vol. 32. Duluth, MN: Association for Consumer Research, pp. 627–632.

Henderson, K.A. (1998). 'Researching diverse populations'. *Journal of Leisure Research*, 30(1), 157–175.

Hill, R.P. and Stephens, D.L. (1997). 'Impoverished consumers and consumer behavior: the case of AFDC mothers'. *Journal of Macromarketing*, 17(2), 32–48.

Jae, H. and DelVecchio, D. (2004). 'Decision making by low-literacy consumers in the presence of point-of-purchase information'. *The Journal of Consumer Affairs*, 38(2), 342–354.

Kaufman, C.F. (1995). 'Shop 'til you drop: tales from a physically challenged shopper'. *Journal of Consumer Marketing*, 12(3), 39–55.

Kaufman-Scarborough, C. (1999). 'Reasonable access for mobility-disabled persons is more than widening the door'. *Journal of Retailing*, 75(4), 479–508.

Kempson, E., Bryson, A. and Rowlingson, K. (1994). *Hard Times? How Poor Families Make Ends Meet*. London: Policy Studies Institute.

Kempson, E., Whyley, C., Caskey, J. and Collard, S. (2000). *'In or Out? Financial Exclusion: A Literature and Research Review'*. London: Financial Services Authority.

Kleinman, M. (2002). 'Fight to end invisibility of UK's disabled consumers'. *Marketing*, 25(July), 15.

Laczniak, R.N., Muehling, D.D. and Carlson, L. (1995). 'Mothers' attitudes towards 900-number advertising directed at children'. *Journal of Public Policy and Marketing*, 14(1), 108–116.

Leyshon, A. and Thrift, N. (1995). 'Geographies of financial exclusion: financial abandonment in Britain and the United States'. *Transactions – Institute of British Geographers*, 20, 312–341.

Miles, S. (2001). *Social Theory in the Real World*. London: Sage.

Monbiot, G. (2000). *Captive State: The Corporate Takeover of Britain*. London: Pan Books.

Moore, L.W. and Miller, M. (1999). 'Initiating research with doubly vulnerable populations'. *Journal of Advanced Nursing*, 30(5), 1034–1040.

Morgan, F.W., Schuler, D.K. and Stoltman, J.J. (1995). 'A framework for examining the legal status of vulnerable consumers'. *Journal of Public Policy and Marketing*, 14(2), 267–277.

Mueller, J.L. (1990). '"Real" consumers just aren't normal'. *Journal of Consumer Marketing*, 7(1), 51–53.

National Consumer Council (2003). *Everyday Essentials: Meeting Basic Needs: Research into Accessing Essential Goods and Services*. London: National Consumer Council.

O'Boyle, E.J. (1998). 'Transitions into and out of poverty'. *International Journal of Social Economics*, 25(9), 1411–1424.

Office of Fair Trading (2006). *Focus Group Research on Consumer Detriment*. London: Office of Fair Trading.

O'Shaughnessy, J. and O'Shaughnessy, N.J. (2002). 'Marketing, the consumer society and hedonism'. *European Journal of Marketing*, 36(5/6), 524–547.

Penaloza, L. (1995). 'Immigrant consumers: marketing and public policy considerations in the global economy'. *Journal of Public Policy and Marketing*, 14(1), 83–94.

Prahalad, C.K. (2006). *The Fortune at the Bottom of the Pyramid*. Upper Saddle River, NJ: Wharton School Publishing.

Reedy, J. (1993). *Marketing to Consumers with Disabilities*. Chicago, IL: Probus Publishing Co.

Reinharz, S. (1992). *Feminist Methods in Social Research*. New York: Oxford University Press.

Ringold, D.J. (2005). 'Vulnerability in the marketplace: concepts, caveats, and possible solutions'. *Journal of Macromarketing*, 25(2), 202–214.

Szmigin, I. (2003). *Understanding the Consumer*. London: Sage.

Taylor, C.R., Landreth, S. and Bang, H. (2005). 'Asian Americans in magazine advertising: portrayals of the "model minority"'. *Journal of Macromarketing*, 25(2), 163–174.

Townsend, P. (1987). 'Deprivation'. *Journal of Social Policy*, 16(2), 125–146.

US Census Bureau (2004). *Poverty Overview*. Available at http://www.census.gov/hhes/www/poverty/overview.html

Viswanathan, M. and Harris, J. (1999). 'A functional illiteracy: the dark side of information processing'. In E.J. Arnould and L.M. Scott (eds), *Advances in Consumer Research*, Vol. 26. Provo, UT: Association for Consumer Research, p. 25.

Viswanathan, M. and Harris, J. (2001). 'Illiteracy and innumeracy among consumers: the dark side of information processing'. In P.M. Tidwell and T.E. Muller (eds), *Asia Pacific Advances in Consumer Research*, Vol. 4. Provo, UT: Association for Consumer Research, p. 274.

Wallendorf, M. (2001). 'Literally literacy'. *Journal of Consumer Research*, 27 (March), 505–511.

Woodliffe, L. (2004). 'Rethinking consumer disadvantage: the importance of qualitative research'. *International Journal of Retail and Distribution Management*, 32(11), 523–531.

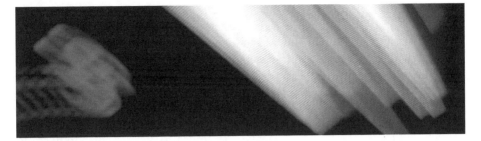

13

Sustainable Marketing: Marketing Re-thought, Re-mixed and Re-tooled

Ken Peattie

Introduction: A 20-Year Prelude

The new millennium is providing many challenges to marketing as a management discipline and an academic field. Old certainties have become strained as markets continue to globalize, as existing mass markets dissolve in a tide of individualism, and as the power of the Internet continues to reshape how we communicate and consume. Perhaps the most profound challenge for marketing lies in playing a role in moving industries and economies towards a more environmentally (and socially) sustainable path. In 1987 the Brundtland Report, *Our Common Future* (WCED, 1987) put forward the case that our current production and consumptions systems were not sustainable, in a way that governments and businesses found hard to ignore. By the early 1990s the majority of the world's governments had committed to pursue sustainability following the Rio *Earth Summit* and the publication of Agenda 21. Most of the world's largest companies followed suit by signing up to the International Chamber of Commerce's Charter, or through their own environmental or corporate social responsibility (CSR) policies. The scale of the challenge has been illustrated in the political arena by the lack of substantive progress observed by the time the second *Earth Summit* was held in Johannesburg in 2002. Within the corporate sector this was reflected by the *Green Wall* phenomenon in which well-intentioned environmental initiatives have stalled in the face of implementational difficulties (Shelton, 1994).

Simple observation of a trip to the supermarket also demonstrates how little two decades of widespread concern about environmental sustainability has changed the products that we consume and the technologies that deliver product benefits to us. The homes we leave and return to, the cars we are likely to use for the journey and the foodstuffs we will buy, will neither look nor be, in any way radically different to those of 20 years ago. There will be some incremental changes beneath the surface (e.g. in the energy efficiency of the car's engine or the density of the food packaging), but these will usually have been offset elsewhere. So for example, the average European home used 22% less energy for heating in 2005 compared to 1985 due to energy efficiency measures. Overall household energy use however increased by 4% due to the growing number of energy using appliances in homes over that period. Since our homes (and particularly household energy), personal travel and food account for 70–80% of the environmental impacts of individuals' consumption in Europe, this represents a disastrous lack of change and progress (Tukker et al., 2005).

Making progress towards sustainability is not just a question of changes to products and technologies. A key barrier to the adoption of sustainable practices by governments, companies and consumers, is that it cannot be achieved without a radical change in how we live and think. The sustainability challenge is forcing management disciplines to confront their own assumptions about the ends towards which they are working, the means they use and the way they measure 'progress' (e.g. the excellent reappraisal of organization studies by Shrivastava, 1994). Sustainability requires those who practice, preach or study marketing, not just to apply a critical eye to the discipline, but also to question and re-examine some of the most fundamental concepts that underpin it.

Sustainability as Re-thinking Marketing Orthodoxy

In 1632, Galileo published his *Dialogue Concerning the Two Chief World Systems*, proving that the earth was not the centre of all things. This laid the foundations of *The Enlightenment* and gave the scientific revolution the necessary momentum to overthrow the entrenched ecclesiastically based scholastic paradigm, and replace it with the Newtonian scientific paradigm. At the time though, Galileo's revelations were not popular, even though he had delayed making them public for nearly 20 years, until he judged society to be ready to accept them. In 1633 he was brought before the Inquisition in Rome, was forced to recant, and spent the rest of his days in exile. The problem for those attempting to promote a more environmentally sustainable (or greener) vision of marketing, is that the changes in perspective required are so unorthodox as to be received as heretical by *The Church of Marketing.*

When entrenched orthodoxies are challenged, they typically try to maintain the status quo by one of three approaches. First comes the **denial** phase; if the challenge cannot be discredited or eliminated it is followed by **concessions** aimed at reducing pressure to a manageable level; if this isn't achieved there follows an attempt at **absorption**, in which an evolutionary compromise is accepted instead of the unpalatable option of revolutionary change. Each of these strategies is visible in the response to the sustainability challenge today. There are many still in denial regarding the environment, who continue to deny the need for change on a number of bases including:

- *The pressure for change comes from the exaggeration of threats by unrepresentative pressure groups*: This argument put forward by Baden (1992), has been maintained through the work of Lomborg (2001), and his subsequent role as ubiquitous sceptical media pundit attacking accepted views about environmental problems. However, it is rather negated by consistent market research demonstrating public concern about the environment and the need for action across countries and social groups. A 2005 TNS/6th Dimension Survey of European countries showed that while almost 60% of Europeans favoured tough international legislation to restrict environmental damage by companies, only 6% believed environmental threats had been 'overhyped'.
- *The need for change is unproven*: The lack of total certainty, and a unified scientific consensus concerning environmental issues such as global warming, has been used by many in politics and business to argue against radical change, and in favour of ever-more research as a precursor to action. This confuses a lack of unanimity with a lack of consensus, and uses uncertainty as a reason for inaction instead of caution. Uncertainty is created in environmental science because of a lack of historical data, deficiencies in the models created to analyse complex systems, and the fact that some elements of natural systems are chaotic and therefore fundamentally unknowable (O'Riordan, 1995). As Naess (1989) concludes about ecology:

  > to the great amazement of many, the scientific conclusions are often statements of ignorance: 'We do not know what long-range consequences the proposed interference in the ecosystem will beget, so we cannot make any hard and fast predictions'. Only rarely can scientists predict with any certainty the effect of a new chemical on even a single small ecosystem.

- *Technology will make the need to change unnecessary*: Although technology is yielding solutions to many environmental problems, it seems unlikely that it can sustain current population and development trajectories. A joint statement issued by the Royal Society of London and the US National Academy of Sciences (two of the most conservative and pro-science organizations imaginable) stated that:

  > If current predictions of population growth prove accurate and patterns of human activity on the planet remain unchanged, science

and technology may not be able to prevent either irreversible deg-
radation of the environment or continued poverty for much of the
world. . . . The future of the planet is in the balance.

- *Sustainable development will disadvantage poorer countries*: This argument
  rather assumes that the status quo benefits poorer countries, when the
  reality is that current trade rules are skewed in favour of the richer countries and multi-national companies. The relationship between trade liber-
  alization and sustainable development is a complex and controversial one
  (Brack, 2005), but the current situation can create pressure on poorer countries to liquidate their environmental resources for short-term economic
  gain, instead of developing them to deliver sustainable benefits.

Although people might assume that we are beyond the denial phase,
Thørgersen (2006) uncovered a tendency within the media to shift their cov-
erage of environmental business developments so that those companies who
were initially newsworthy as heroes, become more interesting later cast in the
role of failures or hypocrites (which very much reflects Body Shop's experience with the media). Similarly the pair of adverts broadcast during 2006 in
the USA about 'global warming alarmism' from the Competitive Enterprise
Institute (a think tank partly bankrolled by many of the major companies pub-
licly committed to tackling global warming) demonstrate that the tendency
towards denial remains alive and well.

For marketers willing to accept the legitimacy of the sustainability concept,
and public environmental concern, it is tempting to aim to reduce the pressure
to change marketing theory and practice through concessions or by absorbing
environmental concern within the existing marketing agenda. Concessions
include a switch to the use of recycled packaging materials, the addition of
'end-of-pipe' environmental improvements (typified by the addition of catalytic converters onto cars), or the implementation of the BATNEEC principle
(using the best available technology not entailing excessive cost). Marketing
academics have also been making concessions through the application of
their own form of BATNEEC (best available teaching not entailing excessive
change), often through the bolting-on of a 'green' lecture into their otherwise
conventional courses (Peattie, 1994).

Steps to absorb environmentalism within the existing marketing paradigm
include the recognition of the environment and concern about it as, an element of consumer behaviour (e.g. Scherhorn, 1993); a potential source of differentiation and competitive advantage (e.g. Porter and van der Linde, 1995)
and a consideration within new product development processes (e.g. Pujari
et al., 2003). These steps represent improvements, but are relatively 'light' green
forms of marketing, as identified by Crane (2000) under labels such as *passive
greening, muted greening, niche greening* or *collaborative greening*. Such changes
fall well short of progress towards the type of 'closed system' vision of sustainable marketing, rooted in the physical systems principles derived from the
field of industrial ecology and promoted by authors like Fuller (1999). Another

facet of the tendency towards absorption that has been apparent recently, has been the absorption of the pioneering and iconic green brands into the brand families of multi-national firms. Body Shop's absorption into L'Oreal, Green & Black's into Cadburys and Ben & Jerry's into Unilever are all symptomatic of this. Although optimists might view this as a signal that the multi-nationals are picking up the agenda and driving it forward, pessimists might view this as a successful strategy for defusing a perceived threat, or for polishing the larger firms' green credentials.

To make substantive progress towards sustainability, business and marketing must move beyond concessions and the grafting of environmental issues onto conventional agendas and models. However, meeting the green challenge and making substantive changes to the way that marketing is practised and taught is an uncomfortable one for marketers to confront for several reasons:

- Many environmentalists have demonized the doctrine of marketing, its holy men and some of its most sacred artefacts (such as branding and advertising). Marketers, in their role as the consumers' champion are used to seeing themselves as the potential saviours of companies from the perils of a product or production focus. Being cast as part of the problem rather than part of the solution is something they are unused to.
- A sustainable marketing perspective requires the dissolving or re-drawing of many boundaries that have helped to define and focus marketing as both an academic discipline and a management function. It requires a much broader focus, and a longer time span, within marketing strategy development.
- Environmental concern challenges some of our most fundamental assumptions about marketing, and like the clerics faced with the revelation that they were aboard a whirling spaceship instead of a stable platform, marketers may find this hard to accept.

It is unsurprising that marketers prefer to deny or minimize the extent of the sustainability challenge, and to try to dismiss environmental concern as faddish or as just one of many 'business pressures' faced by the 21st Century Marketer.

Re-thinking and 'Re-mixing' the Marketing Vision

It was Galileo's innovative telescope that revealed the truth in Copernicus's heretical theory that the Earth was not the centre of the Universe. Marketing theory has acted like a telescope in many ways, and through the reductionalist scientific method, and an emphasis on quantitative research, it has provided an ever-more penetrating analysis of a clearly defined field. This has brought many marketing issues into highly detailed focus, but it has kept other important issues in the darkness beyond the magnified circle of light. To meet the challenge of moving marketing towards sustainability (as opposed to finding ways to reduce the level of environmentally related pressure being experienced

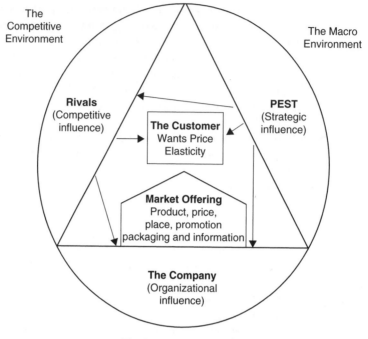

Figure 13.1 Marketing – the orthodox 'telescopic' view.

by companies and marketers) will require the current vision of marketing theory and practice to be broadened and re-focused in a number of areas.

The conventional vision of marketing is represented by the model in Figure 13.1. (Although this is not meant to be an all-encompassing model, e.g. the ability of companies to shape the external environment is not expressed through reciprocal arrows. The model shows where the gaze of marketing usually rests, on the attempt to win over the customer through a superior market offering.) It highlights some of the fundamental marketing principles and assumptions which, although widely accepted, perhaps need to be reconsidered in the light of the need for sustainability.

The conventional 'telescopic' view of marketing has led to the development of six key articles of marketing faith, which a sustainability orientated view requires us to reconsider:

The Sanctity of the Market

Marketers, hardly surprisingly, focus their energies on, and place their faith in, the operation of markets. Worldwide, the perceived superiority of market-based solutions compared to centralist approaches, mean that free-market principles are seen as crucial to the generation and distribution of wealth, and also to meeting an increasing range of social needs. Marketers' understanding of markets is firmly rooted in economics, but conventional neoclassical economics hardly qualifies as 'environmentally friendly'. Economic theory blossomed in the Victorian era of imperial expansion in which vast new continents were being opened up and explored. Then it seemed reasonable to assume that the world and its resources had no practical limits, and that the only costs that needed to be attached to resource exploitation were the cost of extraction.

Economists tend to view markets as the solution to everything, including environmental problems. The gloom of *Limits to Growth* (Meadows et al., 1972), perhaps the first environmental warning of the modern era to be taken seriously, was lifted when rising oil prices in the mid-1970s appeared to bring a whole new range of oil reserves into being. Seeing a supposedly finite resource being almost magically expanded by the simple mechanism of rising prices produced a comforting illusion that the power of markets could overcome the physical constraints of the planet. The conventional counterargument to concern about dwindling resources, that rising prices will protect them (Cairncross, 1991), didn't help the dodo amongst others, and it suffers from several fundamental flaws:

- Markets don't recognize ecological distinctions between natural resources. Therefore a particular species of tree will be liquidated according to global timber prices.
- It assumes that property rights will be respected. The increasing rarity of the rhinoceros simply raises the black market price of rhino horn and makes poaching even more potentially rewarding.
- Environmental systems work to thresholds, so that the population may fall below its sustainable level before the price for the remaining stock becomes high enough to encourage preservation.
- While market pricing failures can be reversed, environmental system failures are often difficult to correct. Once rainforest is cleared, the land rapidly becomes incapable of supporting rainforest growth, whatever price or value is placed on it (Naess, 1989).
- Markets cannot predict the future demand for species and other resources. The Pacific Yew, which reached the brink of extinction after the forestry industry burned it in massive numbers because it obstructed the harvesting of economically valuable species, went on to prove invaluable in the fight against cancer as the source of the drug Taxol.

The argument that pricing can save the environment suffers from its focus on resource inputs for which there is a market. Many ecosystems are threatened, not by direct overexploitation, but from accidental damage by pollution or competition from other economic activity. Other vital elements of the environment cannot be protected by market mechanisms because they exist outside the market framework. Without a market, economics views a resource such as the ozone layer (upon which all life depends) as 'worthless'. In practice, 'the vast majority of the biosphere is . . . not covered by price (air, water, common land, habitat, species, ozone layers, etc.)' (Gray, 1990).

f a product usually covers the direct and indirect internal costs plus a profit margin to reward investors and for reinvestment. vironmental costs of production, product use and disposal are ded from the price that consumers pay. These costs are treated as 'externalities' to be met by governments through the taxes that the company, its investors, customers and employees pay. In practice (most) governments actively seek to reduce tax burdens, resulting in many costs of protecting, restoring and sustaining the environment remaining unmet. Although marketers might not see this as relevant to them, the reality is that companies are not politically neutral and often lobby hard against the imposition of measures proposed by elected governments to protect the environment or meet the costs of market externalities.

Environmentalists' distrust of markets is often dismissed as simply the expression of outdated left wing, centralist tendencies. The reality is that if markets worked with perfect efficiency, so that all costs associated with production and consumption were covered by the price paid, then there would be no sustainability challenge to meet. However, economics is what Woods (1991) labels an 'IF' doctrine:

> IF there are no costs of production not reflected in price . . . IF competition is perfectly free . . . IF information is full, accurate and readily available . . . IF there are no unresolved concerns for human rights or social justice . . . IF, IF, IF.

The fact that markets are imperfect, particularly in terms of purchasers' lack of information about the environmental implications of their decisions and behaviour, and in creating many unresolved externalities, means that blind faith in market solutions is misplaced.

The Sovereignty of the Consumer

Central to marketing is the customer (either the final consumer or the organizational buyer), who they are, what they buy and how much they are willing to pay. This is as it should be, but the current vision of customers is perhaps flawed by a myopic view of them, and by an unswerving devotion to the tenet that 'The Customer is King'. The pioneering management theorist Henri Fayol once quipped about sending out for workers, but human beings turning up instead. Marketers face a similar situation. The textbook consumer tends to be a simple and consistent being, whose purpose is to consume and who tends to be preoccupied with individual and non-conflicting wants or needs, one at a time. The reality is that people are complex, individualistic and inconsistent. They typically want both the convenience and freedom of owning a private car, and to live and raise their children away from traffic. They want to lose weight, but not to eat less. They want the environment to be protected, but not to consume less. These contradictions were very visible in the consumer research undertaken by Mohr et al. (2001) who found that American consumers felt that the consumer lifestyle had enriched them in so and impoverished them in others. They also had faith that mar would move firms and their strategies towards social responsibility, and yet were not changing their own consumption behaviour to achieve this, instead relying on someone else's invisible hand to do the work.

Consumer sovereignty and choice is a sacred article of faith within marketing, to the point that we equate it with other values such as democracy or freedom (or as Hutt, 1936, puts it 'the only grounds on which consumer sovereignty may be attacked, is by a refutation of our conception of liberty'). However, freedom to consume needs to be balanced against the rights of non-consumers, and against freedom from the consequences (individual or collective) of others' consumption. Dedicated smokers will claim smoking as their right, but often without equal consideration to the non-consumer's right to breathe unpolluted air. Ultimately consumers are not sovereigns. They are not unique individuals with a God-given right to rule the fate of others, whom the marketer must obey. A more enlightened and contemporary view of consumers is as a constituency whose members will vary in their needs and priorities, and who have rights and responsibilities which must be balanced against the rights and responsibilities of others.

The conventional faith placed in consumer choice as a means of guiding companies' strategies and activities also assumes that the consumer is faced with a full and free choice and complete information. In reality consumer freedom of choice may be more illusory than real because choices are often carefully constructed by others (Tomlinson, 1990). Returning to our car trip to our 'local' food retailer (which in reality is likely to be an out-of-town superstore after planning policy decisions rendered the smaller local retailers unable to compete) it will involve choosing between the products and brands that the retail gatekeepers have allowed onto the shelves, and which have previously managed to fight their way through the manufacturer's internal political and financial decision-making processes in order to be brought to market. Given the lack of general environmental literacy within the population, and the incomplete and often misleading information provided about many products (such as food products), expecting consumers to be able to make the decisions that will lead us towards sustainability is extremely optimistic.

The Overwhelming Importance of the Product, the Purchase and the Price

Theoretically, the marketing orientation should prevent too myopic a focus on the product itself, and should instead focus attention on the needs of the consumer and the delivery of benefits to them. The reality is that the product continues to be the focus of a great deal of practical marketing effort, and of much marketing research and scholarship. Marketing theory has helped to broaden marketers' concept of 'the product' beyond the core product to encompass all the tangible dimensions of the product (such as packaging) and the augmented dimensions (consisting of supporting services and products). Environmentally concerned customers have shown that they will also take an interest in the externalities involved in production, and may reject a technically excellent product because they become aware of the environmental harm caused in production or disposal. They may also avoid a product because of activities of a producer, its suppliers or investors. Therefore customers may differentiate in favour of rod-and-line caught tuna or FairTrade coffee or against Nescafè coffee because they disapprove of Nestlè's marketing of infant formula milk.

The conventional marketing vision maintained a focus on the product as a market offering, while leaving the production system and the rest of the company in shadow.

However, as customer satisfaction becomes more likely to be influenced by the acceptability of the production process and all the other activities of the producer, we are approaching the situation where the company itself is becoming the product consumed (or the *total* product; Peattie, 1995). Drucker's (1973) famous concept that 'Marketing is the whole business seen from its final result, that is from the customers' point of view', will become a reality within a more sustainable economy, because green concern means that customers (or those who influence them) will be actively looking at all aspects of a company.

Although consumption is a multi-stage process, it is the actual purchase which is the focus of marketers' attention, and which is the focus of the majority of the literature dedicated to marketing (Kotler and Armstrong, 2004). This is not surprising, since the purchase is where the money changes hands, but the emphasis given to actual purchasing tends to obscure a good deal of consumer behaviour which is important in the debate about sustainability. Whether or not products are efficiently used, how they are maintained and disposed of, and whether they are repaired, recycled or re-used greatly affect their overall eco-performance. Gradually research is beginning to focus more on the impact of other elements of the consumption process (e.g. Pieters, 1991; Wiese et al., 2004) and their implications for sustainability. This process will need to go much further to allow consumption as a process to become the focus of marketing's attention more than purchase as an activity.

The third key area of focus, is on the monetary price paid for a product when it is purchased. This also seems entirely logical, because it is the way that we are used to thinking. However, if we purchased durable products such as cars, buildings and equipment on the basis of the lifetime cost (including disposal) it would encourage different purchase and product design priorities, and would also encourage progress towards sustainability. A further step forward would be to consider costs of consumption which go beyond the conventional monetary dimensions to consider the full set of transaction costs involved in consumption. These could include the time and effort or any psychological 'wear and tear' involved in the acquisition, use and disposal of products.

The Pursuit of Satisfaction in the Face of Insatiability

Marketing assumes that, providing that the marketing mix is correctly configured, that satisfaction will flow from material consumption. The generation of customer satisfaction (and profit as a by-product) is seen as the raison d'être of marketing, and an unassailable justification for everything done in its name. The concept that genuine satisfaction is derived from material consumption is one that has regularly been challenged by philosophers (e.g. Illich, 1981), and evidence from psychology demonstrates that the relationship between material consumption and satisfaction is complex, non-linear and dependent on a wide range of psychological and social factors (Jackson et al., 2004). As Robert Lane (2000) summarizes in his book *The Loss of Happiness in Market Economies*, the risk is that societal pressures to maintain levels of material consumption actually keep us away from more intrinsically satisfying activities such as spending time with friends and family. This is not to argue that that being a 'have-not' is more satisfying than being a 'have', but it does mean that more consumption does not necessarily bring more satisfaction. The continued 'flat-lining' of satisfaction levels in the face of rising material living standards in industrialized countries during the past 50 years is evidence of this.

One of the fundamental principles of sustainability is 'need' and the requirement to meet the needs of the global poor in particular. This again takes marketers into relatively uncharted territory. The conventional 'telescopic' view tends to focus only on those people who have sufficient money to be actual or potential customers. Those unable to afford a product are excluded, and the impact of marketing activity on non-consumers is rarely discussed. Therefore the satisfaction that a new and heavily advertised luxury product generates amongst customers, is never set against any dissatisfaction created amongst the many people who can be made to desire the product, even if they cannot aspire to afford it. It is a sobering thought that currently some 3 billion people (or almost half the global population) exist on under $2 per day, and lack the discretionary spending power to be embraced within the consumer economy and the world of conventional marketing. One aspect of the sustainability debate concerns the extent to which 'base-of-the-pyramid' approaches can include the world's poor within markets through new and innovative products, business models and pricing approaches (Kirchgeorg and Winn, 2006). Tackling deprivation and poverty through such initiatives is a laudable objective, and eliminating poverty is an important aspect of progress towards sustainability. However, embracing a further 3 billion people into the consumer society will simply worsen current problems of environmental unsustainability, unless we also learn how to reduce over-consumption in richer countries, and radically improve the material efficiency (and environmental harmony) of the technologies that underpin our consumption and production.

Although marketing talks about both 'wants' and 'needs', in practice it shares with economics a tendency to:

- distinguish between them only rather vaguely, if at all;
- fail to define what 'satisfaction' really means;
- devote almost all its attention to issues of consumer choice and the satisfaction of 'wants'.

Jackson et al. (2004) provide an excellent and detailed critique of our under-standing of the relationship between wants, needs, consumption and sat-isfaction. Amongst the many valuable insights that can be drawn from this critique, is the irony of a marketing discipline orientated around the satisfac-tion of wants, which is rooted in the discipline of economics that assumes that wants are insatiable. It also explains the evolution of theoretical perspectives on consumption and living standards beyond utilitarian concepts of whether or not we gain subjective pleasure from our consumption choices, to instead consider the 'capabilities' that consumption delivers in terms of the freedoms or opportunities it provides for us. Thus in meeting our short-term wants through increasing material consumption, we may actually be impoverishing ourselves in terms of reducing our capabilities in terms of future choices and opportunities. Viewing consumption in terms of the provision of opportun-ities and freedoms, rather than the satisfaction of insatiable wants, allows for more meaningful inclusion of issues including poverty, deprivation and sustainability; 'The capability approach directs us to investigate whether soci-eties, and societal consumption patterns, would permit people to live healthy lives, in harmony with each other and with nature' (Jackson et al., 2004).

A Belief in Competition

The conventional vision of marketing is set in a competitive market in which companies' marketing strategies and actions are designed to secure some form of competitive advantage. Much of the debate about the environment and marketing has therefore centred around whether good eco-performance can generate and sustain competitive advantage. Authors such as Porter and van der Linde (1995) have argued that 'win–win' strategies exist which are environmentally superior and which, by stimulating innovation and tapping consumer concern, can create competitive advantage. Others argue that this is difficult to achieve in practice (e.g. Walley and Whitehead, 1994). Products marketed on an environmental platform have often proved vulnerable to competitor tactics such as discounting, or attacks on the level of technical per-formance offered, or on the credibility of the environmental claims. The reality is that substantive progress towards sustainability will not be made because some companies within a given market provide greener products, to meet the needs of those consumers with greatest environmental concerns, whilst the others compete on different bases. This may even prove counterproductive by effectively reducing the pressure for change within the industry as a whole. For a sustainable future, good eco-performance needs to evolve from one means by which companies may choose to generate competitive advantage, to an entry pass into the game as a whole.

In practice many companies in the environmental front line are part of global industries such as cars, chemicals and electronics which are character-ized by networks of international strategic alliances. These can assist in devel-oping industry-wide solutions to common environmental problems as is the case with the elimination of Chlorofluorocarbons (CFCs) as solvents in the electronics industry or the development of alternative fuels in the automotive industry.

The Abstraction of the Environment

The 'telescopic view' model shows the conventional definition of the macro-marketing environment as made up of the political, economic, social and technical (PEST) environments which influence the actors within a market, and their strategies and behaviours. Books on the marketing environment dedicate whole chapters to these and to other environments (such as the international and legal), but the physical 'green' environment is generally neglected by comparison. At best environmental concern is fitted into the conventional model as a social concern, or a driver of legislation in the political environment. This perpetuates a view of the physical environment as existing within one or more parts of the PEST framework, rather than the reality of the PEST environments being underpinned by the physical environment. Or as Capra (1983) expressed it, the mechanistic economic models which have dominated the last century of our development ignore the ecological contexts in which economic activity occurs. The view of our planet which suffuses marketing is as a form of economic hyperspace, which only imposes limits on business in terms of creating physical distances between customers and producers.

Similarly the view of the relationship between firms and their macro-environment as relatively unidirectional, which tends to pervade marketing thinking, will need to be amended. Belz's (2006) vision of the evolution of sustainable marketing ultimately requires:

> ... ultimately requires 'transformational sustainability marketing' explained as '... the active participation of companies in public and political processes to change the existing framework in favour of sustainability. ... Within the present institutional framework the successful marketing of sustainable products is possible, but limited. The institutional design fails to set positive incentives for sustainable behaviour, both for producers and consumers ... Changes in institutions are necessary to expand the intersection between socio-ecological problems and consumption, and to set up the conditions for the successful marketing of sustainable products beyond niches.

Re-tooling Marketing for Sustainability

One of the difficulties that marketing practitioners and marketing students have had in trying to relate to the debate about reconciling marketing and sustainability, is that it has largely been held within scholarly journals and academic conferences. Although companies and students have been exposed to, and involved in, progress towards the greening of marketing, it has largely been at the 'light green' end of the spectrum, involving incremental changes that sit comfortably within the existing marketing worldview. Amongst marketing academics, there has gradually been a shift of emphasis beyond the initial 'managerialist' stream of work on marketing and sustainability, to new more critical and more challenging work, which questions some of the fundamental assumptions of the marketing academy (Kilbourne and Beckman, 1999). This evolution in academic marketing thought has yet to make a significant impact on marketing practice, marketing education or the mainstream of marketing scholarship. To do so will require concern about sustainability (and particularly environmental sustainability) to go beyond being viewed as a particular issue that marketing must respond to, to being recognized as an alternative approach to marketing theory and practice (just as in politics it needs to be recognized as an approach to policy making, not an area for making policy or in education as an approach to learning, not an issue to be accommodated within the curriculum). A summary of some of the implications of this evolution of the marketing mindset towards sustainability is presented in Table 13.1.

Table 13.1 Towards more sustainable marketing.

From being . . .	To becoming . . .
Myopic – with a focus on people as consumers and on their wants and needs considered individually	Holistic – focusing on customers as people and on their welfare and on putting their consumption in its social and environmental context
Fixated on purchase as an activity	Focused on consumption as a process
About linear market structures and an ever-more globalized economy	About market loops and networks and an increasingly re-localized economy
Orientated towards providing products at a particular price	Orientated towards providing benefits involving a set of (transaction) costs
Increasingly short term	Inter-generational in outlook
About insatiable material wants and acquiring more and more	More about meeting needs, generating opportunities, achieving lasting satisfaction and desiring less
Concerned with appealing to a dedicated minority of green consumers to generate differentiation and competitive advantage	Concerned with the greening of mass markets through collaborative efforts to ensure the survival of entire markets and industries
About customers' perceived willingness to pay a premium for greener products	About a refusal to buy cheap products that are effectively subsidized because their social and environmental costs remain unmet
Based in socio-economic hyperspace where socio-environmental costs are 'externalized'	Grounded within the physical limitations of a finite planet in which socio-environmental costs are internalized and met

Moving marketing and marketers towards sustainability is going to require a range of new ideas, new tools and a new vocabulary. As a simple example, marketers who are intimately familiar with the concept of a 'product life cycle' in terms of the evolution of sales levels, will need to understand the concept of a physical 'cradle-to-grave' life cycle of the product as a physical, rather than purely economic, entity. Gradually resources to support this transformation are evolving, with the development of new design tools, guides aimed at practitioners, case studies illustrating good practice and a range of educational resources (many of which have been gathered together and made available via the Sustainable Marketing Knowledge Network: http://www.cfsd.org.uk/smart-know-net/index.htm).

Conclusions: Re-focusing the Marketing Telescope

The heretical revelations of Galileo, which so affronted the clerical establishment, ushered in *The Enlightenment* and from this sprang the modern, industrial paradigm which follows Newton's mechanistic view of the world. This paradigm places faith in the principle of **reductionism**; it is **technocentric** in its emphasis on the ability of technology to control and harness nature; it is **econocentric** in its emphasis on markets and monetary values; and it is **anthropocentric** in seeing the environment as something which only exists to support human activity. The initial response to the sustainability challenge has reflected this prevailing paradigm by emphasizing the development of new cleaner technologies, attempting to improve market mechanisms to protect the environment and assigning monetary values to environmental resources. It has been about minimizing, and not maximizing, change.

The truth behind Galileo's observations may have been inconvenient at the time, but it was also inescapable and the same principle applies to sustainability. Sustainability is an inescapable proposition through the simple truism that, if a process or system is not sustainable, then it cannot be sustained. Sooner or later, and more or less traumatically, change will have to occur and a more sustainable state reached (and generally speaking, the longer the delay, the greater the trauma of adjustment). A loss-making firm can continue with 'business as usual' for as long as the patience of creditors endures, but not indefinitely. Environmentally unsustainable systems of production and consumption can over-stretch environmental systems in the short term, but cannot endure indefinitely.

Many marketers, tend to view topics like sustainal
relatively peripheral and not as 'real' marketing. I w
Baker (1991) suggests that 'real marketing' has four es

1 Start with the customer.
2 A long-run perspective.
3 Full use of all the company's resources.
4 Innovation.

Sustainable marketing is 'real' marketing because it centres itself around the customer, not just as a consumer, but as a person with needs and interests beyond material consumption and temporary gratification. Whether it must still start with the customer is a moot point. Belz's (2006) vision of sustainable marketing for the 21st century, involves an analysis of the socio-ecological context as a precursor to analysing consumers and their needs and behaviours. Sustainable marketing will also require a long-run perspective to consider the needs of customers and stakeholders, not just of the present, but also of future generations. It will also require not only full, but also efficient, use of all the company's resources to ensure there is no waste of effort, energy or materials. In terms of innovation, it is at the heart of attempts to move towards sustainability in terms of clean technology, new products and services and new marketing approaches. It also requires innovative thinking within the marketing academy, but this is not so easily achieved.

Ottman (1992) makes the point that sustainable marketing issues are 'real' issues. Instead of talking about consumer 'needs' such as whether our clothes are 'whiter than white', sustainable marketing means tackling issues which affect the fundamentals of peoples' quality of life (and which may ultimately threaten the lifestyles or even lives of future generations of consumers). Given the almost universal concern about the environment being shown by consumers all around the world, it is the companies who are not doing all that they can to make genuine progress towards sustainability (subject to the limitations of cost, technology, information and consumer understanding) that are not practising real marketing. To quote the great American author Henry Miller (from Chapter 9): 'The world has not to be put in order: the world is order incarnate. It is for us to put ourselves in unison with this order.'

References

Baden, J.A. (1992). 'Business, science and environmental politics: towards a political economy of hope'. *Columbia Journal of World Business*, 27(3/4), 27–35.

Baker, M.J. (1991). 'One more time – what is marketing?' In M.J. Baker (ed.), *The Marketing Book*, 2nd edition. London: Butterworth-Heinemann.

Belz, F.-M. (2006). 'Marketing in the 21st century'. *Business Strategy and the Environment*, 15(2), 139–144.

Brack, D. (2005). 'The World Trade Organization and sustainable development: a guide to the debate'. *Energy, Environment and Development Briefing Paper* 05/03, Chatham House.

Cairncross, F. (1991). *Costing the Earth*. London: Economist Books.

pra, F. (1983). *The Turning Point*. New York: Bantam.

e, A. (2000). 'Facing the backlash: green marketing and strategic reorien-
n in the 1990's'. *Journal of Strategic Marketing*, 8, 277–296.

P.F. (1973). *Top Management*. London: Heinemann.

Fuller, D. (1999). 'Marketing mix design-for-environment (DFE): a systems approach'. *Journal of Business Administration and Policy Analysis*, 309–339.

Gray, R. (1990). 'The accountant's task as a friend to the earth'. *Accountancy*, 105(1192), 65–69.

Hutt, W.E. (1936). *Economists and the Public*. London: Jonathon Cape.

Illich, I. (1981). *Vernacular Values*. Marian Boyers. London.

Jackson, T., Jager, W. and Stagl, S. (2004). 'Beyond insatiability: needs theory, consumption and sustainability'. *Sustainable Technologies Programme Working Paper* (2004/2). Centre for Environmental Strategy, University of Surrey.

Kilbourne, W.E. and Beckman, S. (1999). 'Review and critical assessment of research on marketing and the environment'. *Journal of Marketing Management*, 14(6), 153–532.

Kirchgeorg, M. and Winn, M.I. (2006). 'Sustainability marketing for the poorest of the poor'. *Business Strategy and the Environment*, 15(3), 171–184.

Kotler, P. and Armstrong, G. (2004). *Principles of Marketing*, 10th edition. Upper Saddle River, NJ: Pearson Education.

Lane, R. (2000). *The Loss of Happiness in Market Economies*. New Haven, CT: Yale University Press.

Lomborg, B. (2001). *The Skeptical Environmentalist*. Cambridge: Cambridge University Press.

Meadows, D.H., Meadows, D.L., Randers, J. and Behrens, W.W. (1972). *The Limits to Growth*. New York: Universe Books.

Mohr, D., Webb, D.J. and Harris, K.E. (2001). 'Do consumers expect companies to be socially responsible? The impact of corporate social responsibility on buying behavior'. *Journal of Consumer Affairs*, 35(1), 45–72.

Naess (1989). *Ecology, Community and Lifestyle: Outline of an Ecosophy*, trans. D. Rothenberg (ed.). Cambridge: Cambridge University Press.

O'Riordan, T. (1995). *Environmental Science for Environmental Management*. Longman, Harlow, Essex.

Ottman, J.E. (1992). 'Industry's response to green consumerism'. *Journal of Business Strategy*, 13(4), 3–7.

Peattie, K. (1994). 'A green light for business education?' *European Journal of Business Education*, 3(2), 39–47.

Peattie, K. (1995). *Environmental Marketing Management: Meeting the Green Challenge*. London: Pitman.

Pieters, R.G. (1991).' Changing garbage disposal patterns of consumers: motivations, ability and performance'. *Journal of Public Policy and Marketing*, 10(2), 59–76.

Porter, M.E. and van der Linde (1995). 'Green and competitive: ending the stalemate'. *Harvard Business Review*, 73(5), 120–133.

Pujari, D., Wright, G. and Peattie, K. (2003). 'Green and competitive: influences on environmental new product development performance'. *Journal of Business Research*, 56(8), 657–671.

Scherhorn, G. (1993). 'Consumers' concern about the environment and its impact on business'. *Journal of Consumer Policy*, 16, 171–191.

Shelton, R.D. (1994). 'Hitting the green wall: why corporate programs get stalled'. *Corporate Environmental Strategy*, 2(2), 5–11.

Shrivastava, P. (1994). 'CASTRATED environment: GREENING organizational studies'. *Organization Studies*, 15(5), 705–726.

Thørgersen, J. (2006). 'Media attention and the market for 'green' consumer products'. *Business Strategy and the Environment*, 15(3), 145–156.

Tomlinson, A. (1990). 'Consumer culture and the aura of the commodity'. In A. Tomlinson (ed.), *Consumption, Identity and Style*. London: Routledge.

Tukker, A., Huppes, G., Guinée, J., Heijungs, R., de Koning, A., van Oers, L., Suh, S., Geerken, T., Van Holderbeke, M., Jansen, B. and Nielsen, P. (2005). *Environmental Impact of Products (EIPRO): Analysis of the Life Cycle Environmental Impacts Related to the Total Final Consumption of the EU25*. Brussels: IPTS/ESTO, European Commission Joint Research Centre.

Walley, N. and Whitehead, B. (1994). 'It's not easy being green'. *Harvard Business Review*, 72(3), 46–52.

WCED (1987). *Our Common Future, The Brundtland Report of the World Commission on Environment and Development*. Oxford: Oxford University Press.

Wiese, B.S., Sauer, J. and Üttinger, B.R. (2004). 'Consumers' use of written product information'. *Ergonomics*, 47(11), 1180–1194.

Woods, D. (1991). 'Toward improving corporate social performance'. *Business Horizons*, 34(4), 66–73.

14

Journeying Beyond Marketing's Collective Consciousness

Ingrid Kajzer Mitchell

Introduction

Today we are faced with a whole series of global problems of both ecological and social nature which have detrimental effect on the biosphere and human life. There is no polite way of saying that Marketing practice to date has taken very little interest in examining its role in constructing and maintaining unsustainable business practice and 'have continued to ignore or respond inadequately to the worsening ecological crisis currently being witnessed around the globe' (Fitchett and McDonagh, 2000, p. 210). Indeed, according to a worldwide research study carried out by ESOMAR in collaboration with the United Nations Environmental Program (UNEP) social and environmental welfare issues are still off the radar for most marketing practitioners (2003). This tendency towards inertia and maintenance of the status quo in Marketing pose the critics with an inescapable challenge: how can we affect change through critique, and what happens when we do so?

Against this background, this chapter sets out to illuminate our understanding of some of the change processes that occur as we as critical marketing scholars seek to rethink our practice in light of contemporary environmental and social problems. The writing here is the outcome of cumulative reflections from interventions carried out in research and consultancy projects between 1999 and 2005, which all sought to affect change through critique. As we have seen by other authors in earlier chapters, there are naturally various ways to affect change through critique. However, the particular change efforts drawn upon on here specifically refers to interventions where professionals were invited to suspend concerns for economic actualities, and to temporarily subvert dominant marketing logic in order to think differently about products, consumers and the role of marketing itself. These change initiatives were informed by a social constructionist argument whereby affecting change through critique may be realized if we attempt research as an *activity* seeking to move beyond accepted realities (Gergen, 1999). They were also informed by the idea of seeing the individual as a 'signifier of change', as a 'change agent', a concept which occupies a central position in organizational change theory (Cummings and Huse, 1989; Senior, 2002). As a 'change agent' the marketer actively instigates change and positively contributes to the creation of alternative futures. In this context, *being critical* does not mean standing *outside* marketing exposing its many flaws and weaknesses, rather it involves an *active* commitment to improving the abilities of those practising marketing to question the status quo and envisioning alternatives. Thus, I have sought to affect change through practice as well as through theory and analysis. If following the logic of Buchanan and Huczynski (1997), critique is then not something that is opposed to Marketing, but rather seeks to encourage participation and involvement in change by those who are affected.

This chapter is organized as follows: First, there is a brief review of how my interventions accounted for here build on the extant criticism directed towards marketing. Second, I introduce the reader to the idea of seeing individuals as 'change agents', and I will elaborate on the consequences of adopting this kind of thinking, both on practice and research. Third, I will reflect upon my own experiences of what happens when we seek to affect change through critique. My reflections are organized under three headings related to processes that occur as we seek to rethink our practice: 'addiction to reality', 'rationalizing our way out of change' and finally 'a question of legitimacy'. This chapter will conclude by offering some final reflections upon the extent to which we can affect change through critique and how we can journey beyond, what Emile Durkheim would refer to as marketing's 'collective consciousness' (1966), and create images of our own discipline without having to cover it in decorative paint.

Affecting Change through Critique

There has been no shortage of criticism directed towards marketing theory and practice both from within (Feldman, 1971; Fisk, 1974; Kilbourne et al., 1997;

Van Dam and Apeldoorn, 1996) and outside the discipline (Haug, 1986; Packard, 1957). In order not to repeat, a by now potentially familiar argument with the reader, I will only briefly review some of the criticism directed towards marketing, with the purpose of illustrating how this extant criticism has influenced the interventions accounted for here.

As a 'marketer', inhabiting an academic 'Marketing Department', I have grown increasingly critical towards the practice and theory of my own discipline. The inquiries accounted for here are manifestations of my own continuously growing urge to challenge the underlying assumptions driving the marketing doctrine. Subsequently, I have sympathized with other critical scholars, from early writings by Wolfgang Haug, who by referring to marketing as the 'illusion industry' (1986, pp. 120–121) argued it played havoc with consumers' minds, and more recent writing by Kilbourne et al. (1997), who in their now seminal article in *Journal of Macromarketing* argued that marketing as a discipline has 'contributed to the existence of a patriarchal society and to the destruction of the natural world' (1997, p. 11). Being well aware of the supposed 'evils' of marketing, well publicized by writers such as Naomi Klein (2001) in her book *No Logo*, by anti-consumerist magazines like *Adbusters*, and by on-line communities such as *Commercial Alert* who seek to prevent marketing 'from exploiting children and subverting the higher values of family, community, environmental integrity and democracy' (http://www.commercialalert.org/), I have over the years become increasingly impatient with the present. Despite criticism raised some time ago by both Feldman (1971) and Fisk (1974), marketing has yet to show that this critique is central to professional marketing practice. The potential problem with marketing is that it lacks *objectivity* and, to borrow the term from Peter Senge (1990), suffers from a learning disability. First, by being (1) too close to the problem, (2) part of the problem and (3) part of the capitalist system creating the problem, marketers frequently lack the necessary objectivity required to re-examine its own unsustainable beliefs and habits. Second, because the most important consequences of our actions as marketers occur elsewhere in the system, we have difficulty in learning from our experiences. Consequently, here I follow scholars (Kilbourne et al., 1997) who argue that the solution to environmental and social problems lies in the changing of our current social organization, the 'dominant social paradigm' (DSP). The DSP is defined by Milbrath (1984, p. 7) as '. . . the metaphysical beliefs, institutions, habits, etc. that collectively provide social lenses through which individuals and group interpret their social world'. Kilbourne et al. (1997) suggest that the more confidence people have in their belief structure and the current economic, political and social institutions, the less concerned they are with the natural environment. Thus, it is only through a transformation of the way we as individuals think, feel and act, that there can be lasting improvements in our behaviour towards the environment.

Critically important in leading and inspiring deeper change in our marketing practice, and to avoid the accusation of exploiting and manipulating consumers' needs, a radical alternative approach to what obligations and tasks marketers could and should perform in a more sustainable market place is needed. Marketer, in whatever disguise, have to rethink their identity to an extent that they have perhaps never had to do before. This is a task of grand proportions, requiring us marketers to be more demanding of ourselves (Kajzer-Mitchell, 2005). In order to assist the creation of new form of marketing it is crucial to adopt an alternative persona, one that is not associated with the marketer as a talented pusher, dedicated to make use compulsive consumers (Brown, 1995, p. xvi). I propose here that we seek to recast ourselves as 'change agents', as signifiers of positive change towards sustainable living patterns.

The Change Agent

The concept of 'change agent' occupies a critical position in organizational change theory and in order to explore the critical role of the individual marketer as an *agent of change* I draw from the writings of Cummings and Huse (1989), Paton and McCalman (2000), Friedman (2001) and Senior (2002). The consequences of adopting this kind of thinking is that *first*, as change agent, the marketer adopt a more proactive persona, that is, actively instigates change and attempts to consciously move beyond current capacity as opposed to merely reacting to events as they occur (Cummings and Huse, 1989). Since change agents are not complainers who simply sit back to be judged by others (Friedman, 2001), as a signifier of change, the marketer can address its current negative persona and play an important role in creating a vision of a desired future. As Cummings and Huse suggest they could 'energise movement in this direction' (1989, p. 57) by playing a crucial role in setting these change processes in motion. As a facilitator of change (Senior, 2002) the key challenges for the marketer would be to find creative ways to assist organizations to offer alternative sustainable solutions, and provide directions in the implementation of these alternatives (Paton and McCalman, 2000). In short, the marketers would seek to help both organizations and other stakeholders to devise strategies for managing the transition from the present to the future.

Adopting a 'change agent' perspective has implications not only for marketing practitioners but naturally also for *marketers* residing in the world of academia. I have speculated elsewhere on this (Kajzer Mitchell, 2005), and whilst taking a change agent approach to our research we might find that as researchers we assume the role of provocateurs; thus using our intellectual curiosity to ask radical questions, to rise above presuppositions, and to turn marketing assumptions and existing perspectives around. As 'change agents' we risk security, and abandon the notion of the researcher as a passive observer, an immobile spectator, prying into the secret lives of customers or organizations. By positioning the researcher as an agent of change we begin to acknowledge our academic abilities not only to interpret, and respond to the circumstances around us, but our role in shaping those interpretations. As scholars we, in the words of Law and Urry (2003), are not just describing the world as it is but also involved in enacting it.

An Invitation to Act Differently

In the interventions which I draw from in this chapter, I assumed the role of an academic 'change agent'. In my early interventions this was a more unconscious process and later more conscious and deliberate. What all the encounters had in common was that they were designed as invitations to act (Beech, 2002) where current assumptions were temporarily subverted. I designed creative situations (i.e. circumstances conducive to creativity (Amabile, 1983)), where a diverse range of participants, not just from marketing, but also design and product innovation, were encouraged to suspend concerns for economic actualities and existing assumptions of the marketplace. Through the use of various creativity techniques such as brainstorming, role playing (Stein, 1974, 1975), provocations and other lateral thinking techniques (De Bono, 1996), I stimulated participants to *think* differently about products, consumers and marketing itself, and to *do* something differently. The selected individuals' accounts which I will refer to were obtained in various ways, either through conversations during or after workshops, some of which were in-house company sponsored, and some which were set up independently with other workshop facilitators. Other accounts are based on informal creative discussions with individuals.

In seeking to affect change through critique, my thinking and subsequent empirical work has been informed by a constructionist argument and an action-research epistemology whereby affecting change through critique may be realized when we attempt to approach research as an *activity* seeking to move beyond accepted realities. It refers to finding ways to open ourselves to different sort of realities and create opportunities to explore new modes of understanding and action (Gergen, 1999; Reason, 2003). The word *action* here refers to 'not just doing things to obtain specific results, but to doing things in a way that also questions assumptions and potentially reframes future activity' (Reason and Torbert, 2001, p. 10). In contrary to other efforts seeking to affect change through critique, my efforts were not guided by analytical *what-is* type of thinking, that is *What is this situation? What is the truth?*, but by *what-if* type thinking. *What-if* type of thinking encourages us to focus attention on questions such as: *What happens if we think of marketing differently? What would happen if we envisioned an alternative future? What new images would we create?* As such my role as a researcher was not pry into organizational life to unravel 'bad behaviour' of corporates but to play an active facilitating role in creating these new images and challenge our assumptions of products, customers and the role of marketing. As Morgan (1993, 1997) argues, images and ideas that we hold of ourselves and our world have fundamental impact on how our realities unfold.

What Happens When We Seek to Affect Change through Critique?

So what happens when we seek to affect change through critique? The following section outlines illustrations drawn from my interactions with individuals and organizations under headings related to processes that occur as we seek to rethink our practice in light of contemporary and social problems. Conceptual contribution to inform this discussion comes from organizational behaviour and change theory (e.g. Lewis, 2000; Senge, 1990; Westenholz, 1993) but I will also make reference to writings by social theorists (e.g. Agger, 1991; Bergen and Luckmann, 1966; Watzlawick, 1976). Turning to these authors illuminates our understanding of how change occurs and doesn't occur and help us expand our understanding of the tension inherent in the change processes at work when se seek to be critical and rethink assumptions about marketing.

'The Way Things Simply Are': An Addiction to Reality

I use the term *addiction* here to signal the complex ways in which I experienced individuals are unable to give up the current status quo, 'the way things simply are'. Through many of the interventions which I reflect upon here, I experienced a continuous dialectic tension between what is perceived as reality; *what-is*, and what could be; *what-if*? This tension, which resides in the shadow between the alternative and our perception and understanding of commonly accepted marketing logic, appears habitual (i.e. it becomes a recurrent norm and a mental attitude towards the usual practice of things). This tension feeds on a general assumption about reality, that there is a reality that *ought to be* (i.e. that there is *one* reality out there which is acceptable). This addiction to the real world is problematic, particularly since it becomes a source of justification and determines what we should focus our attention on, and ultimately sets the stage for non-change to take place. Consequently, as we are allowing ourselves to continue life within our comfort zone, we limit our abilities to look beyond preconceptions and to envision and accept alternative realities.

This dependency upon existing realities expressed by participants is evident in the following stories. I begin with Eva, who runs her own marketing consultancy business. This illustration draws from interactions with Eva two weeks after she attended one of my innovation workshops. In her reflections on the workshop she is keen to be portrayed as someone who is sympathetic towards change, and someone who has made a shift in her thinking. However, she continuously refers to need to have an understanding of what the real world is:

> **Eva:** I mean I am down to earth person. I think it is entirely right to be sustainable. I think that it needs to be talked about in acceptable terms. Very down to earth, yes have the ideology behind it, but always link it to something that people can relate to . . . The answer to all of this is not about being revolutionary. The answer is about looking at how we live in society at the moment and coming up with ideas that work together with society. You know, rather an evolutionary approach . . . And I think, how we evolve towards more sustainable way of living is to say, "well let's look at what we are doing at the moment."

This commitment to what is real is further articulated in Brian's account, a business development manager. In a post-workshop discussion he clearly states his position:

> **Brian**: You know, my approach to all this, is that it has got to be based, or it has got to include an understanding of what the real world is for some people . . . A lot of it [sustainability] has been sort of intellectualised, as it is actually, from my point of view, who is working in a business and has done so for many years, it is difficult to see the relevance of some of it, for the way that things really are.

Like many other participants Eva and Brian argue that change need to be grounded in a parallel commitment for the way 'that things really are'. In, another account provided by John, a regional marketing manager with a car manufacturer, the need to make the potential alternative 'real' is used an excuse to interrupt the change process:

> **John**: I think the key to all this is real-life examples of someone who has [done it]. If you don't give me real life models who have taken an alternative approach to business I will not understand what you mean. I am being honest with you, I need someone to show me example, real world examples.

Paradoxically, John is setting an ultimatum to the facilitator, arguing that if he is given what is real (i.e. examples of what already exists, then he will envision alternatives). However, John's persistent reference, to borrow the term from Watzlawick, 'the perennial now', the constant and everlasting now, risks of becoming a delusion 'of which we spend substantial parts of our daily life shoring up to, even at the considerable risk of trying to force facts to fit our definition of reality' (1976, p. pxii). Westenholz (1993) research on 'frame of reference' helps us understand the underlying processes behind both John's, Eva's and Brian's addiction to the real. In the words of Westenholz:

> Because we are social beings, we contribute to create the world that adherents of the modern myth think lies beyond themselves. This does not imply that a reality, which both sets limits to our behaviour and offers us possibilities, does not exist. Rather it implies that reality is chaotic and unstable to such an extent that it cannot be represented by unambiguous pictures. It also indicates that our way of constructing our pictures (frames of reference) of the world is decisive of our world view. As social beings, we are creating these pictures to defend our identity against a chaotic world . . . At the same time, however, the pictures become a prison into which we are locked, so that we cannot view the world 'afresh' (1993, p. 39).

Although my experience is that individuals may challenge their existing frames of references by creating alternative mental pictures, for example through role play and design of scenarios, yet this (1) occurs for only *a moment in time* and (2) is but a minor alteration of status quo. Thus, it is questionable whether deep change is actually taking place, and whether the new alternative is simply not just the old covered in decorative paint. Westenholz argues that we as individuals relapse into our old frames of reference before we get the time to construct new understandings of a situation. The individual may experience being left in a void so frightening that he or she returns to their known frame. We may have sympathy for the alternative; however, the expectations and demands of existing realities are overpowering (Kajzer, 2004). Language plays a key role here in reinforcing existing frames of reference. Common to the stories told so far is that the language used articulate that there are 'rules or structures underlying the surface features of the world', and that there exists 'a "right" way of doing things' which can be discovered (Burr, 1995, p. 12), or perhaps I should rather say, delivered by external actors. I will return to this discussion later in this chapter. However, if we accept the constructionist argument that language and thought are inseparable, mutually dependent (Burr, 1995), then this kind of language play an important role in producing and constructing our experiences. Speech that is not contested eventually becomes the rule of precedent that hides future behaviour of speech (Watzlawick, 1976). By continuously making reference to, and not contesting, the 'real', Eva, Brian and John act as servants of existing realities addicted to a reality *out there* which is assumed to operate according to unquestionable rules. An unlikely originator of this kind of passive thinking came from the artists during the Renaissance, who through their reliance on geometry promoted a linearity of thought that argued we could know the world through distanced seeing. Consequently, the world is a distant spectacle where they as viewer take the person of immobile spectator (Purser et al., 1995). I find the legacy of this kind of thinking still very present in many of my own change interventions, and this addiction to reality and servant mentality has proven to be habits almost impossible to break free from.

However I have also found it is not only the addiction to reality outlined above, but also individual's tendency to *rationalize* their way out of change that interrupts change. This process of rationalizing ones way out of change, which I will elaborate on next, is very much a by-product of our addiction to reality, and the linear ways of looking at the world it fosters.

'Yes to Change, But No to Change': Rationalizing Our Way Out of Change

Whilst I found that participants were sympathetic towards alternative marketing realities at the same time they were finding increasingly elaborate justifications as not to change, and continue servicing the marketing machine. As Senge notes in the *5th Discipline* we tend to blame outside circumstances for our problems (1990). Commonly, this is manifested through a process of externalization, whereby changing the status quo and envisioning alternatives is made dependable on external factors such as the customer and the employer.

To illustrate my argument I will first return to Eva, the marketing consultant. As we saw earlier, Eva is keen to be portrayed as someone who is sympathetic towards change. In our conversation she is suggesting that the lack of change in Marketing is due to lack of companies willing to 'stick their head above the parapet', and to be prepared to 'fail or stand by what they feel'. When being asked a few weeks after the workshop, to what extent she has been able to act upon the outcomes of the workshop, she explains:

> **Eva**: No, not yet – too early . . . There has not been the opportunity. These things evolve, and having the right client really, is the most important thing . . . when you go and get a client, you have to really match what you can do with what they need – as a starting point. Then you build a certain level of trust, and then you can introduce new ideas. And at the moment, my relationships with my clients are so early, that you know it wouldn't help at this stage, to distract . . . But later down the line, yes of course.

Whilst arguing that the lack of change is due to organizations and individuals not being prepared to stand up for their alternative ideas, Eva is herself guilty of externalizing the initiative to enact change, by blaming, in this case, the potential client. Consequently, she is also guilty of not acknowledging her own role as a marketer in this process of change. Similarly to Eva, George, an experienced product designer with a sports shoe manufacturer, justifies his own inability to enact change by externalizing the responsibility to the customers. George, however also blames other colleagues within the organizations as reasons to not enact change. The account below is taken from a follow-up conversation a few weeks after the workshop he attended:

> **George**: In all honesty I have not really applied this kind of thinking in how I am currently approaching more sustainable products. Why? A myriad of reasons. And it is too bad, because I really do like the perspective shift the ideas conveys . . . It just feels like it would be too big . . . I like it on one side but it feels awfully intimidating, it feels like "oh my God we have to worry about so much!, in other words it is too much to take on. Especially at the stage that we are, where shoes are not typically something people worry about, like how it is disposed of for instance.
>
> When I say too much to take on I am probably thinking about: 'how much can a company accomplish?' I am looking for what we can start doing. I think we are looking for a catalyst, some things that we can do that really turn some internal momentum on sustainability with our products. I think we all hope that this will change the way we manufacture, sell and you know deal with our products, all of them.

But we have to start kind of small, if you will. You want to get a couple of wins; you want to get a little bit of momentum behind things . . .
Because then you will have to worry about every single aspect of it
and we would run the risk of maybe not getting anything done! . . . I
am really worried getting things off on the right foot, being successful . . . because I am worried if it is a failure then we will jump off it . . .
We want to demonstrate internally that we can build this product
and it is going to perform like it should perform, we are not going to
compromise performance on it.

At various points in his account, George justifies his own inertia and reluc-
tance to enact new ideas by blaming customers, as well as his other colleagues
within the organization. Once again Westenholz (1993) writing on frame of reference, introduced earlier, helps us understand both Eva's and George's efforts
to rationalize their way out of change. She explains that individuals when
returning to their own organizational milieu will be afraid to express new
attitudes as 'he or she has committed some kind of treason, viewed from the
perspective of the old reference group' (1993, p. 55). An individual who then
seeks to implement alternatives may experience being isolated from others
frame of reference and what ever new attitudes they will show will be interpreted and incorporated into the old patterns by remaining part of the organization. Building on this, an alternative way to make sense of what is going
on in Eva's and George's accounts is to apply the logic of self-censorship.
According to Williams (2004) self-censorship includes the conscious choice to
withhold or the unconscious inhibition of one's creative ideas. This implies
that an individual, who judges his or her ideas to be infeasible, ineffective
or strange, may consciously choose to withhold them (Parloff and Handlon,
1964). It also suggests that an individual may censor ideas on a subconscious level (Meichenbaum, 1975), that is the perceived threatening climate
for unconventional thinking, the perceived expectation of negative evaluation may create unconscious mental blocks for creativity. This is captured in
George's account where he simultaneously expresses optimism and fear about
change, and where getting on with the 'real job' intensifies the tension. The
alternative is perceived as 'a noble future goal', but not really something he
feels he can disclose to the rest of the organization.

Yet, another way of rationalizing ones way out of change is provided by
Kim, a marketing manager for a science centre, and Dennis, a product designer
with an electronics manufacturer. Similarly to the earlier stories, they both
externalize the responsibility to enact change, however in this case they refer
to one of the most fundamental marketing assumptions of all – the sovereignty
of the customer. The science centre where Kim works takes great pride in
promoting themselves as a sustainable enterprise, using state of the art environmental technology to reduce the ecological impact of their activities. The
particular account below relates to an incident where Kim is provoked to challenge the inherent tension residing in the practice of a sustainable business;
the need to consume less versus the need for continuous raise in sales.

> **Kim:** Somewhere along the line I think we have too much faith in marketing. Maybe one can fool people during short periods to buy unnecessary things . . . Where should one draw the line of what an individual needs? Does a child need 1 or 4 toys? That must be people's own responsibility, to put things in a bigger perspective. . . . Well, and then everything is built upon some sort of commercial activity! Then I think that in a way it is better that people by a high quality environmentally adapted toy from us rather than from one of the big toy chains that maybe do not have the same criteria as us.

Significantly, in this first passage we witness Kim externalizing change by shifting the responsibility away from himself towards the customer, in this case, the parents who bring their children to the science centre. He then defends his inability to enact change by referring to the assumption that 'everything is built upon some sort of commercial activity'. The kind of individual defensiveness expressed in Kim's account risks of becoming habitual, which in turn may become not only a protection of the individual, but of the maintenance and perpetuations of an organization or society at large (Vince and Broussine, 1996). Next, we see him become increasingly creative in finding justifications for non-change to take place. Even though he temporarily, for a moment in time, recognizes his own role in the construction of reality, he does in the end resorts to escapism:

> **Kim:** This type of question really require that one create an understanding amongst consumers [and] maybe this is part of our responsibility . . . I think that maybe what we want to try and do is communicate the information and generate interest for people to go and find out more for themselves and make up their own mind about thing. We do not have the ambition to tell people what is right and what is wrong . . . Also we do not take a stand like other more commercial organisation can do . . . We communicate scientific facts, but making value propositions is not within our remit.

If following the argument by Horkheimer and Adorno (1972) Kim is, whilst seeking to avoid making a value commitment, making the strongest value commitment of all that we can have it both ways – we can consume and conserve at the same time. Next, Dennis, a product designer with an electronics manufacturer, is provoked to question the role the company he works for have in creating a more sustainable society.

> **Dennis:** I think it would possibly be very dangerous to turn all our marketing information around to say 'buy [our product] because it is a sustainable product' . . . It is absolutely customers' choice . . . what we do is a by-product of human nature, people like collecting things. If you are a car enthusiast you want it to go faster, if you are a bicycle enthusiast you want a lighter bike that has got better gears on. That improvement process is always going to have redundancy.

As both Kim's earlier account and Dennis narrative above suggest, individuals use the assumption of consumer choice to legitimize a no-change situation. Ford and Ford (1994) argue that we as human beings distinguish phenomena by placing boundaries around it. We create these boundaries around phenomena in order to provide us with a sense of being, as well as sense making-abilities. Confined to the boundaries of existing marketing ideology Kim and Dennis rationalize their way into a non-change situation by refereeing to popular marketing wisdom where customer choice is perceived as the ultimate truth. Lewis (2000, p. 762) notes these 'distinctions become objectified over time, giving actors the impression that their perceptions are distinct and immutable entities'. The following final illustration is yet another example of this. In 2005 I was asked to design and facilitate two in-house workshops with a manufacturing organization, which for the purpose of this chapter will be referred to as *SustainBiz*. Participants were all employees related to *SustainBiz* marketing function. The two workshops, which were designed to encourage participants to examine day-to-day marketing realities from different perspectives and to critically examine extant roles of marketers, generated a wealth of new ideas. The traditional marketing tools such as the 4Ps were challenged and replaced with alternatives, and the participants embraced a much more proactive role as marketers. After the two workshops had taken place I had the opportunity to attend a 2-day business plan review meeting where the purpose was for *SustainBiz* marketers to show how they had integrated the new ideas and alternative marketing perspectives generated at previous workshops into the business plans for the following financial year. Expectations were very high however it quickly became apparent that it was back 'to business as usual'. Marketers at *SustainBiz* seemed unable to let go of conventional marketing models and it was becoming apparent that, as Fitchett and McDonagh point out, this dominant discourse not only 'furnish us with a way of reporting and discussing any given issue but actually go some way to constructing the issue' (2000, p. 211). Frustration was building up as the meeting progressed. Participants started questioning 'what is holding us back?' It quickly transpired that, similarly to Kim and Dennis, the marketers at *SustainBiz* treated existing marketing logic as an immutable entity, and blamed it for lack of change. As one marketing manager explained: 'what I am guilty in some respect is that I am so customer focused . . . I have had to prioritize . . . We just do not have the time to single-handily trying to make a difference'. What is captured in the narrative above is how extant marketing logic, specifically the use of the 4Ps is used as a culprit against change.

'Is it Legitimate?': A Question of Legitimacy

Next our discussion will turn political, in other words we will move beyond the individual to consider social structures. Attachment to the status quo, to *what-is*, is not only about a continuity in the structure of meaning within the individual, but it also involves the ways in which the current order and the routines supporting it is reinforced by the ontological security that it provides for both individuals and groups. Social theory has informed my thinking here, particularly Berger and Luckmann's (1966) writings on the sociology of knowledge. According to these scholars social reality is precarious, although how precarious depends on the social structural position of the group espousing the conception of reality. By this it is suggested that some versions of reality have more strength than others 'by virtue of their authors' right of appeal to an institutional power base' (p. 308). Affecting change through critique becomes pre-eminently a political task to the extent that the alternative gains legitimacy if it acquires endorsement from other powerful actors (Hayagreeva et al., 2000).

The often subconscious political forces define the boundaries of individual marketers and organizations at large, legitimizing certain interpretations, attitudes and reactions over others. As a facilitator of many of the change initiatives described in this chapter, I often experienced the feeling of being 'pulled back' by many of the participants, and the organizations they were representing. With this I mean: they formed their perception of me, and the day itself, to fit their own individual norm and/or the organization they represented, resulting in a 'nice day out'. I have realized from experience that alternative thinking, for example in line with an ecological paradigm, can therefore be appropriated not necessarily as a source of cultural transformation, but as an instrument for leaving prevailing social orders unchanged (Merchant, 1992). As Parker writes alternatives 'do not need to be suppressed or burnt on the street, merely labelled as utopian' (2002, p. 4). There is a real danger of the alternative being perceived as an utopia, and expression of desire, and imaginary good place (Carey, 2000) as this often is associated with unobtainable, not realistic or practical. When utopian means impractical or unrealistic then as Parker (2002, p. 3) suggest it is by definition the opposite of sensible managerial strategies to organize the world, and 'of course, who would want to be impractical and unrealistic'.

By assigning the alternative with a sense of impracticality, unrealism and ideals, we encourage myopic behaviour and close off opportunities to push boundaries and explore alternative through critique. It becomes very difficult to think beyond current orders, or to, as Gergen (1994a) suggests we do, vivify possibilities of new modes of action, when we are faced with practicalities and a constant search for market legitimacy. What we as marketers seem to forget is that our collective marketing doctrine is but one alternative among many, yet we perceive it the ultimate truth. Is it perhaps as Parker suggests 'an odd trick of marketing' that our current order itself is not labelled utopian? Our current order is a reality that is political, it is an utopia that matters' (2002, p. 4). As we have seen earlier, this reality is perceived to be *outside* and above us; it constrains the individual and shapes their daily lives (Kajzer, 2004). Mathew, an environmental manager with a car manufacturer expresses this in his account below:

Mathew: We are force fed that everything is consumable, it is throw away, we are a throw away society [and] manufacturers deliver to that philosophy to make themselves an economically sustainable business. It is about 'replacing' all the time, otherwise companies would not exist . . . I am so entrenched in the fire-fighting in the reactive mechanisms within the business . . . it is like an oppression industry that does not allow [alternative thinking] . . . You do not want to be seen out of the mainstream itself. It is about acceptability and what spheres of influence that you have, and how to better increase those.

In the case above Mathew clearly expresses he does not have the freedom to act according to his own wishes and desires. It can be argued that this is paradoxical, in the sense that our human species has come to the verge of dominating everything that happens on the surface of the planet (McKibben, 2000). Or as the Czech-born philosopher Vilém Flusser (1999, p. 37) writes:

We cook up worlds in any form we wish, and we do this at least as well as the Creator did in the course of the much celebrated six days. We are the master witches' brewers, the designers, and this makes it possible, now that we have outsmarted God, to sweep away all can't about reality.

However my experience is that people often are unaware of the mental models they hold on to, that is the deeply ingrained assumptions, generalizations that influence how we understand the world and how we take action (Senge, 1990). I am inclined to agree with both Gladwin et al. (1995) who argue that our mental models often are incomplete, fragmented and often not even recognized, nor appreciated by their holder. This is problematic, specifically as if we are not able to embrace and enact upon alternatives how are then to be reminded that social beliefs are constructions, and that other constructions are also possible? Those familiar with Marx famous analysis of commodity fetishism and the notion of 'false consciousness' will find the empirical encounters discussed earlier illustrate individuals inability to experience and recognize social relations as historical accomplishments that *can* be transformed. Instead, if following Ben Agger's (1991) argument marketers 'falsely' experience their lives as products of an unchangeable social nature. In sociological terms this would mean that marketing professional have internalized certain values and norms that causes them to participate and reinforce existing systems. We apply a form of formal logic, that is we will be driven towards internal consistency, and polarize the elements (change and non-change) to stress distinctions and insurmountable differences rather than independencies (Lewis, 2000). To complicate matters further, by rewarding individuals servicing the existing system, we ensures a degree of conformity and passivity amongst people (Chomsky and Herman, 1979, Vol. 2).

Concluding Reflections: Can We Change Our Collective Consciousness?

A key task of this chapter has been to illuminate our understanding of some of the change processes that occur as we as critical marketing scholars seek to affect change through critique. The change efforts elaborated on here specifically referred to creative situations where individuals were invited to suspend concerns for economic actualities, and temporarily subvert dominant marketing logic in order to think differently about products, consumers and the role of marketing itself. Whilst reflecting upon these empirical encounters it became clear that individuals experience their lives as products of a certain unchangeable social nature. More specifically, as servants of existing realities we act as if reality is *out there*, holding the answers to our questions, influencing us, rather than us being part of it. In this way we are servants of a reality that is assumed to operate according to certain predetermined norms and values. This is not dissimilar to Emile Durkheim's term 'collective consciousness' suggesting that there is a set of common values and belief that is held important in the minds of all members of a particular community and which influence our ways of acting, thinking and feeling. These values and norms metaphorically act as glue, keeping the existing marketing order intact, and are given permanence by being repeated in our verbal language, transmitted by education, and fixed even in writing (Durkheim, 1966). As we have seen in this chapter this 'collective consciousness' is expressed in a variety of formal and informal ways, ranging from the use of established marketing tools such as the 4Ps, to everyday informal marketing discourse whereby individual consumer choice is celebrated as universal truth. To challenge this collective consciousness becomes problematic for a number of reasons. First, as Durkheim (1966) argued himself, this collective consciousness takes a persona of it is own scrutinizing every act which offends it and offering resistance against every individual efforts that seeks to violate it. In his own words:

> If I attempt to violate the law, it reacts against me . . . if I tried to escape . . . my attempts would fail miserably . . . Even when I free myself from these rules and violate them successfully, I am always compelled to struggle with them.
>
> Durkheim (1966, pp. 2–3)

Second, as Agger (1991) suggests, individuals believe that they can achieve modest personal betterment by complying with social norms and that large-scale social changes beyond this are impossible. Following Durkheim and Agger's line of thought, extant marketing values function ideologically to foreshorten people's imagining of what is possible. In other words, the shared values and norms ensure that individuals intentionally and unintentionally act in coherent and agreed-upon ways. In writing this chapter, accounting and reliving the inquiries that I was a part of, I have come to conclude that *critique* in itself does not give us guidelines for how to enable individuals to overcome these constraints, and does not provide us with mechanisms to help us cope with the challenges arising as we seek to affect change through critique. How, then do we journey beyond our 'collective consciousness' and create images of our own discipline without having to cover it in decorative paint. Do we as marketers have the ability to re-evaluate, to contest old truths and initiate an open dialogue amongst our contemporaries? In order to conclude this chapter and provide avenues for future directions I will offer some reflection on how we can creatively change marketing's 'collective consciousness'. The following suggestions are by no means conclusive; rather serve as an initial tentative ideas that are open for debate.

A Matter of Free Movement

As we saw earlier individuals have a tendency to blame the *other* (i.e. other individuals and outside circumstances for the inability to enact change). These external barriers are frequently perceived as insurmountable obstacles which individuals experience they do not have the power to change. I imply here that in order to affect change through critique it is crucial that individuals develop an alternative relationship to their environment. At the heart of this lies the individuals amount of what one might call 'space of free movement', introduced by Kurt Lewin in his book *Resolving Social Conflicts* (1948, p. 5), which he refers to as 'one of the most important facts of social life' (p. 150). Following his logic lack of free movement creates for a group, as for an individual, high tension which in turn may result in conservatism and lack of development. However, the more 'individuals recognize their own role in creating their images of reality and in shaping the context in which learning occurs the more proactive they can be in determining their space of free movement' (Friedman, 2001, p. 411). Organizational change theory tells us that whilst seeking to expand individuals space for free movement we are required us to assess their 'change agent power', meaning we are invited to evaluate the individuals own source of power (Cummings and Huse, 1989, p. 57). This will in turn allow the individual marketer to identify areas in which they might need to enhance their sources of power, and determine how to use it to influence others to support change.

A Matter of Generative Capacity

However, the cure lies not only in our relationship with the 'other'. Equipped with an inability to challenge agreed-upon realities individuals often lack the capacity to challenge the guiding assumptions of our dominant marketing ideology. In the words of Gergen (1994b, p. 109) individuals lack generative capacity: 'the capacity to challenge the guiding assumptions of the culture, to raise fundamental questions regarding contemporary social life, to foster reconsiderations of that which is "taken for granted" and thereby to generate fresh alternatives for social action'. Yet somehow if we are to alter our 'collective consciousness' and affect change, individuals must cultivate the habit of perceiving reality as precarious and changeable, and thus challenge their enacted role as spectators. As I have argued elsewhere, there is a need for a better understanding of how our day-to-day activities draw upon and reproduce unsustainable social systems (Kajzer, 2004). In other words, it is imperative to heighten marketers' awareness of the connection between patterns in their own lives and the wider system. This is perhaps the real challenges of marketing education where the task becomes to liberate future marketers; discover ways in which we simultaneously have the freedom to conserve the past and to create new futures. As Csikszentmihalyi and Rochberg-Halton (1981, p. 246) suggest, this process of liberation does not happen spontaneously:

> because the wisdom of the past has trained us to hold on to goals that have been of service before. But the wisdom of the past must constantly be reinterpreted and cultivated in order to create the wisdom of the future.

Ultimately, following the logic of Adams' 'blockbusting' skills (1987) critical marketers need address the perceptual blocks that inhibit this liberation process and encourage individuals to develop scepticism towards existing answers, techniques and approaches. As Csikszentmihalyi and Rochberg-Halton argue 'it is through the outcomes of perception that new patterns of thought and emotion emerge' (1981, p. 246).

A Matter of New Knowledge and Old Knowledge

Our ability to effect change through critique is heavily reliant on individuals extant knowledge base. As change agent, the marketer 'must have the expertise and information needed to persuade stakeholders that the changes are logical way to meet their needs' (Cummings and Huse, 1989, p. 118). However, my experience is that individuals do not necessarily possess this kind of knowledge. Thus, they are not 'knowledge agents' (Giddens, 1984, p. 281), who know about the consequences of what they do in their day-to-day lives, rather they possess a limited ability to articulate what they do and the reason for it. As we saw from some of the participants' accounts earlier, whereas some individuals feel they can sympathize with, and possess knowledge about the alternative, they cannot enact it. Argyris and Schön (1974, pp. 6–7) make a helpful distinction between 'espoused' theory representing what people or organizations say about their behaviour, and 'theories-in-use' which are implicit in their behaviour. Addressing theories-in-use becomes a matter of discarding obsolete and misleading knowledge – unlearning is as important part of understanding as adding new knowledge (Hedberg, 1981). In concluding this chapter I argue that in order to effect change through critique we need a better understanding not only of how existing knowledge impede the performance of new behaviour, but also how individuals create new knowledge (i.e. unlearn the old and learn the new). By taking an organizational learning perspective (see Argyris, 1990; Senge, 1990) we could then devise interventions that seek to allow individuals to develop a more systemic world view and learn how to reflect upon their current mental models; allowing prevailing assumptions to be brought into the open.

A Matter of Thinking Paradoxically

Furthermore, challenging marketing's collective consciousness may require a particular set of attributes and skills for dealing specifically with the conflict and resistance that change often causes. I argue here that as marketers we need to learn to think paradoxically. Westenholz (1993) defines it as a process through which we establish a new relationship with the situation we are in. In her own words:

> To establish a new relationship with the situation means to realise that one does not know in advance what the situation is about. Once has no fixed model of the reality and of one's own identity in this context. Possession of a paradoxical understanding in this situation helps one recognise that the situation is not what it seems to be. A paradoxical understanding of one's previous identity leads to the loss of meaning – a deframing – that makes one open to other lines of thought. This opens up the prospect of mutually constructing the social definition necessary to bridge old prejudices in order to handle recurring problems differently (1993, p. 56).

By identifying, and even go as far as creating paradoxes we can begin to locate important points of leverage. Lewis and Kelemen (2002, p. 265) write that 'preserving opposition invokes creative tension', and in our case it may inspire us to break free of traditional *what-is* and *what-if* dualities. O'Conners (1995), writing from an organizational change perspective, provides us with some further useful advice, suggesting that by not confronting the paradoxical tensions inherent in change we will be unable to learn. By failing to 'recognise limits and to reflect upon the effects of these limits' we may 'restrict the creativity and integrity of the change of "transformation" process' (p. 791). Jung, too, emphasized the role of tension of the opposites in attaining an archetypal balanced wholeness. In order to arrive at creative new solutions to old problems we must according to Jung not only tolerate, but actively seek to bring out the painful and maddening opposites in our lives (Harris, 1996). By immersing ourselves in the opposing views, applying divergent thinking as opposed to convergent thinking (Westenholz, 1993), we can then begin to foster an appreciation of the limitations of our current marketing wisdom (Kajzer, 2004). As marketing professionals and academics, we would then continuously strive to entertain conflicting knowledge simultaneously (Lewis and Kelemen, 2002). Naturally, it is not an easy task to begin thinking paradoxically, as Watzlawick (1976) argues it requires, first, a very high degree of maturity with the individual, and second, tolerance for others to live with relative truth. However, 'if we cannot develop this ability we will, without knowing it, relegate ourselves to the Grand Inquisitor's world, in which we will live the lives of sheep, occasionally troubled by the acrid smokes rising from some auto-da-fé or chimneys of crematoria' (Watzlawick, 1976, p. 222).

References

Adams, J.L. (1987). *Conceptual Blockbusting*, 3rd edition. Harmondsworth: Penguin Books.

Agger, B. (1991). 'Critical theory, poststructuralism, postmodernism: their sociological relevance'. *Annual Review of Sociology*, 17, 105–131.

Amabile, T.M. (1983). 'The social psychology of creativity: a componential conceptualization'. *Journal of Personality and Social Psychology*, 45(2), 357–376.

Argyris, C. (1990). *Overcoming Organizational Defences. Facilitating Organizational Learning*. Boston: Allyn and Bacon.

Argyris, C. and Schön, D. (1974). *Theory in Practice: Increasing Professional Effectiveness*. San Francisco: Jossey Bass.

Beech, N. (2002). 'An exploration of identity as a paradoxical factor in organizational change/inertia', in *Proceedings of the 5th International Conference on Organizational Discourse*, King's College, London, July.

Berger, P. and Luckmann, T. (1966). *The Social Construction of Reality*. New York: Doubleday.

Brown, L.R. (1995). 'Ecopsychology and the environment revolution: an environmental foreword'. In T. Roszak, M.E. Gomes and A.D. Kanner (eds), *Ecopsychology Restoring the Earth Healing the Mind*. Sierra Club, Los Angeles, pp. xiii–xvi.

Buchanan, D. and Huczynski, A. (1997). *Organizational Behaviour*, 3rd edition. London: Prentice Hall.

Burr, V. (1995). *An Introduction to Social Constructionism*. London: Routledge.

Carey, J. (2000). *The Faber Book of Utopias*. London: Faber and Faber.

Chomsky, N. and Herman, E. (1979). *After the Cataclysm: Postwar Indochina and the Reconstruction of the Imperial Ideology, the Political Economy of Human Rights*, Vol. 2. Boston, MA: South End Press.

Csikszentmihalyi, M. and Rochberg-Halton, E. (1981). *The Meaning of Things: Domestic Symbols and the Self*. New York: Cambridge University Press.

Cummings, T.G. and Huse, E.F. (1989). *Organization Development and Change*, 4th edition. St. Paul: West Publishing Company.

De Bono, E. (1996). *Serious Creativity: Using the Power of Lateral Thinking to Create New Ideas*. London: HarperCollins.

Durkheim, E. (1966). *The Rules of Sociological Method*. London: Collier Macmillan Publishers.

ESOMAR/UNEP (2003). 'Sustainable motivation'. Available at: http://www.mpgintl.com/sustain/english/MPG_Intl_Sustainable_Motivation_Report.pdf (accessed January 3, 2006).

Feldman, P.L. (1971). 'Social adaptation: a new challenge for marketing'. *Journal of Marketing*, 35(July), 54–60.

Fisk, G. (1974). *Marketing and the Ecological Crisis*. New York: Harper & Row.

Fitchett, J.A. and McDonagh, P. (2000). 'A citizen's critique of relationship marketing in risk society'. *Journal of Strategic Marketing*, 8, 209–222.

Flusser, V. (1999). *The Shape of Things: A Philosophy of Design*. London: Reaktion Books Ltd.

Ford, J.D. and Ford, L.W. (1994). 'Logics of identity, contradiction, and attraction in change'. *Academy of Management Review*, 19, 756–795.

Friedman, V.J. (2001). 'The individual as agent of organizational learning'. In M. Dierkes, A. Berthoin, J. Child and I. Nonaka (eds), *Organizational Learning and Knowledge*. New York: Oxford University Press.

Gergen, K.J. (1994a). *Realities and Relationships: Soundings in Social Construction*. Cambridge, MA and London: Harvard University Press.

Gergen, K.J. (1994b). *Towards Transformation in Social Knowledge*. London: Sage.

Gergen, K.J. (1999). *An Invitation to Social Construction*. London: Sage.

Giddens, A. (1984). *The Constitution of Society: Outline of the Theory of Structuration*. Oxford: Polity Press/Blackwell Publishing.

Gladwin, T., Kennelly, J. and Krause, T.S. (1995). 'Shifting paradigms for sustainable development: implications for management theory and research'. *The Academy of Management Review*, 20, 874–907.

Harris, S., A. (1996). *Living with Paradox: An Introduction to Jungian Psychology*, Brooks/Cole Publishing Company, Pacific Grove.

Haug, W.F. (1986). *Critique of Commodity Aesthetics*. Minneapolis: University of Minnesota Press.

Hayagreeva, R., Morill, C. and Zald, M. (2000). 'Power plays: how social movements and collective action create new organizational form'. In B. Staw and R. Sutton (eds), *Research in Organizational Behavior*, Vol. 22. JAI Press, Greenwich, CT, pp. 237–282.

Hedberg, B.L.T. (1981). 'How organizations learn and unlearn'. In P.C. Nystrom and W.H. Starbuck (eds), *Handbook of Organizational Design: Vol 1. Adapting Organisations to Their Environments*. Oxford: Oxford University Press, pp. 3–27.

Horkheimer, M. and Adorno, T. (1972). *Dialectic of Enlightenment*. Herder & Herder, New York.

Kajzer, I. (2004). *An Inquiry into the Taken-for-Granted and Emergent Paradoxes: Exploring the Idea of the 'Living Product'*. Unpublished Doctoral Thesis, University of Strathclyde, Glasgow.

Kajzer-Mitchell, I. (2005). 'The marketer as a change activist: confessions of a marketing academic'. *Academy of Marketing Conference*, Dublin Institute of Technology, Ireland, July, pp. 5–7.

Kilbourne, W.E., McDonagh, P. and Prothero, A. (1997). 'Sustainable consumption and the quality of life: a macroeconomic challenge to the dominant social paradigm'. *Journal of Macromarketing*, 17, 4–24.

Klein, N. (2001). *No Logo*. London: Flamingo.

Law, J. and Urry, J. (2003). 'Enacting the social'. Published by the Department of Sociology and the Centre for Science Studies, Lancaster University. Available at: http://www.comp.lancs.ac.uk/sociology/papers/Law-Urry-Enacting-the-Social.pdf

Lewin, K. (1948). *Resolving Social Conflicts: Selected Papers on Group Dynamics*. New York: Harper & Row.

Lewis, M.W. (2000). 'Exploring paradox: towards a more comprehensive guide'. *Academy of Management Review*, 25, 760–776.

Lewis, M.W. and Kelemen, M.L. (2002). 'Multiparadigm inquiry: exploring organizational pluralism and paradox'. *Human Relations*, 55, 251–275.

McKibben, B. (2000). 'Humans supplant God; everything changes'. *Harvard Design Magazine*, Winter/Spring, 10. Available at: http://mitpress.mit.edu/HDM

Meichenbaum, D. (1975), 'Enhancing creativity by modifying what subjects say to themselves'. *American Educational Research Journal*, 12, 129–145.

Merchant, C. (1992). *Radical Ecology: The Search for a Livable World*. New York: Routledge.

Milbrath, L.W. (1984). *Environmentalists: Vanguard for a New Society*. Albany, NY: State University of New York Press.

Morgan, G. (1993). *Imaginization, the Art of Creative Management*. Newbury Park, California: Sage.

Morgan, G. (1997). *Images of Organization*. California: Sage.

O'Connor, E.S. (1995). 'Paradoxes of participation: textual analysis and organizational change'. *Organization Studies*, 16, 769–803.

Packard, V. (1957). *The Hidden Persuaders*. New York: D. McKay Co.

Parker, M. (2002). 'Utopia and the organizational imagination: outopia'. In M. Parker (ed.), *Utopia and Organization*. Oxford: Blackwell Publishing, pp. 1–8.

Parloff, M.B. and Handlon, J.H. (1964). 'The influence of criticalness on creative problem solving in dyads'. *Psychiatry*, 27, 17–27.

Paton, R.A. and McCalman, J. (2000). *Change Management: A Guide to Effective Implementation*. London: Paul Chapman Publishing.

Purser, R.E., Changkil, P. and Montuori, A. (1995). 'Limits to anthropocentrism: toward an ecocentric organization paradigm'. *Academy of Management Review*, 20, 1053–1090.

Reason, P. (2003). 'Choice and quality in action research practice'. *World Congress of Participatory Action Research*, Pretoria, South Africa. Available at: http://www.bath.ac.uk/carpp/

Reason, P. and Torbert, B. (2001). 'The action turn: towards a transformational social science'. *Concepts and Transformations*, 6, 1–37. Available at: http:www.bath.ac.uk/carp/

Senge, P.M. (1990). *The Fifth Discipline*. London: Bantam Doubleday Dell Publishing.

Senior, B. (2002). *Organisational Change*, 2nd edition. Essex: Pearson Education Ltd.

Stein, M.I. (1974). *Stimulating Creativity*, Vol. 1. New York: Academic Press Inc.

Stein, M.I. (1975). *Stimulating Creativity*, Vol. 2. New York: Academic Press Inc.

Van Dam, Y. and Apeldoorn, P. (1996). 'Sustainable marketing'. *Journal of Macromarketing*, 16(2), 45–56.

Vince, R. and Broussine, M. (1996). 'Paradox, defense and attachment: accessing and working with emotions and relations underlying organizational change'. *Organizational Studies*, 17, 1–21.

Watzlawick, P. (1976). *How Real Is Real? Confusion, Disinformation, Communication*. New York: Random House.

Westenholz, A. (1993). 'Paradoxical thinking and change in the frames of reference'. *Organization Studies*, 14, 37–58.

Williams, S.D. (2004). 'Self-esteem and the self-censorship of creative ideas'. *Personnel Review*, 31(4), 495–503.

15

Relevance of Critique: Can and Should Critical Marketing Influence Practice and Policy?

Robin Wensley

Within the critical approach, the issue of relevance and impact is frequently seen as problematic. This is particularly true of fields such as management and marketing, where relevance itself has often been defined in a restricted manner to imply usefulness as measured by a sub-group of either practitioners or self-selected intermediaries. Other writers however have provided more useful approaches, such as Burawoy (2004) with his analysis of differing audiences and purposes and Eldridge (1986) with his notion of differences between congenial and critical relevance. Developing on these approaches and the related notion of audience, we can recognize there are also questions to be asked about the basis and purpose of critical approaches in marketing.

In exploring these key questions related to the nature of consumer choice, the collective rationale of such choice processes and the assumptions of those who practice marketing it is clear that there is a basis for critical marketing to influence both policy and practice as well as to achieve what might be called indirect impact via what is both taught directly and also codified in textbooks.

The other four chapters in this section of the book have generally focused on four different and distinct ways in which critical studies particularly in marketing can influence policy and practice. At the risk of over-summarizing they broadly cover: focusing attention on the process of influencing choice through social marketing (Gordon et al. Chapter 11); identifying the multiple dimensions of consumer disadvantage (Hamilton of Chapter 12); privileging issues of sustainability over those of consumption (Peattie of Chapter 13); and, at a more individual level, using the direct encounter with empirical evidence as learning opportunities to change individual frame of reference rather than to reinforce the current dominant mode (Kajzer Mitchell of Chapter 14).

Each of these approaches represent important ways in which a more critical perspective on the nature of the marketing activity can have an impact on either or both practice and policy. In this final chapter we will add to these mechanisms by considering two further perspectives on the underlying issue that also relate to the four previous ones. These two further perspectives both focus in different ways on the nature of the audience for our research and scholarship both in terms of the nature of our discourse with them and the nature of our relationship. In so doing we will show that they also provide a more general context within which to consider some further issues related to each of the four perspectives.

Broadly speaking the two approaches consider, respectively, the nature of the engagement itself with, what might be termed, the broader political economy and the much more focused question of the way in which the engagement itself with a particular audience is defined as achieving relevance.

The Nature of the Engagement

Burawoy (2004) argues that various forms of sociological inquiry and commentary need to co-exist, based on whether the knowledge generation process is instrumental or reflexive and the audience is intra- or extra-academic. He typifies four forms that he labels (Figure 15.1) professional, policy, public and

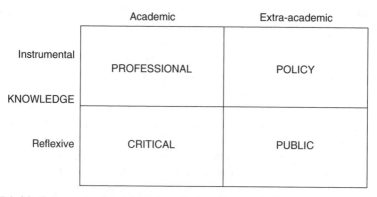

Figure 15.1 A basic taxonomy of sociological enquiry from Burawoy (2004).

critical sociology but also notes that such an analysis can be readily applied to other social science disciplines.

His analysis is particularly useful for two reasons but also potentially misleading in the wrong hands. The two good reasons are that it provides an important basis for the co-existence of the different modes of enquiry and engagement and that he further develops his analysis to consider the way in which the key characteristics differ between the modes (Figure 15.2). The danger is that in the wrong hands it can be used to try and stereotype the work of one individual or group: even worse to identify the 'best' way.

	Academic	Extra-academic	
Instrumental	Theoretical/empirical Scientific norms Peers Self-referentiality Professional self-interest	Concrete Effectiveness Clients/patrons Servility Policy intervention	The nature of knowledge Form of legitimacy Mechanism of accountability Key pathology Essential politics 'governance'
Reflexive	Foundational Moral vision Critical intellectuals Dogmatism Internal debate	Communicative Relevance Designated publics Faddishness Public dialogue	

Figure 15.2 Key elements of four sociological types from Michael Burawoy (2004).

Burawoy's approach also helps to focus renewed attention on the contentious issue of incommensurability. Ever since the Burrell and Morgan (1979) the issue of incommensurability has been a challenging topic in management and organizational studies. Whilst it remains a topic of lively debate (see for instance Hassard, 1988; Weaver and Gioia, 1994) we would argue that in fields such as management research more broadly and, a fortiori, particular aspects such as marketing, we are required to ensure forms of debate and dialogue across different perspectives and assumptions about the nature and purpose of empirical enquiry.[1] This inevitably means that we cannot just define differing perspectives as incommensurate but need to engage in more fine grained analysis as to the specific nature of the incommensurability, whilst recognizing that at least some of these differences will not, for instance, be susceptible to resolution merely through further empirical enquiry.

---

[1] This is not to deny the importance of underlying questions of ontology and epistemology. We somehow need to manage a dialogue in which we both discuss substance and definition as two parallel but interacting activities.

Congenial or Critical Relevance?

It is also not really possible to discuss the issue of audience without also considering the current issue of relevance. When we do so we inevitably find there are strong echoes of earlier debates. John Eldridge, who himself was involved in disputes around the research of the Glasgow University Media Group in the late seventies and early eighties (see Eldridge, 1995), consider the history of some key areas of management research in a paper in 1986. In particular he drew attention to the key management research in the fifties by Joan Woodward (1986, p. 173):

> From her survey of 203 manufacturing firms she concluded that different technologies imposed different kinds of demand on individuals and organisations and that these demands had to be met through an appropriate form of organisation . . . This was of obvious practical interest to managers. Her work came to be treated as an effective demolition job on the 'one best way' of management myth . . . (and) the so-called principles of scientific management were challenged . . .

> Here, then, was an answer to sceptical managers who wanted to know what use social science was to them. It could replace arid abstract principles of management by a situational approach which was more realistic. Not only did this make it relevant to them, but in some respects, they could even be reassured by a concrete situational approach which was more realistic.

At this stage we have what might be termed from a more conventional perspective, an ideal case: sound empirically based social science which is also seen as relevant, but there is a sting in the tail:

> What one finds in British sociology after Woodward is that research investigations frequently built into their design her classification of types of technology . . . Woodward and her colleagues at the Imperial College Industrial Sociology Unit did come to accept the operational difficulties that were involved in measuring technical variables. One response to this was to introduce the concept of the 'control system'. The control system is offered as an intervening variable between task and organization structure . . . Again one can see the managerial implications. In so far as this kind of approach attempts to understand organizations in order that managers may more effectively control uncertainty, it may be regarded as highly relevant to management yet the analysis takes place on the assumptions that the existing distribution of power remains unchanged (p. 174).

Eldridge concludes:

> It is perhaps the questions that are not asked that in part enable one to distinguish between a sociology which is congenially relevant to an

interested party and one which is critically relevant. If we neglect to ask what a particular form of technology is designed to do, in whose interests and with what consequences, it does save a good deal of unpleasantness. If we do not inquire into the structure of domination within which typologies of technology and control systems are embedded, then the critical relevance of the theory is diminished (p. 175).

As Eldridge himself recognizes, in introducing the distinction between congenially or critically relevant, he is also assuming that the general topic of study is of some importance to a wider community and hence that in the end there can be said to be, in his terms, 'a general relevance for society'. The notion of relevance therefore in management research can be seen as flawed if it is defined solely as, to use Eldridge's terms, congenially relevant to a partial group, community or indeed representatives of the same within society.

Many more recent advocates of critical marketing would no doubt echo such claims. Yet is there an implicit assumption that in being critical of the position of one or more particular groups, the analysis becomes again congenial to others or can we be critical of all? Second, if our aim is to be critically relevant there are further questions of both audience and method.

Some of the practitioners of critical marketing have a very clear sense of the group or groups to which their analysis is congenial. In some cases we might define the group concerned as the 'direct' beneficiaries, such as say the poor, in other cases key intermediaries such as policy-makers interested in problems of exclusion. There is undoubtedly an important role for such activities but we should also ask about the extent to which any degree of engagement is actually achieved with the concerns and interests of the intended audience or beneficiaries. When asked a number of academic critical marketers identify, perhaps not surprisingly, their students as one, and sometimes the only important, audience. Undoubtedly they represent a potential audience, which can be both intellectually stimulating and responsive, but maybe particularly so if they are to be examined on the topics under discussion as well.

There are two other questions that we need to consider: the nature of the actual relationship between the researcher and the audience and the extent to which our very notion of 'being critical' can be addressed at various levels of analysis. The problem with the initial Eldridge analysis is that it sees the question of congenial or critical as decontextualized in terms of the relationship between researcher and audience. This may sometimes be a reasonable assumption but it is also true that the effective transmission of a more critical analysis can often depend on a longer term and secure relationship between the two parties. Hence from the advocates of action research onwards, there have been those who argued that the very process of engagement over an extended period made it feasible that difficult and challenging lessons and insights could be realized.

In his description and critique of the Woodward research on work organization, Eldridge described a process which we can see repeated in other domains of management research, and which itself can be seen as a critical process but framed within rather than outside a set of relatively traditional assumptions about the nature of managerial knowledge and the role of management. He describes an initial empirical research study which establishes a pattern which can be interpreted in terms of managerial relevance and action, followed by more detailed and systematic work which establishes severe doubts about the validity of the early study, followed by further elaboration of the original work which introduce more complex contingencies and hence sustain apparent managerial relevance but rarely withstand further empirical scrutiny.[2] Key examples would be the history of research on the so-called strategic importance of market share and the related development of such management tools as the market share/market growth matrix (Morrison and Wensley, 1991), and more recently the work related to the so-called generic strategies debate, in which Michael Porter originally asserted that effective strategies required firms to avoid the performance trap of being 'stuck in the middle' between cost competition and differentiation, yet later more systematic research established that there is little empirical evidence for such the assertion that such a trap exists (Campbell-Hunt, 2000) let alone how any such outcome might be linked to the strategic intentions of any particular firm (Wensley, 2003).

Being Critical about the Critical

The analysis above helps to emphasize that if we are to espouse a critical approach to our own field of study, we must to some degree at least apply this to ourselves as well. In particular we need to consider how any intervention in practice or policy is legitimized in terms of our intentions and our own knowledge claims. In general, we can distinguish between interventions that are intended to support one or more of three general groups: consumers, policymakers and marketing practitioners.

From a marketing perspective it is perhaps easiest to deal with the situation in which the principle intention is to support consumers. Traditionally we have justified such interventions on the basis of either lack of (or misleading)

---

[2] This form of process has been described by Oaksford and Chater (1998) as a key characteristic of, what they call, 'folk theories' in that they generate inferences that are defeasible, in other words capable of being readily defeated by further information. This they contrast with the nature of scientific inference that requires, they claim, a much higher level of robustness to further information. Hence they argue that judged against normal criteria, folk theories will always be bad science in domains that are well understood scientifically. In a somewhat similar manner but from a rather different perspective, the redoubtable Richard Feynman noted 'What happens is that you get all kinds of statements of fact about education, about sociology, even psychology – all kinds of things which are, I'd say. Pseudoscience. They've done statistics which they say they've done very carefully. They've done experiments which are not really controlled experiments' (1999: 242).

information and/or supplier dominance in terms of the degree or nature of the choice provided. As Lynch and Wood (2006, p. 1) observe such actions:

> center on three key interventions to public policy that are drawn from economics and that are intended to benefit consumers in the marketplace: 1. Offering more choices, 2. Providing better information to consumers about options they might consider, and 3. Providing incentives for consumers or sellers to change their behaviour.

To this list, however, needs to be added interventions designed to enable consumers to actually use any information that is provided in a more effective manner. Certain marketing scholars (see Adkins and Ozanne, 2005) have noted that we need to appreciate that even projects directed to consumer literacy must recognize the particular context and coping strategies of the intended audience.

Hence, effective interventions of the 'better information' sort have a clear underlying legitimacy yet can often have limited efficacy. Additionally we may need to be cautious about the underlying policy intent: at what stage does an information campaign in France for the Euro, as described in Chapter 11, for instance become seen more as propaganda rather than purely the provision of public information? How far does an attempt to redefine grocery store options so as to retain the 'High Street' (Peattie) become more about land use planning[3] and general issues of transport and less about reinforcing the choices made by individual customers?

The Rationality of Consumer Choice

In many cases, we find the justification is moving towards a policy perspective in one way or another. As critical marketers we should not be necessarily against such a move but we should be very clear about the basis for the shift and the underlying evidence. It is worth noting a number of general considerations. First there is the question of consumer choice rationality. Shugan (2006, p. 5) in his review of this general area notes that, 'consumers are becoming more rational because we are becoming better able to predict their behaviour'. Whilst this may sound a rather perverse way of measuring rationality,[4] Shugan's approach reminds us of two key issues: if we are to argue the case for intervention we must first be able to show that the particular impact that is being asserted is indeed empirically evident, and, to borrow a concept from

---

[3] and hence about competing property rights claims such as embodied in particular instruments such as 'the green belt'.

[4] However rather less perverse than this bald representation. In general terms Shugan is considering the extent to which rationality can be linked to explicability and hence predictability. His notion of rationality might be better sub-titles: 'consumer rationality, as understood by the researcher'!

our legal colleagues, one of material effect and also that the rationale which might underlie such an effect is itself inappropriate or perverse.

Whilst this is quite a strong test, there do remain some crucial candidates. One lies in the general area of individual time discounting of costs and benefits or, as Lynch and Zauberman (2006) summarize:

> 'underweighting outcomes in the distant (compared with the near) future and of overweighting outcomes in the present compared with any point in the future'. Such well established behaviour provides a legitimate basis on which to intervene in domains as different as unprotected sexual activity to the provision of personal pensions.

Aggregate Effect of Individual Choices

Beyond the question of individual choice, there is the issue of the aggregate effect of individual choices. In complex economic and social systems, we have recognized since Keynes the possibility of the so-called 'fallacy of composition', when in the General Theory he emphasized 'the vital difference between the theory of the economic behaviour of the aggregate and the theory of the behaviour of the individual unit'. Is there then also some sort of consistent collective failure in time discounting as well as an individual one? If so this would be a powerful rationale for marketing to intervene in broader areas such as the promotion of sustainability. One of the standard ways of addressing this question empirically is to compare imputed time discount rates in terms of various forms of choices, under either experimental or actual conditions with the so-called Social Time Preference Rate (STPR) as determined by policy. In the UK the generally accepted STPR is 3.5% equivalent to a discount factor of 0.035. Table 15.1 below is from Frederick et al. (2002), which summarizes the results

Table 15.1 Result of empirical studies during 1975–2000 (from Frederick et al. (2002)).

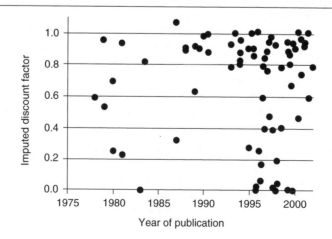

of many empirical studies, the majority being experimental but a number also being so-called 'field' studies.

Despite a few studies clustering around the desired rate the overall result is a general and strong tendency to over-discount the future. Frederick et al. (2002, p. 388) argue that there is a range of confounding factors which are not directly to time preference and assert that:

> [The Table] also reveals a predominance of high implicit discount rates – discount rates well above market interest rates. This consistent finding may also be due to the presence of the various extra-time-preference considerations listed above, because nearly all of these work to bias imputed discount rates upward – only habit formation and anticipatory utility bias estimates downward. If these confounding factors were adequately controlled, we suspect that many intertemporal choices or judgments would imply much lower – indeed, possibly even zero – rates of time preference.

However, others might argue that in the face of such a substantial overall bias towards high discount factors, it might be reasonable to assume that at least a precautionary principle would still suggest that public policy interventions are appropriate in areas such as sustainability. However, where possible it might be appropriate to focus on measures which enable the 'presentiation'[5] of future costs and benefits and hence the continued opportunity for individual and collective choice. Whether such developments would be adequate to deal with broader issues such as those clustered around the impact of the culture of consumption is another matter but we would be well advised to recognize the complex social and historical context of the phenomenon (Trentmann, 2005) before assuming that a particular form of intervention is justified let alone efficacious.

Our Role As Active Agents

When we come to consider the impact not only on practitioners but also on ourselves, Kajzer Mitchell rightly points to the tendency to rationalize the problem as that of the 'other'. In so doing there is a tendency to deny or ignore the extent to which all participants have a possible role as actors within actor-network theory (Latour, 1987) or indeed the interactive process of 'structuration' (Giddens, 1986), in that actions within structures recreate or modify the structure itself and the potential for future action. However, there is an exactly equivalent oversight when it comes to our own role as researchers and teachers.

---

[5] 'presentiation' is a concept from contract law. MacNeil (1980) defines it as: 'Presentiation' describes the process by which executory contracts allow parties to plan the future by making future obligations immediately binding; it is 'the bringing of the future into the present' (p. 60).

When we engage in such joint learning and development we have to recognize that we are likely to be as least as much changed by the experience as the practitioners or policy-makers with whom we engage.

There is perhaps a danger in some of the writing on critical marketing that it is somehow assumed that the academic commentator has greater insight that either the practitioner or the policy-maker in such matters.[6] If we return to the issues raised by Buroway (2004) then it seems reasonable that if we are to critically engage with an extra-academic audience then we might be expected to do so in a reflexive manner.

Finally we come to the nature of our textbooks and the ways in which marketing knowledge is codified and disseminated.[7] Here we face a significant further challenge: mainstream marketing texts have remained clearly focused on the so-called 'marketing management' perspective (Priddle, 1994) and look set to remain so for the foreseeable future despite the valiant attempts of various scholars, including a number of contributors to this volume, to try and encourage a new direction. Catterall et al. (2002) provide a full and well-argued analysis of the pedagogic and pragmatic challenge involved: it is clear that there is still quite a long way to go.

---

[6] Indeed one can ask rather similar questions about the espousal of 'double loop learning' to those used by Argyris and Schon (1978). Chris Argyris (1999) has asserted that this often does not take place because of the defensive routines adopted by the participants but we need to recognize that academics or observers often also exhibit such 'defensive routines'!

[7] Indeed in marketing as elsewhere in much of the social sciences there is a disjunction between notions of research or scholarly impact via article citation analysis and issues of wider impact via text or trade books (see Wensley (2006) in general, and Skrbis and Germov (2003), and Gläser (2004)) in the specific case of sociology texts.

References

Adkins, N.R. and Ozanne, J.L. (2005). 'Critical consumer education: empowering the low-literate consumer'. *Journal of Macromarketing*, 25(2), 153–162.

Argyris, C. (1999). *On Organisational Learning*. Oxford: Blackwell.

Argyris, C. and Schon, D. (1978). *Organizational Learning: A Theory of Action Perspective*. Reading, MA: Addison-Wesley.

Burawoy, M. (2004). 'Public sociologies: contradictions, dilemma and possibilities'. *Social Forces* (June), 1603–1618.

Burrell, G. and Morgan, G. (1979). *Sociological Paradigms and Organizational Analysis*. London: Heinemann.

Campbell-Hunt, C. (2000). 'What have we learned about generic competitive strategy? A meta-analysis'. *Strategic Management Journal*, 21(2), 127–154.

Catterall, M., Maclaran, P. and Stevens, L. (2002). 'Critical reflection in the marketing curriculum'. *Journal of Marketing Education*, 24(3), 184–192.

Eldridge, J. (1986). 'Facets of "relevance" in sociological research'. In F. Heller (ed.), *The Use and Abuse of Social Science*. London: Sage.

Eldridge, J. (ed.) (1995), *Glasgow University Media Reader*, Vol. 1. Oxford: Routledge.

Feynman, R.P. (1999). *The Pleasure of Finding Things Out*. Cambridge, MA: Perseus Books.

Giddens, A. (1986). *The Constitution of Society: Outline of the Theory of Structuration*, Reprint edition. University of California Press.

Gläser, J. (2004). 'Why are the most influential books in Australian sociology not necessarily the most highly cited ones? ' *Journal of Sociology*, 40(3), 261–282.

Hassard, J. (1988). 'Overcoming hermeticism in organization theory: an alternative to paradigm incommensurability'. *Human Relations*, 41, 247–259.

Latour, B. (1987). *Science in Action: How to Follow Scientists and Engineers through Society*. Milton Keynes: Open University Press.

Lynch Jr., J.G. and Zauberman, G. (2006). 'When do you want it? Time, decisions, and public policy'. *Journal of Public Policy and Marketing*, 25(1), 67–78.

Lynch Jr., J.G. and Wood, W. (2006). 'Special issue editors' statement: helping consumers help themselves'. *Journal of Public Policy and Marketing*, 25(1), 1–7.

MacNeil, I. (1980). *The New Social Contract: An Inquiry into Modern Contractual Relations*. New Haven, CT: Yale University Press.

Morrison, A. and Wensley, R. (1991). 'A short history of the growth/share matrix: boxed up or boxed in?' *Journal of Marketing Management*, 7(2), 105–129.

Oaksford, M. and Chater, N. (1998). *Rationality in an Uncertain World*. Hove, UK: Psychology Press.

Priddle, J. (1994). 'Marketing ethics, macromarketing, and the managerial perspective reconsidered'. *Journal of Macromarketing*, 14(2), 47–62.

Shugan, S. (2006). 'Editorial: Are consumers rational? Experimental evidence?' *Marketing Science*, 25(1), 1–7.

Skrbis, Z. and Germov, J. (2004). 'The most influential books in Australian sociology (MIBAS) 1963–2003'. *Journal of Sociology*, 40(3), 283–303.

Trentmann, F. (ed) (2005). *The Making of the Consumer: Knowledge, Power and Identity in the Modern World*. Oxford: Berg Publishers Ltd.

Weaver, G.B. and Gioia, D.A. (1994). 'Paradigms lost: incommensurability vs structurationist inquiry'. *Organization Studies*, 15(4), 565–590.

Wensley, R. (2003). 'Strategy as intention and anticipation'. In D. Wilson and S. Cummings (eds), *Images of Strategy*. Oxford: Blackwell.

Wensley, R. (2006). 'Beyond rigour and relevance: the underlying nature of both business schools and management research'. Working Paper, London: AIM.

Index

Learning Resources
Centre